The CALVIN INSTITUTE OF CHRISTIAN WORSHIP LITURGICAL STUDIES Series, edited by John D. Witvliet, is designed to promote reflection on the history, theology, and practice of Christian worship and to stimulate worship renewal in Christian congregations. Contributions include writings by pastoral worship leaders from a wide range of communities and scholars from a wide range of disciplines. The ultimate goal of these contributions is to nurture worship practices that are spiritually vital and theologically rooted.

PUBLISHED

The Pastor as Minor Poet: Texts and Subtexts in the Ministerial Life
    M. Craig Barnes

Arts Ministry: Nurturing the Creative Life of God's People
    Michael J. Bauer

Touching the Altar: The Old Testament and Christian Worship
    Carol M. Bechtel, Editor

Resonant Witness: Conversations between Music and Theology
    Jeremy S. Begbie and Steven R. Guthrie, Editors

God against Religion: Rethinking Christian Theology through Worship
    Matthew Myer Boulton

From Memory to Imagination: Reforming the Church's Music
    C. Randall Bradley

By the Vision of Another World: Worship in American History
    James D. Bratt, Editor

Inclusive yet Discerning: Navigating Worship Artfully
    Frank Burch Brown

What Language Shall I Borrow? The Bible and Christian Worship
    Ronald P. Byars

A Primer on Christian Worship: Where We've Been, Where We Are, Where We Can Go
    William A. Dyrness

Christian Worship Worldwide: Expanding Horizons, Deepening Practices
    Charles E. Farhadian, Editor

Gather into One: Praying and Singing Globally
    C. Michael Hawn

The Touch of the Sacred: The Practice, Theology, and Tradition of Christian Worship
    F. Gerrit Immink

The Substance of Things Seen: Art, Faith, and the Christian Community
    Robin M. Jensen

Our Worship
    Abraham Kuyper, Edited by Harry Boonstra

For the Common Good: Missional Worship for the Sake of the World
    Ruth A. Meyers

Wonderful Words of Life: Hymns in American Protestant History and Theology
    Richard J. Mouw and Mark A. Noll, Editors

Discerning the Spirits: A Guide to Thinking about Christian Worship Today
    Cornelius Plantinga Jr. and Sue A. Rozeboom

Evangelical versus Liturgical? Defying a Dichotomy
    Melanie C. Ross

Voicing God's Psalms
    Calvin Seerveld

My Only Comfort: Death, Deliverance, and Discipleship in the Music of Bach
    Calvin R. Stapert

A New Song for an Old World: Musical Thought in the Early Church
    Calvin R. Stapert

An Architecture of Immanence: Architecture for Worship and Ministry Today
    Mark A. Torgerson

A More Profound Alleluia: Theology and Worship in Harmony
    Leanne Van Dyk, Editor

Christian Worship in Reformed Churches Past and Present
    Lukas Vischer, Editor

We Have Seen His Glory: A Vision of Kingdom Worship
    Ben Witherington III

The Biblical Psalms in Christian Worship:
A Brief Introduction and Guide to Resources
    John D. Witvliet

Worship with Gladness: Understanding Worship from the Heart
    Joyce Ann Zimmerman

The Touch of the Sacred

The Practice, Theology, and Tradition of Christian Worship

F. Gerrit Immink

Translated by
Reinder Bruinsma

WILLIAM B. EERDMANS PUBLISHING COMPANY
GRAND RAPIDS, MICHIGAN / CAMBRIDGE, U.K.

© 2014 F. Gerrit Immink
All rights reserved

First published in Dutch under the title
Het heilige gebeurt. Praktijk, theologie en traditie van de protestante kerkdienst,
by Uitgeverij Boekencentrum, 2011.

This English edition published 2014 by
Wm. B. Eerdmans Publishing Co.
2140 Oak Industrial Drive N.E., Grand Rapids, Michigan 49505 /
P.O. Box 163, Cambridge CB3 9PU U.K.
www.eerdmans.com

Library of Congress Cataloging-in-Publication Data

Immink, Gerrit.
　　The touch of the sacred: the practice, theology, and tradition of Christian worship /
　　F. Gerrit Immink; translated by Reinder Bruinsma.
　　　　pages　　　cm.　　　— (Calvin Institute of Christian Worship liturgical studies series)
　　Includes bibliographical references and index.
　　ISBN 978-0-8028-6915-9 (pbk.: alk. paper)
　　1. Theology, Practical.　2. Worship.　3. Spiritual life — Christianity.
　　4. Salvation — Christianity.　5. Jesus Christ — Person and offices.　I. Title.

BV3.I4613　2014
264 — dc23

　　　　　　　　　　　　　　　　　　　　　　　　　　　　　　　　2014003476

Unless otherwise noted, the Scripture quotations in this publication are from the Revised Standard Version of the Bible, copyrighted 1946, 1952 © 1971, 1973 by the Division of Christian Education of the National Council of Churches of Christ in the U.S.A., and used by permission.

Contents

Introduction	vii
1. Worship as Religious Praxis	1
Worship as a Communal Act	1
The Agenda and Script of Worship	10
The Performance of Worship	22
Worship as True Mediation?	33
2. Sharing in Salvation	38
Salvific Facts and Spiritual Participation	39
The Christian Year	47
The Prayer for the Presence of the Holy Spirit *(Epiclesis)*	52
The Participation	57
3. The Mystery of Christ	68
The Resurrection of Christ	68
The Ontological Character of the Resurrection	78
A Liminal Event and an Independent Person	85
4. Backgrounds and Dilemmas	93
The Lord's Supper: A Departure from Tradition?	94
The Word of God and the Sermon	106
Baptism and Confession	123

CONTENTS

5. Prayer — 140
   Prayer as a Religious Praxis — 140
   Liturgical Prayer — 146
   The Prayers in the Worship Service — 152

6. Preaching — 163
   The Act of Participation — 163
   The Scriptures in the *Performance* — 183
   The Rhetorical Form of the Sermon — 201

7. Celebrating the Lord's Supper — 224
   Protestant Communion Practices — 224
   The Origin of the Reformed Liturgy of the Lord's Supper — 227
   Theology and Piety in the Reformed Communion Praxis — 235
   Comparison with the Sacrifice of the Mass — 238
   Contemporary Praxis — 245

   Bibliography — 252

   Index of Subjects and Names — 264

Introduction

All over the world, Christian communities meet on Sunday morning for worship. They come together to sing and pray. They read from the Bible and listen to a sermon. They greet each other,[1] give their offerings, and celebrate the Lord's Supper. These assemblies show considerable variation, depending on cultural diversity and ecclesial traditions. Some churches follow fixed patterns, based on established scripts, while other churches are characterized by spontaneity, emphasizing freedom of expression. In some denominations, celebrating the Eucharist is an intrinsic part of the main service on Sunday morning, while in others the sermon plays a prominent role. This book deals with the worship service as the concrete practice of the Christian church on Sunday morning. The focus is on the worship service as it developed in the Protestant tradition. What happens during a service? How does it happen? And how do we come to a proper understanding of what happens?

To begin with, we must understand that a worship service is a religious *practice*. A practice is more than an incidental act: it comprises multiple acts that form a coherent unity.[2] Moreover, these acts are performed by a group of people with a common interest. This is certainly true of a worship service. Praying, singing, preaching, celebrating the Lord's Supper — together these

---

1. The Bible mentions that the church members greet one another: "Greet one another with a holy kiss" (Rom. 16:16); "Greet one another with the kiss of love" (1 Pet. 5:14). The liturgy has several moments of greeting — e.g., the greeting of peace, immediately before the communion of bread and wine.

2. James Nieman, "Why the Idea of Practice Matters," in *Teaching Preaching as a Christian Practice: A New Approach to Homiletical Pedagogy*, ed. Thomas G. Long and Leonora Tubbs Tisdale (London/Louisville: John Knox Press, 2008), pp. 18-40; Dorothy C. Bass and Craig Dykstra, *For Life Abundant: Practical Theology, Theological Education, and Christian Ministry* (Grand Rapids: Wm. B. Eerdmans, 2008).

INTRODUCTION

activities constitute the worship service, and the congregation is the acting subject. Two aspects are important if we want to understand the worship service as a practice. First, practices are *saturated with theories*. We are dealing with human activities that are embedded in a particular tradition, and with acts that have been thought through. Those who participate in worship do not act merely as a matter of routine, but are spiritually involved. Second, practices are forms of *coordinated* social action.[3] The collective character does not emerge spontaneously, but is coordinated. The worship service follows a *script*, a liturgical agenda. This script evolved over time and must adapt itself constantly to changing circumstances.

We must also emphasize that the worship service is a *religious* practice. Broadly speaking, this means that the congregation is practicing its communion with God. In more specifically Christian terminology, we would say that a worship service is about the encounter with the crucified and risen Christ. In this book the theological analysis of the practice of the worship service occupies an important place. Our attention will be directed toward the concrete practice as a human activity. The question, then, is this: How can we arrive at a theological elucidation of the religious dimension of this activity?

The worship service is not the only form that may be used to express the Christian faith. Faith is expressed in a variety of ways in our everyday existence — in the moral aspects of our lives, in our contacts with others, and in the social and societal relationships that surround us. There also is a more personal, subjective expression in devotion and spirituality. However, in addition to these forms of expression, the worship service has a significance of its own. In its worship the church becomes visible to the external world. The community of faith assembles in a public space for a public service.[4] Moreover, in worship the personal, social, and societal elements are integrated in a collective public act. In this sense the Sunday worship service provides a comprehensive view of faith.

---

3. Craig Dykstra and Dorothy C. Bass, "A Theological Understanding of Christian Practices," in *Practicing Theology: Beliefs and Practices in Christian Life*, ed. Miroslav Volf and Dorothy C. Bass (Grand Rapids: Wm. B. Eerdmans, 2002), pp. 13-32.

4. In Hellenic culture, the word "liturgy" originally referred to a *public service* of a city. In the New Testament, the word is not used for the worshipping community. Cf. Peter Brunner, "Zur Lehre vom Gottesdienst der im Namen Jesu Versammelten Gemeinde," in *Leiturgia*, vol. 1, ed. Karl Ferdinand Müller and Walter Blankenburg (Kassel: Stauda, 1954), pp. 101-2; Irénée Henri Damais, "The Liturgy as Celebration," in *Primary Sources of Liturgical Theology*, ed. Dwight W. Vogel (Collegeville, Minn.: Liturgical Press, 2000), pp. 18, 19.

Introduction

A great deal of the literature on the practice of the worship service deals with the task of the minister. This is understandable, since preaching and worship are important elements of a pastor's task. Schleiermacher, for instance, developed his theory of praxis mainly to promote the professionalism of church leaders.[5] In this study, however, I will direct my primary attention not to the minister,[6] but rather to the communal act. I will pay special attention to worshippers, since their actions are also theory-laden and offer insights into the practice of the worship service. This focus will result in the following questions: How do worshippers participate in the service? What does it mean to sing, pray, and celebrate the Lord's Supper together? And what do worshippers do when they listen to a sermon?

The Content of This Book

In considering the worship service as a religious practice, there are three angles to be discussed. They are referred to in the subtitle of this book: *The Practice, Theology, and Tradition of Christian Worship*. The first angle is thus the *practice*: the concrete celebration of the Sunday-morning worship service. *That is where and when it happens.* This practice is ultimately the heart of the matter for both worshippers and the worship leader. Prayers are said and hymns are sung in appropriate wording. The sermon is delivered in a specific style and rhetorical form. This sermon inspires worshippers and carries them along (or fails to do so). The Lord's Supper is celebrated with specific formulas and actions, and the congregation practices the communion with Christ in celebrating the communion of bread and wine. Hence, worship unfolds in the concrete actions of the congregation. Essential to this practice is the communicative and social infrastructure of the worship service. It is therefore not surprising that traditionally the liberal arts play an important role in the

---

5. Friedrich Schleiermacher, *Die Praktische Theologie nach den Grundsätzen der Evangelische Kirche im Zusammenhang Dargestellt* (Berlin: Jacob Frerich, 1850; photographic reprint, 1983), p. 12.

6. In the English language, the term "minister" is a gender-neutral word. However, this is not the case for the personal and other pronouns that refer to the minister. In this English edition, I'm most often using the feminine form of these pronouns, not for any feminist reason, but solely to avoid the suggestion that the church still lives and operates in an exclusively male world. For the same reason, I have attempted to vary the word "man" with such terms as "humanity" and "humankind." When direct quotations are used, the original wording is, of course, maintained.

implementation of the service. The sermon benefits from the art of rhetoric. The church hymn benefits from poetry and musicality. (Since practices are theory-laden, this implies that other disciplines besides theology provide insight into the worship service as a religious practice.)

The second angle is that of *theology*. Practices are saturated with theory and infused with *theology*. The shape of the liturgy is determined by religious convictions. It would even be possible to say that practices breathe faith. They are the expressions of faith, and they nurture faith. The religious dimension of worship becomes accessible through *theological discourse*. It is, for example, not a coincidence that worship services are held on Sunday. Sunday is celebrated as the day of the resurrection of Christ, and Easter is the pivot of the church calendar. The congregation gathers on Sunday and confesses that Christ has truly risen. What does this mean? How is the faith in the resurrection of Christ expressed in the prayers, the sermon, and the Lord's Supper? In addition to the specifically Christian nature of the worship service, there are also aspects of it that may be compared with those of other religions. Prayer, for instance, is widely practiced in many religions. And there are rites and rituals, such as greeting ceremonies, which have a universal human background.[7] This implies that we should relate theological considerations and arguments to insights from religious studies.[8] We arrive at a better understanding of Christian practices when we discover the similarities and dissimilarities with the practices of other religions.

The third angle is that of *tradition*. Practices develop over time, and this certainly applies to the worship service. Renewal takes place, sometimes even through a breach with history. But some traditions have survived the centuries. The worship service itself is a centuries-old institution. Particularly when celebrating the Lord's Supper, tradition plays a major role. Was the Reformation a breach with long-established liturgical models? What effects do *historical* arguments have on the way in which we shape our worship service? In order to obtain a better understanding of the practice of the Sunday worship service, we will therefore need to look at historical developments.

---

7. Gerard Lukken, *Rituals in Abundance: Critical Reflections on the Place, Form, and Identity of Christian Ritual in Our Culture* (Leuven: Peeters, 2005).

8. G. van der Leeuw understood the art of simultaneously attending to the dimensions of both theology and religious studies. It is striking that his theology of the sacraments consists of three parts: (1) a historical part; (2) a phenomenological part; and (3) a theological part. In his introduction to the phenomenological part, he states that he will attempt to "present the sacrament as it shows itself to the world, i.e., as a phenomenon." See G. van der Leeuw, *Sacramentstheologie* (Nijkerk: Callenbach, 1949), p. 133.

Introduction

The Title of This Book

Any reflection on worship that fails to include the specifically religious dimension is inadequate, says H. C. Schmidt-Lauber.[9] I share this view, and in this book I will attempt to provide an adequate theological understanding of the specifically religious dimension of worship. However, this is not a simple task for two reasons. First of all, *human faith as well as divine action remain mysterious.* They are complex phenomena with many diverging aspects. And the divine reality and acts are not easily accessible to us. God is holy and gracious, august and near. Second, it remains difficult to find the right words to describe the specifically religious impact of the worship service. As a performance, it is a dynamic process. *Something happens* when the congregation speaks and acts. *It is touched by the sacred.* But what is this religious event that occurs? Is faith brought to life? Is divine grace actualized? Do love and mercy flourish? Is compassion toward others stimulated?

What is the performative nature of the worship service? The answer to this question is often wrapped in the language of theology, such as "Worship has a liturgical impact," or "The Lord's Supper is sacramental in nature," or "Preaching is administering God's Word." In Protestant circles the religious impact is intimately related to the power of the Word *(Predicatio verbi dei, est verbum dei),* while in Roman Catholic circles the mystery of Christ is directly linked to the Eucharist. J. D. Crichton says, "By the liturgical mystery we are actualizing the past event, making it present so that the saving power of Christ can be made available to the worshipper in the here and now."[10] Although there may be differences, the same theme is at the core: the *actual* communion with Christ.

It is my intention to provide an understanding of the religious dimension. The worship service is a religious practice. This religious dimension is a unique reality that should not be reduced to processes of hermeneutical interpretation, or to social, psychological, or ritual processes. The encounter with God and the communion with Christ are religious realities. In worship *the sacred occurs.* This is not to say that the sacred is readily available. In

---

9. *Handbuch der Liturgik. Liturgiewissenschaft in Theologie und Praxis der Kirche,* ed. H. C. Schmidt-Lauber and Karl Heinz Bieritz (Göttingen: Vandenhoeck & Ruprecht, 1995), p. 35: "Every theory of liturgy remains inadequate, if it does not address the question of what happens in a Christian worship service that goes beyond the interaction of the participants and in their meetings."

10. J. D. Crichton, "A Theology of Worship," in *The Study of Liturgy,* ed. Cheslyn Jones, Geoffrey Wainwright, and Edward Yarnold, S.J. (London: SPCK, 1987), p. 14.

worship we reach the limits of our speaking and knowing. Nevertheless, the encounter with God is a living reality. The veil is torn. The sacred is present. It touches us.

The Outline of This Book

This book consists of two major parts. In the first part (Chapters 1-4), I discuss three fundamental themes: the worship service as religious praxis, participation in salvation, and the mystery of Christ. In order to gain some insight into the tradition of Christian worship, I outline in the fourth chapter some backgrounds and dilemmas with respect to Word and sacrament. In the second part of the book (Chapters 5-7), I discuss three major components of the Sunday worship service: praying, preaching, and celebrating the Lord's Supper. In these chapters I deal directly with the practice of the worship service.

In Chapter 1 I explain my views on worship as a religious practice. I deal with three components. The first is the active involvement of the congregation itself, which is evidenced in Protestant worship by the fact that the congregation is a singing community. However, the second and most characteristic aspect of worship is that the communal activity is based on an *agenda* and a *script*. This is where the liturgy comes into view. The third point is that the worship service can best be described as a *religious performance* in which the congregation meets God. In this connection I discuss the so-called liturgical dimension of worship and the suspicion of modern Protestantism regarding this point.

In Chapter 2 I deal with the manner in which the congregation that has gathered shares in Christ's salvation. In response to the sixteenth-century Roman Catholic liturgy of the mass, the Reformation strongly emphasized the unique and decisive sacrifice of Jesus Christ on the cross. In Protestant worship the communion with Christ is practiced as well. However, the connection between salvation history and the here and now is understood as the work of the Holy Spirit. In the service this is expressed in the prayer for the presence of the Holy Spirit *(epiclesis)*. (In this chapter I also discuss the Christian Year.)

In Chapter 3 I elaborate on the mystery of Christ. Here, Paul's interpretation of the cross and the resurrection are central issues. I argue that the resurrection is essential to the worship service, since the congregation shares in this new life in Christ through the Spirit. Chapter 4 is concerned with the

Introduction

contours of Protestant worship as I discuss some dilemmas relating to the celebration of the Lord's Supper, to preaching, and to baptism.

In Chapter 5 I focus on prayer. In their prayers, people speak with God about their concrete experiences of daily life and of faith. The worship service brings order to the prayer life of the people: thanksgiving, adoration, confession of sin, Kyrie Eleison, the burning desire to see the kingdom come, intercession — all these expressions are structured by the liturgy.

In Chapter 6 I deal with the sermon. How does a sermon "work"? I primarily focus on worshippers *listening to the sermon* rather than on preaching as an activity of the minister. I treat the preaching process from three angles. First, I look at it from the perspective of worshippers. What part do they play in the sermon? How do ministers relate their sermons to the lives of the listeners? Next, I ask how Scripture functions in the sermon. What happens in the work of homiletic exegesis? Finally, I discuss the rhetorical structure. How is a sermon constructed and built strategically? And what does this mean for worshippers as participants in the preaching process?

In Chapter 7, the final chapter, I deal with the celebration of the Lord's Supper. I distinguish three types of celebration: classical Reformed, Protestant ecumenical, and a form of "blended worship" found in the Reformed evangelical tradition. I pay special attention to the origin of the Reformed form of the Lord's Supper and to the devotion and the theology of the classical Reformed formulas for the communion service.

Finally, I should mention that the italics in the citations I have used are mine. Quotations from sources that do not exist in English or could not be located in any English translation have been translated by the translator of this book.

CHAPTER 1

Worship as Religious Praxis

Worship as a Communal Act

The stereotypical image of a Protestant worship service is that of a minister who preaches from the pulpit while wearing a robe. This may be compared with a priest in the Roman Catholic Church who, in his priestly garments, performs sacramental acts behind the altar. These descriptions are correct to the extent that the Word has a central role in the Protestant tradition, while the Eucharist is central in the Roman Catholic Church. But in some ways they also offer, with regard to both traditions, a kind of caricature. They fail to do justice to the communal or the ecclesial character of the worship service. For the worship service is a gathering of the church community, and the worshippers are active participants rather than passive observers. If we want to have a clear picture of the worship service, we must therefore pay attention not only to the minister in the pulpit, but also to the church members in the pews. What is the role of the congregation?

The worshippers perform different kinds of verbal and nonverbal acts: they greet one another, pray together, read from the Holy Scriptures, listen to the Word of God, give their offerings, and eat bread and drink wine. They do so as a community while a minister leads them in these communal acts.[1] The minister may primarily function as the voice of the community, but at other moments she speaks on behalf of God — as, for instance, in the call to worship. At other moments, however, the church members lift their voices — as, for instance, in the congregational singing.

According to Bruno Bürki, the communal hymn-singing is an impor-

---

1. The New Testament refers to elders and bishops (Titus 1:5, 7).

tant aspect of the active participation in the worship service.[2] A Protestant congregation is a singing community:

> The Reformation does not know of a "silent mass"; in every worship service the people sing in the Lord's presence. We do not leave the singing exclusively to a choir or a professional musician; no, the entire church lifts its voice in praise to God. Nor is it a performance, to be enjoyed by those who love music. All who are present are part of "the performing audience."[3]

The communal hymn-singing underlines the fact that the worshippers are *actors* in a performance. The singing is not intended as a pause or as entertainment; it is an essential part of the liturgy. (Christoph Albrecht states that, at the time of the Reformation, the church members were freed from their role as observers.)[4] Through the communal singing, notes Wim Kloppenburg, the worshippers become active participants in the worship service. Thus the congregation itself becomes "the performing audience." Kloppenburg explains how the Reformation effected this change:

> Luther and Calvin once again gave a voice to the church members by providing them with hymns in their own languages. It should be noted that they were not the first to do so. Hymns in the vernacular were already sung in the Reform movements around John Hus in Bohemia and Geert Grote in the Netherlands. But it was only with Luther and Calvin that congregational singing was systematically practiced and promoted.[5]

When the Reformation began, a singing congregation was a novelty.[6] Upon arriving in Strasbourg, Calvin found a German-speaking congregation

---

2. Bruno Bürki, "Gottesdienst im Reformierten Kontext," in *Handbuch der Liturgik. Liturgiewissenschaft in Theologie und Praxis der Kirche,* ed. Hans Christoph Schmidt-Lauber and Karl Heinz Bieritz (Göttingen: Vandenhoeck & Ruprecht, 1995), p. 161.

3. Wim Kloppenburg, "Het kerklied," in *De weg van de liturgie. Traditties, achtergronden, praktijk,* ed. M. Barnard and F. G. Immink (Zoetermeer: Meinema, 2008), p. 266.

4. Christoph Albrecht, *Einführung in die Liturgik* (Göttingen: Vandenhoeck & Ruprecht, 1989), p. 27.

5. Kloppenburg, "Het kerklied," p. 268.

6. John D. Witvliet, *Worship Seeking Understanding: Windows into Christian Practice* (Grand Rapids: Baker Academic, 2003). Witvliet notes, "In the Reformation era, the entire congregation sang — men, women, and children together — an innovation in an era in which women's voices could otherwise be heard in worship only in a convent" (p. 211).

that already used a repertoire of psalms and spiritual hymns. Many of these hymns originated in Wittenberg. Some letters with comments from visitors have been preserved; one of them states,

> The sermon is accompanied by hymns that have been translated from the Hebrew Psalter into the vernacular. The female voices mix in a wonderfully beautiful way with those of the men. It is a joy to listen to this. After the meal, four hours later, there is another service in the same church building. Once again, the hymns before and after the sermon are not absent. It is as if, through these hymns, they ask for the grace that enables them to receive the seed of the gospel, and, having received it, to express their gratitude for it.[7]

Praise and prayer have received an independent place in the Protestant worship service, not as the contribution of clergy and choirs, but of the congregation. Luther expressed this in a concise manner when he spoke at the opening of the Schlosskirche (Castle Church) in Torgau: "The only thing that needs to happen in this new church is that the sweet Lord himself speaks to us through his Holy Word, and that we respond by speaking to Him through prayer and praise."[8]

But, in the course of the twentieth century, this communal aspect of church worship also received much more emphasis in the Roman Catholic Church. After Vatican II, we noticed much stronger attention paid to the congregation as "the people of God." As a result, the active participation of the congregation was strongly developed through communal singing. According to the *Constitution of the Sacred Litury* of the Second Vatican Council, "In the liturgy God speaks to his people; Christ proclaims His gospel. The people respond to God with hymns and prayers."[9]

Liturgical Styles

For centuries, the congregational singing in the Protestant worship service was accompanied by organ music. The organ became a standard accessory

---

7. T. Brienen, *De liturgie bij Johannes Calvijn* (Kampen: De Groot, 1987), pp. 60, 61.

8. Martin Luther, Weimarer Ausgabe (W.A.), 49, 544.

9. "In liturgia enim Deus ad populum suum loquitur; Christus adhuc evangelium annuntiat. Populus vero Deo respondet tum cantibus tum oratione." *Vaticanum ii, Constitutio de Sacra Liturgia Sacrosanctum Consilium,* 33 (Rome, 1963).

in a church building; sometimes there would also be a piano or a grand piano. The organ has greatly contributed to the development of the ecclesial hymnody and musical culture and has thereby also exerted an influence on the style of the worship service. Since the emergence of the evangelical movement within the traditional denominations, however, organ and piano are no longer the standard instruments for musical accompaniment. An explanatory remark in the Dutch Evangelical Hymnal suggests that optimal justice is done to the "evangelical hymns if other instruments are used in the accompaniment" besides the organ.[10] Robert Webber points out how, in addition to the liturgical renewal that was stimulated in an ecumenical context, a new evangelical-liturgical renewal emerged, giving rise to a new musical genre: "These churches introduced new instruments, such as the guitar, drums, and synthesizers, and new forms of communication, such as drama and congregational dance. Congregations became more involved in worship through uplifted hands, prayer circles, and times of testimony."[11] This new approach to singing and hymnody has also been widely accepted in traditional Protestant churches. While the ecumenical liturgical renewal placed major emphasis on the poetic quality of the church hymn, the more recent evangelical renewal is characterized by the use of more common language and is rather uncomplicated and one-dimensional. Debra Rienstra and Ron Rienstra refer to this type of language in the worship service as "Chatter and Patter."[12]

Communal singing in its various forms demonstrates how the worship service, as a performance of the congregation, is a human activity. It demands discipline and human creativity. Skill and creativity are required with regard to language and poetry, to musicality and ability in accompaniment. Aristotle already pointed out that human artistic activity requires both *pathos* and *poiesis*. This human activity also implies a technical dimension, which may be learned.[13] (This is true not only with regard to church hymns, but also, for example, with regard to the writing and the delivery of a sermon.)

Hymns and music may touch us very directly. Among the arts, music in particular has the ability to touch us emotionally, and to almost automat-

---

10. *Evangelische liedbundel* (Zoetermeer: Boekencentrum, 1999), p. 706.
11. Robert Webber, *Planning Blended Worship: The Creative Mixture of Old and New* (Nashville: Abingdon Press, 1998), pp. 15-16.
12. Debra Rienstra and Ron Rienstra, *Worship Words: Discipling Language for Faithful Ministry* (Grand Rapids: Baker Academic, 2009), pp. 61-74.
13. Manfred Josuttis, *Religion als Handwerk. Zur Handlungslogik Spiritueller Methoden* (Gütersloh: Kaiser Verlag, 2002).

ically evoke desire and ecstasy. This also happens during congregational singing, and precisely there the combination of singing, text, and music makes the difference. In its singing the congregation expresses its various emotional states: joy for Christ's atonement for human sin and his victory over death, but also despondency and regret as it observes the needs of the world and realizes its guilt. The New Testament already indicates that the church is a singing church, as we read in Colossians 3:16:

> Let the word of Christ dwell in you richly, teach and admonish one another in all wisdom, and sing psalms and hymns and spiritual songs with thankfulness in your hearts to God.

Protestant churches have considerable variety in liturgical styles. Those denominations that stand in the tradition of the liturgical movement emphasize liturgical order and look for high quality in the poetic content of their hymns. In the second half of the twentieth century, the Netherlands saw a renewed interest in church hymnody. This renewed appreciation for the church hymn combined with an intense theological interest. In the selection of the hymns, the "treasure of the ages" was highly valued. The Protestant ecumenical hymnal that was published in 1973 may serve as a good example of this trend. However, this interest in the linkage between church hymns, poetry, singing, and music dates from the nineteenth century. Around that time there was an increasing realization that the actual state of congregational singing was not in step with the ideals that were being espoused. The literature of the period repeatedly refers to "extremely confused and terrible screaming" and to the singing of incomprehensible texts.[14]

In some worship services, praise hymns have become very popular, especially at the beginning of the service. In some cases the minister speaks a few connecting words between the hymns, but it may also happen that hymns in different styles and content are sung without any common theme. We see this most often in "free" churches with an independent character. A worship leader may tie together the various hymns with a few words or a prayer. This constitutes a more or less separate unit in the worship service. In general, in this environment the worship service has a more spontaneous style, and the hymns serve first of all to express the faith experiences of the people. Marcel Barnard points out that in this type of worship, emotion and

---

14. J. H. Gunning, *De gezangenkwestie in de Nederlandse Hervormde Kerk* (Utrecht: Oosthoek, 1910), p. 15.

enthusiasm, as well as community and participation, are quite prominent.[15] The text of the hymns is popular and easy to understand. Often a projection screen is used to enable the people to read the text, and in the accompaniment the organ tends to be replaced by a band with a drummer.

Other worship services follow a classical Reformed pattern. Usually the psalms play a dominant role, and the congregation has an active role only in the congregational singing. But we notice that elements from the evangelical tradition are increasingly absorbed into the liturgy. A more popular collection of revivalist hymns is often preferred over the standard ecumenical hymnal. Robert Webber points out how the term "blended worship" has become common in the United States. This means that liturgies from various traditional currents are "blended" together. In the Netherlands this occurs frequently in Reformed evangelical circles. Their blended worship offers a Reformed structure with praise-and-worship elements.

This short exploration of congregational singing indicates that the worship service is a multifaceted, multicolored event. Even though the service may be defined as a communal performance, it also offers worshippers the opportunity to express very personal experiences and emotions. Apparently, the communal and the existential aspects tend to go hand in hand. The congregational singing already shows us something of the many aspects of the worship service as a religious praxis:

- A worship service allows us to express both joy and sorrow. Singing and music play an important role in this respect. Congregational singing channels human emotions and experiences and expresses these in a well-ordered manner. In this way the worshippers become personally involved, and they can express their life and faith experiences.
- Even though congregational singing is a collective expression, it can be very personal and subjective. Worshippers may, for instance, place themselves in the "I" position when they sing a psalm:

    I praise You, Lord, with all my heart and soul.
    With reverence I kneel before You. (Ps. 138)

    The "I" of the original poet was already made into a "representative I" by inclusion in the Psalter. When the congregation sings, they are asked to identify with this "I." Thus, in the course of the liturgy, worship-

---

15. Marcel Barnard, "Late Modern Rhythm and the Renewal of Worship," in *At the Crossroads of Art and Religion*, ed. Hetty Zock (Leuven: Peeters, 2008), pp. 173-87.

Worship as Religious Praxis

pers are invited to play various roles and to occupy various positions, enabling them to give personal meaning to the prescribed texts.
- Congregational singing also indicates that worshippers follow a *script*. There are prescribed texts and melodies; the songs are not invented on the spot. Therefore, congregational singing may best be described as a *performance based on a script*.
- Congregational singing acquires a certain *form*. As a communal *performance*, congregational singing demands an artistic style. The execution is a complex interplay of sound and tone, poetic texts and spiritual life.

Worship as Communal and Personal

Participants in a worship service join a social community, so they must relate to each other. Because of its stress on personal faith, subjectivity tended to have the upper hand in the Protestant tradition. However, the movement for liturgical renewal in the nineteenth and twentieth centuries took issue with this far-reaching individualization of the faith and the subjectivizing of the liturgy. It advocated the rightful place of institutional forms and the value of collective action. In the Dutch tradition we find these themes in the writings of G. van der Leeuw as well as those of Abraham Kuyper. The Roman Catholic philosopher and theologian Romano Guardini explores how individual worshippers must yield to the community:

> Of particular importance for the liturgical act is the active and full participation of the congregation as a body. The act is performed by every person, not as an isolated individual, but as a member of a body in which the Church is present. It is this body which is the "we" of the prayers.... In the liturgical act the celebrating individual becomes part of this body and incorporates the circumstances in his self-expression. This is not simple, if it is to be genuine and honest. Much that divides us must be overcome: dislikes, indifference towards the many who are of "no concern to me," but who are really members of the same body.[16]

In their expressions, worshippers must consider the community. The "I" of the liturgy is not an isolated individuality, but an "I" that is embedded

---

16. Romano Guardini, "An Open Letter," in *Foundations in Ritual Studies: A Reader for Students of Christian Worship*, ed. Paul Bradshaw and John Mellow (Grand Rapids: Baker Academic, 2007), pp. 6-7.

in contact with others, an "I" that is constituent of the community. This is manifested in our congregational singing. The individual voice becomes part of the choir of the congregation. Prescribed texts may touch the worshipper very personally, but they may also cause him to change his mind, or to focus on other people (or other situations).

By adapting to this community, worshippers receive many things, but at a cost. They must learn how to be part of a group of people they did not select themselves. It may even be that they (sometimes secretly) strongly dislike some of these people. They must overcome their disinterest and dislike. They cannot simply ignore or reject their fellow worshippers. This social dimension is most explicitly tested when celebrating communion. Celebrating the Lord's Supper together does not allow for disagreements, quarrels, or conflict: "For as out of many grains one meal is ground, and one bread baked, ... so shall we all, who by a true faith are grafted into Christ, be altogether one body, through brotherly love, for Christ's sake, our beloved Savior, who hath so exceedingly loved us, and not only showed this in word, but also in very deed towards one another."[17]

Today, even more than in the past two centuries, extreme individualization presents a challenge in the shaping of the worship service. More than in the past, this individualization implies that the focus is on the individual person, and no longer on the family or the social unit to which one belongs. We feel a much greater freedom with regard to collective standards than did worshippers in times past. Also, church members are part of a society that has become extremely diverse — socially, culturally, and religiously. They belong to all kinds of different networks. Henk de Roest points to a change in patterns of belonging: "Whereas older people felt connected to a party, a newspaper, a company, a particular brand or a church, younger people connect in other ways and manifest loyalties that have a much more flexible character."[18] In addition, the options in church life and church attendance have multiplied. It is significant to note how people "hop" from church to church. They feel attached to the larger church and to their faith, but they search for a congregation that they feel comfortable with.

Local congregations have often become more diverse and more complex. This tends to produce tensions with regard to liturgical styles and provokes

---

17. See the following Web site: http://www.reformedalberta.ca/Doctrine/Sections/Confessions/Minor_Confessions/Lord's_Supper.htm.

18. Henk de Roest, *Een huis voor de ziel. Gedachten over de kerk van binnen en buiten* (Zoetermeer: Boekencentrum, 2010), p. 154.

Worship as Religious Praxis

questions. How can we act in unison when we differ in so many ways from each other? From what hymnal shall we sing? What instruments shall we use? What kind of language shall we choose for the liturgical *performance*, for our prayers, and in the sermon? Who may feel excluded? As a community, what approach to our faith do we adopt?

Congregational cultures have also become more dynamic. The diversity leads to discussions between particular interest groups, and these discussions provoke change. Some will leave, others will join, and thus the congregational culture shifts. As a result, congregations may find it difficult to manifest a clear and recognizable identity. Confronted with so many opinions, ministers may face more situations of conflict. But a preacher who wants to please everyone might do better to keep silent.[19]

Thus the worship service as a communal act of the congregation faces its challenges. In the past, how was the communal character of the assembly of the local church theologically anchored? I offer three types of argumentation. In the Roman Catholic tradition, the church comes first, as Romano Guardini attests:

> Nor does the onus of liturgical action and prayer rest with the individual. It does not even rest with the collective groups, composed of numerous individuals. . . . The liturgical entity consists rather of the united body of the faithful as such — the Church — a body that infinitely outnumbers the mere congregation. The liturgy is the Church's public and lawful act of worship, and it is performed and conducted by the officials whom the Church herself has designated for the post — her priests. . . . It is important that this objective nature of the liturgy should be fully understood. Here the Catholic conception of worship in common sharply differs from the Protestant, which is predominantly individualistic.[20]

G. van der Leeuw emphasizes the role of the ordained leaders of the church in the worship of the church: "The liturgy is the formally established manner in which God and the church interact."[21] This interaction between God and the church receives a special form that is not left to human arbitrariness. That we may interact with God, and that this interaction receives

---

19. Joseph R. Jeter, "Preaching in a Diverse World," in *The New Interpreter's Handbook of Preaching*, Paul Scott Wilson, general editor (Nashville: Abingdon Press, 2008), p. 291.
20. Romano Guardini, *The Spirit of the Liturgy* (New York: Crossroad Publishing, 1998).
21. G. van der Leeuw, *Liturgiek* (Nijkerk: Callenbach, 1946), p. 14.

a specific form, flows from this central salvific fact.[22] Van der Leeuw thus points to a primary theological basis for the form of the worship service. A church without ordained leaders is no more than a religious association. The agenda of the ecclesial worship depends on the unique character of the mystery of faith, and the ordained leaders ensure that this mystery is protected as the church worships. Therefore, the communal aspect does not primarily reside in the harmony within the congregation, but in the mystery of Christ: "The worship service is a dialogue — not between God and man in a general sense, nor between God and an individual person, but between God and the human community, i.e., the community of the Church, the body of Christ."[23]

Van der Leeuw does not deny the importance of the interaction between God and the individual, but what is at stake in the worship service is the community of the elect, the *ecclesia*, which finds its reason for existence in Christ, and which is the body of Christ. J. H. Gerretsen formulates it as follows: "The leader in the liturgy must realize that he is the voice of the church and must act accordingly. He must renounce himself and not demand attention for himself. The liturgy resembles a garment that the Church has put on him, under which the person temporarily disappears."[24]

Abraham Kuyper stresses a somewhat different aspect. He approaches the worship service from the angle of the concept of a *gathering*. "Our normal worship services," he says, "are nothing more than *public gatherings known by the corporate body as the congregation*." It is important that the members of that corporation be present; they come in order to act — that is, they come to execute the worship to which they have been called. Referring to memberships in various kinds of associations and clubs, he says, "There is something precious in all this coming together, because it more or less counters individualism, and thereby egotism, and instead encourages expression of the social and sociable among us."[25]

The Agenda and Script of Worship

When attending church on Sunday, we enter into a certain *order of worship*. We might define this order with the term "agenda," in the sense of a script

---

22. Van der Leeuw, *Liturgiek*, p. 16.
23. Van der Leeuw, *Liturgiek*, p. 53.
24. J. H. Gerretsen, *Liturgie* (Nijmegen: Ten Hoet, 1912), p. 20.
25. Abraham Kuyper, *Our Worship*, ed. Harry Boonstra (Grand Rapids: Wm. B. Eerdmans, 2009), p. 9.

in which the acts and formulas which are used in worship are stipulated. In the German language we find the word *Agende*. The worshippers assemble to perform certain communal acts, according to a particular *script*. This means that certain elements have been pre-defined. Certain texts that provide order and structure are available before the service begins. The church's worship is characterized by the fact that some established formulas and texts occur in every service. Thus, there is a *scenario*.

In the liturgy we distinguish between the *ordinarium* and the *proprium*. The term *ordinarium* refers to the prescribed elements of the liturgy. This may apply to texts that are spoken or sung. They have their particular place in the liturgy. Protestant worship will usually begin with a votum and salutation, and will end with the blessing. These are prescribed formulas. For a long time the reading of the Ten Commandments was also a regular part of the *ordinarium*. In Protestant ecumenical worship services, the opening prayer, Kyrie, and Gloria belong to the prescribed pattern in the first part of the service. The Kryrie follows an established formula:

Lord, have mercy.
Christ, have mercy.
Lord, have mercy.

The particular prayer intentions may vary from Sunday to Sunday. In a Protestant ecumenical communion service, the Sanctus and the Agnus Dei also belong to the *ordinarium*. In the classical Reformed communion service, most elements are prescribed in a specific form and thus are part of the *ordinarium* of the communion service.

The term *proprium* refers to the elements that change over time. They are a regular part of the worship service, but their specific wording may vary from Sunday to Sunday. The introit psalm, for instance, always precedes the votum and the salutation, but the actual psalm may vary. This is also true of the Scripture readings, or lessons, which have a set place in the service, but the reading varies, and may, or may not, follow a reading schedule.

So, a worship service follows an established order of service (an agenda), with regular texts that are repeated each Sunday. But even those worship elements that are variable are not just arbitrarily chosen, but fit into a well-established pattern. Several prayers, for instance, have a fixed place in the order of service, while their content varies according to the occasion. The sermon, in particular, is an address that is not prescribed, yet it follows certain rules. First, a Scripture reading precedes the sermon, and the texts that are read play a role in the sermon. In addition, there is the Christian Year, which to some extent, at least, directs the sermon. And, of course, the minister prepares his sermon and usually follows a script when he delivers it.

We may, therefore, conclude that a worship service is executed according to an agenda and follows a script. This textual form does not imply that the worship service cannot be an interaction between human beings, but it channels the participation of the worshippers. Agenda and script come alive in the performance, and both the minister and the congregation find support in this prescribed pattern. The reciprocity between the minister and the congregation is not characterized by arbitrariness, but is shaped by agenda and script. Even though the worship service will not always have a responsive form, there always is an interaction between minister and congregation.

In the Protestant service, the sermon is an intrinsic part of the liturgy. The sermon is not just a spiritual address that could also be delivered without a liturgical context. The fact that the sermon is embedded in a liturgical framework allows it to function in a unique way. Accordingly, in recent homiletics the sermon is rightly defined as *Ereignis,* as an *event in time.* Martin Nicol comments, "The preaching process culminates in the spoken and heard experience of the sermon (Performance)"; he refers to the sermon as a dramatic event.[26] The use of the word "drama" in liturgical discussions has elicited much criticism among Protestants, because they do not believe that the worship service is a dramatic repetition or re-presentation of the Christ event. However, this is not what Nicol intends to say. In using the term "dramatic event," Nicol wants to underline that the sermon, as a linguistic act, has an actualizing effect. In its *performance,* something happens. The word "performance" reminds us of the theater. Indeed, Jana Childers defines preaching as a *performing art.*[27]

According to David Plüss, the Reformers were convinced that the biblical texts should function not only in the sermon, but also in the liturgy. In Reformed worship, he says, scriptural texts function as *Skripte der Inszenierung* — "scripts for staging."[28] The Scriptures are able to touch people, even change them. This applies in particular to the hymns and the prayers that we find in the Bible:

26. Martin Nicol, *Einander ins Bild Setzen. Dramaturgische Homiletik* (Göttingen: Vandenhoeck & Ruprecht, 2002), p. 114.

27. Jana Childers, *Performing the Word: Preaching as Theater* (Nashville: Abingdon Press, 1999).

28. David Plüss, *Gottesdienst als Textinszenierung. Perspektiven einer Performativen Ästhetik des Gottesdienstes* (Zurich: Theologischer Verlag, 2007), p. 227.

Worship as Religious Praxis

In these prayers and hymns the texts are staged in an extremely effective way. The praying person and the singer become part of a dramatic scene, through their performance of the prayer or their song, from which they cannot easily withdraw. They become part and parcel of the scene, and they seem, without noticeable spiritual effort, to identify pre-reflectively with the "I" and the "we" of the prayer. They sing, as if they are singing the hymn spontaneously for the first time, and thereby they establish in a dramatic manner contact with God. As they sing and pray, they allow themselves to be addressed by God and to respond to Him.[29]

The composition of the classical form for the Lord's Supper demonstrates how powerful these dramatized texts may become. In Chapter 7 we will see why the Reformers, with their criticism of the manner in which the mass was celebrated in their day, had to initiate a totally new approach to the celebration of the Lord's Supper. They eliminated the prayer from the *Canon Missae* (which contained a lot of sacrificial terminology). Where did they find a new approach? We notice how they focus on the Scriptures. Thus the classical "Form for the Administration of the Lord's Supper" begins with a powerful quotation from Paul's letter to the Corinthians:

Beloved in the Lord Jesus Christ, attend to the words of the institution of the Holy Supper of our Lord Jesus Christ, as they are delivered by the holy apostle Paul. 1 Cor. 11:23-30: "For I have received of the Lord, that which also I delivered unto you, that the Lord Jesus, the same night in which he was betrayed, took bread; and when he had given thanks, he brake it and said, Take, eat; this is my body which is broken for you, this do in remembrance of me."[30]

The liturgical acts are preceded by an extensive instruction, which is introduced with this quotation from the Bible. The participants hear these Bible texts with some explanation, which enables them to implement these texts when they celebrate the sacred rite together. The didactic aspect is not a catechetical part that found its way into this document by chance; it belongs to this view of what liturgy is. The sole intention is to ensure that the wor-

---

29. Plüss, *Gottesdienst als Textinszenierung*, p. 228.
30. "Form for the Administration of the Lord's Supper," in *The Psalter: With Doctrinal Standards, Liturgy, Church Order, and Added Chorale Section*, rev. ed. (Grand Rapids: Wm. B. Eerdmans, 1947/1984), p. 60.

shippers may participate in a correct way in the celebration as a *symbolic* act. In this act the event takes place. Consequently, the *participants* in the Lord's Supper play an essential role in this sacred act. The Reformed liturgy for the Lord's Supper may well be described as an act that follows a script. This is also evident in the words that are spoken as the bread is broken at the table where the worshippers have been seated as guests for a meal:

> The bread which we break is the communion of the body of Christ. Take, eat, remember, and believe that the body of our Lord Jesus Christ was given for the complete forgiveness of all our sins.[31]

It should be noted that in the Reformed tradition the emphasis is not on the elements (bread and wine), but on the participation in faith. For that reason the distribution of the bread is not accompanied with words like "the body of Christ."

In the Protestant ecumenical version of the Lord's Supper, the Table Prayer functions as script. But here also, quotations from the Bible and from the church's tradition play a crucial role. The main prayer of thanksgiving *(prefatio)* is concluded with the biblical words from the Sanctus and the Benedictus:

> Holy, holy, holy Lord,
> God of power and might,
> Heaven and earth are full of your glory.
> Hosanna in the highest.
> Blessed is he who comes in the name of the Lord.
> Hosanna in the highest.

After prayerfully citing the words that were used at the Last Supper, the congregation responds:

> We remember his death,
> And proclaim his resurrection.
> We await his coming in glory.
> Maranatha.[32]

---

31. See http://www.crcna.org/resources/church-resources/liturgical-forms-resources/lords-supper/form-celebration-lords-supper-ii.

32. *Dienstboek een proeve: Schrift, maaltijd, gebed* (Zoetermeer: Boekencentrum, 1998), pp. 211-12.

Worship as Religious Praxis

Baptism likewise is an act that follows a script. In the baptismal act the command of Jesus is implemented: "Go therefore and make disciples of all nations, baptizing them in the name of the Father and of the Son and of the Holy Spirit" (Matt. 28:19). Within the framework of instruction, prayer, and confession of faith, the actual baptismal act is performed (by immersion or sprinkling) while these words are spoken:

I baptize you in the name of the Father,
and of the Son,
and of the Holy Spirit. Amen.[33]

In this act of baptism, the acts being performed and the script are intimately connected.

It may happen that, in some circles, such a heavy emphasis is placed on the instructional aspect (the didactic part of the form) that the actual liturgical event is diminished in significance. However, the instruction is intended to highlight the meaning and value of the liturgical act. To avoid getting into a mere teaching mode and a desacralizing of the sacrament, it is important to affirm the value of the prayers that are part of the baptismal liturgy: ". . . we beseech Thee, that Thou wilt be pleased of thine infinite mercy, graciously to look upon these children, and incorporate them by the Holy Spirit into Thy Son Jesus Christ, that they may be buried with him into his death, and be raised with him in newness of life. . . ."[34] This gives rise to the question of what actually happens in the baptismal act. We will return to that question in Chapters 4 and 7.

In the world of the theater and the stage, the performance is all-important. That is the moment when things happen and the audience gets involved. Something similar occurs in a worship service. Even though we cannot put a theater performance on a par with a worship service, they are similar, because in that service, things also happen in the performance. In fact, even more happens in the worship service, because the worshipper is already acquainted with the script. In addition, here we see precisely the difference with the theater. The worshipper is herself the actor and not merely a spectator. That applies to all parts of the worship service. This role of participant is not apparent only in the congregational singing and in the responses. We also see it in the sermon,

---

33. http://www.crcna.org/resources/church-resources/liturgical-forms-resources/baptism-children/service-baptism-2013.
34. "Form for the Administration of Baptism," *The Psalter*, p. 56.

in the Lord's Supper, and even in baptism. The godparents (at the baptism of a child) and the baptismal candidate (at a faith baptism) confess their faith in communion with the congregation. In the baptismal service the minister says to the congregation, ". . . all you, who have gathered together here around this baptismal font to witness the baptism of [name] and to be reminded of your own baptism, raise your voice and answer me. . . ." The faith in the Father, the Son, and the Holy Ghost is confessed in communion with others. We certainly have reason to say that the worship service is a performance in the sense that the communication and interaction that take place are far more than an exchange of thoughts and opinions. It is a drama of interaction in which the worshippers become emotionally involved.[35]

The Role of Salutations

The worshipper in a Protestant service does not enter a sacred space. If there is no spatial demarcation, no threshold between the profane and the sacred, can we nonetheless point to a moment when the service begins? Is that when a prosaic word of welcome is spoken? Or when the introit hymn is sung? Is there a word or an act that marks the formal beginning of the worship service?

Usually at the very beginning the votum is pronounced:

Our help is in the name of the LORD, who made heaven and earth,
Who remains faithful forever
and doesn't forsake the works of his hands.

This declaration may be understood as a dedication. It expresses our trust in divine help. The opening line is from Psalm 124:8. Often, as in the dedication above, a few words are added from Psalm 146:6 ("Who keeps faith . . .") and from Psalm 138:8 ("And doesn't forsake . . .").

Abraham Kuyper, who quotes the phrasing above, suggests that the votum functions like the blow of a hammer: "The votum, as an opening statement, turns a casual get-together of individuals into a united assembly and is intended to confirm 'the presence of God' in the midst of his people."[36]

---

35. Richard F. Ward, *Speaking of the Holy: The Art of Communication in Preaching* (St. Louis: Chalice Press, 2001), p. 23.
36. Kuyper, *Our Worship*, p. 110.

Three aspects stand out. In accordance with the fashionable individualism of the nineteenth century, Kuyper states that separate individuals come together, but that they gather as a community, and that the worship service is characterized by the divine presence.

What happens when the votum is spoken? Is it a sacramental formula or a prayer? Or is a certain consciousness addressed? Kuyper maintains that the votum marks the moment that the worshipper becomes aware of God's presence in the "assembly."[37] It is the moment when the thoughts of the worshippers are joined together and directed towards the Eternal One.

However, one may also describe the votum as a confession and a prayer. Marten Micron begins the service with this: "As you, Christian brethren, have gathered to learn from God's Word about the salvation of your souls, so let us before anything else call upon the Lord for his divine grace."[38]

The orders of service of the Reformation era did not all start in this way. In Strasbourg, a Trinitarian votum was used: "In the name of the Father, and of the Son, and of the Holy Ghost." But Calvin begins his service with "Our help . . ." and regards this as a prayer. In the Netherlands, the provincial Synod of Dordrecht (1574) extended the original short version of "Our help" with the words of Psalms 146 and 138. Going back further in history, we learn that the votum first appeared in the service around the year 1000, but it was a silent prayer by the priest.

Ever since the early church period, the salutation of the congregation has played an important role in the worship service. The leader says, "The Lord be with you [*Dominus vobiscum*]." The congregation responds, "And with your spirit" (or "The Lord be with you also"; *et cum spiritu tuo*). We encounter this mutual salutation already with Chrysostom.[39] The bishop had the authority to say *Pax vobiscum*. We know that the church father Augustine also used this form of greeting before he offered prayer and prior to the celebration of the Lord's Supper. This custom was maintained in the liturgy of the Middle Ages. Each time that something important was about to happen during the service, the priest offered a salutation. The wording is derived from Ruth 2:4, where Boaz meets the reapers with the words "The LORD

---

37. Kuyper, *Our Worship*, p. 112.

38. Marten Micron, *De Christlicke Ordinancien der Nederlantscher Ghemeinten te Londen (1554)*, republished and newly introduced by Dr. W. F. Dankbaar (The Hague: M. Nijhof, 1956), p. 58; A. F. N. Lekkerkerker, *Kanttekeningen bij het Hervormde Dienstboek*, 1 (The Hague: Boekencentrum, 1952), p. 48.

39. *Leiturgia*, vol. 2, ed. Karl Ferdinand Müller and Walter Blankenburg (Kassel: Stauda, 1955), p. 575.

be with you," with the reapers reciprocating. In the early years of the Reformation, this responsive greeting was still in use. (Calvin also introduced the prayers initially with "The Lord be with you.") Gradually, however, this form of salutation disappeared.[40] Meanwhile, the salutation from the letters of Paul became more and more commonly used after the votum:

Votum: Our help . . .

Salutation: Grace to you and peace from God our Father and the Lord Jesus Christ. (Rom. 1:7; 1 Cor. 1:3; 2 Cor. 1:2; Gal. 1:3)

Sometimes the salutation drew on other biblical passages:

The grace of the Lord Jesus Christ and the love of God and the fellowship of the Holy Spirit be with you all. (2 Cor. 13:14)

Grace to you and peace from him who is and who was and who is to come, and from the seven spirits who are before his throne, and from Jesus Christ the faithful witness, the first-born of the dead, and the ruler of kings on earth. (Rev. 1:4-5)

But is the use of both the votum and the salutation not an unnecessary duplication? Simply put, the answer is no. The votum is a confessional formula in the form of a prayer: the church gathers expecting the presence of God. The salutation has another focus: the congregation is addressed on the basis of the communion with Jesus Christ. When the salutation is pronounced, usually a hand is lifted, while the votum is spoken and received with closed eyes.

Other early Christian liturgies begin the service with the singing of a hymn (the *introitus*). This tradition probably dates from the days of Pope Gregory I (590-604). With a long entourage of clergy, the pope strides to the altar while the introit hymn is sung.

The Freedom of the Minister

A number of liturgical books were published in the early stages of the Reformation to describe the order of worship. These contain the prayers to be

---

40. *Leiturgia*, vol. 2, p. 577.

said not only during the administering of the sacraments, but also before and after the sermon. These are usually referred to as the formulary prayers. But by the eighteenth and nineteenth centuries, they were hardly used any longer. When, in 1817, the Dutch Reformed Church published its "Regulations for Public Worship" ("Verordeningen Omtrent den Openbaren Eredienst"), the question was raised whether it might not be time to draft new liturgical documents. The reasoning behind the question was clearly stated:

> These liturgical documents were created for the benefit of those ministers who were still inexperienced in all aspects of their sacred ministry, and therefore needed certain instructions in order to become accustomed to an appropriate and uniform order. This need no longer exists.[41]

Apparently, these liturgical forms had become obsolete, and it was felt that the church could do well without them. Various factors played a role. The resistance against the old was due not only to a liberal theology, which found it difficult to relate to old theological ideas, but also to an increasing individualization, in liberal as well as in Pietistic circles. Within these circles there was much opposition to the enforcement of such prescribed documents. Later, however, the movements for liturgical renewal would criticize this individualism in the worship service and would plead for ecclesial objectivity and a clearly defined liturgical format. J. H. Gunning offered this comment:

> Faced with the *individualism* that always wants to make the worship service "free," which means the minister can do as he wishes — whether, like the rationalists, people break with "all those old forms," and leave everything to the "unrestrained piety," or that, like some English Presbyterians, they expect everything from the inspiration of the Holy Spirit, while rejecting all established forms, such as even the Decalogue, Our Father, and the Apostolicum; faced with the formalism into which Roman Catholicism degenerates, without leaving hardly any personal freedom for those who lead out — the minister in the Reformed Church must ever be reminded that our worship knows of a free as well as of a prescribed element.[42]

---

41. J. H. Gunning, *Onze eredienst. Opmerkingen over het liturgisch element in den gereformeerden cultus* (Groningen: Wolters, 1890), p. 24.
42. Gunning, *Onze eredienst*, p. 29.

The Protestant worship service is characterized by this tension between the free and the prescribed elements. The strong emphasis on the influence of the Holy Spirit ensures that human responsibility and freedom receive adequate room. It is not by accident that the Protestant Reformed tradition has not been able to enforce a uniform liturgical tradition. The *Dienstboek* (Service Book) that was published in 1955 never went beyond a preliminary status.[43] The new Service Book, released by the Dutch Reformed Church, the Christian Reformed Churches, and the Lutheran Church in 1998, mainly follows a Protestant ecumenical agenda, while also giving room to the more classical Reformed order of service. But even this publication was not considered final.[44] The view of G. van der Leeuw, who regarded the liturgy as the "formally established pattern of the interaction between God and the Church," has been realized only in part.[45] Local congregations have a large degree of freedom in how they organize their worship.

How can the communal element best be expressed? How can the minister indicate that worship concerns a *communal intention* and act? Will prescribed forms be most appropriate, or might the subjective expression of the minister provide the bridge whereby the participants can themselves become involved? One of the rules of classical rhetoric maintains that the pathos of the speaker is an important communication tool. Accordingly, some ministers do not utilize traditional texts in their prayers; they prefer to speak spontaneously. The question is this: How might the interpersonal contact and the communal spirit best be realized? What will touch worshippers at the deepest level — free expression or pre-established formulas?

In the nineteenth century in particular, the emerging subjectivism and the individual freedom it engendered played an important role in the order of the worship service. E. F. Kruijf, a professor at the University of Groningen, made this assertion in 1901: "To the extent that the instructions of the apostles are not general, but specific, they apply to local situations and are therefore not binding for us."[46] For Kruijf this means that every part of the Christian church has a degree of freedom and does not have to follow tradition. In determining the format of our worship, we may therefore consider needs and circumstances. Kruijf strongly favors maintaining this freedom

---

43. *Dienstboek voor de Nederlandse Hervormde Kerk in ontwerp* (The Hague: Boekencentrum, 1955).

44. *Dienstboek een proeve.*

45. Van der Leeuw, *Liturgiek*, p. 14.

46. E. F. Kruijf, *Liturgiek* (Groningen: Wolters, 1901), p. 58.

in the way we organize our worship. He feels it is an important Protestant principle.⁴⁷

Around this same time, Abraham Kuyper warns against the danger of too much freedom. The spontaneous prayer, he says, will easily tempt the minister to deliver a short sermon in the form of a prayer. The liturgical prayer may, however, guide him back to the right standard of prayer.

> Such a liturgical prayer is therefore not composed in just a few moments. In fact, it should come to us from the past and from the bosom of the church. The forms and expressions that through the centuries have given voice to the deepest and holiest promptings of the heart must be passed on from generation to generation and speak to the soul. Tone, language, and content should rise above any sponaneous prayer, and immerse us in the deep stream of the communion of saints.⁴⁸

Kuyper also recognizes the tension in the Reformed tradition between what he refers to as spirit and form. He anchors the prescribed form in the church as assembly; such a prayer is a corporate prescribed prayer, on which the ecclesial authorities have agreed. The Psalter also contains many hymns which are, in fact, prayers. "They are and always will be prayers that we have in printed form, and that have been composed *beforehand by someone else.*"⁴⁹

In worship services the ordained leaders have a prominent role. Typically, in Protestant Reformed worship the consistory (or some of its members) enters the church hall at the beginning of the service. The elder shakes the hand of the minister. Prior to this there was a meeting in the consistory room, during which the officiating elder offered a short prayer. At least three church offices are represented in the worship service: elder, deacon, and minister. They represent the congregation, and the handshake that the elder gives to the minister signifies that the minister will lead in worship. After the service, another handshake signifies a communal responsibility. In addition, there are other instances when members of the consistory have an active role. For example, during the service the deacons take up the collections that are destined for diaconal purposes. During the celebration of the Lord's Supper, each office has its own specific duty.

Besides these offices that require ordination, there are scores of other

---

47. Kruijf, *Liturgiek*, p. 57.
48. Kuyper, *Our Worship*, p. 36.
49. Kuyper, *Our Worship*, p. 33.

roles and assignments, varying from custodian to organist, from leaders in the children's department to sound technicians. But these roles and functions are of a different nature. Many of these assignments are pragmatic and technical, while some are linked to the unique nature of the assembly. The latter is true of the ordained leaders, who have a *representative* function.

The minister has a prominent role in the service. The relationship between the minister's role and the role of congregational members is important. A minister has her own responsibility, but she must follow the agenda and the script. She will develop her own approach with regard to the *proprium* of the worship service. Nonetheless, even there she cannot ignore the expectations of the church members. In actual practice, a social relationship exists between the worshippers and the minister, and this relationship presupposes a particular behavior. The worshippers expect the minister to act in a certain way.

The worshippers may, for instance, expect the minister to implement the agenda and the script, and to take a pastoral approach when she addresses questions of faith and daily life. These expectations vis-à-vis the minister also pertain to, for instance, knowledge and understanding of the Bible and the faith tradition. Those who function as ministers may have their own perspective, but they will have to conform to these expectations to a significant degree.

The Performance of Worship

The Performative Process

The main theme of this chapter is that religious practices have a performative function. The question is this: What does that mean? The worship service is an act of the congregation, an act that puts something in motion in the lives of the worshippers. The worshippers are involved in the prayers that are said, in the sermon, and in the celebration of the Lord's Supper. During the service the human self — the sum total of all thinking and considering, of all inclinations, intentions, and feelings — becomes active. And precisely because various aspects of life and faith are addressed in the worship service, the worshippers themselves are actively involved with these. They concern not only their personal life but the entire context in which they live. The liturgical agenda provides the necessary structure, while the script is available to express the contradictory elements of life.

Worship as Religious Praxis

But there is more. It is in the very nature of the assembly that the worshippers will expect God's activity. May we therefore say that God also actively involves himself in this assembly? Or would this be too bold an assertion? Perhaps we may say that the worshippers experience the presence of divine love. Even though this results from the acts performed by the congregation, nonetheless the worshippers are on the receiving end. This receptive character is an intrinsic element of the worship service. Are the worshippers, however, justified in understanding this as being caused by the divine presence? Today, theologians tend to approach such questions with care. Nonetheless, Christian worship is based on the conviction that the cross and the resurrection have a powerful impact on the present. That is why the congregation continues to assemble on Sunday morning, the day of the resurrection. In the final analysis, the worship service is anchored in the faith that Christ himself, the living Lord, meets with the church.

Christians believe that there is a dual process at work in the worship service. The worshippers themselves are involved, existentially and personally. The human self is activated, and this includes the faith perceptions and life experiences of the worshippers. But more is at stake. Manfred Josuttis maintains that the participants also are touched by the energetic presence of the Spirit.[50] This occurs, for instance, in the singing of the hymns and the saying of the prayers. Ninian Smart speaks of a *re-enactment:*

> Why then do hymns and prayers so often continue to say things about God? Things, moreover, that are usually very well known to the hearers and presumably also to the Lord? The reason lies in the performative character of these descriptions; for their function is to praise and to celebrate. In telling God at Easter that He has raised His Son up from the dead, the worshipper is not reminding God or the congregation, but re-presenting the event. . . . If a hymn or liturgy re-enacts some primary sacred event, and does so in part by the use of words, the role of those words is to mimic the original.[51]

A decisive and salvific event from the past is brought to life in the performance. The worship service, however, is about more than the historic impact of an important past event. It is about the renewing reality, which is pre-

---

50. Manfred Josuttis, *Die Einführung in das Leben. Pastoraltheologie zwischen Phänomenologie und Spiritualität* (Gütersloh: Kaiser Verlag, 1996), pp. 85-101.
51. Ninian Smart, *The Concept of Worship* (London: Macmillan, 1972), p. 27.

sented in and through the performance. The various ecclesial traditions use different words for this phenomenon. But in whatever way the phenomenon is described, the worship service focuses on the connection with the decisive salvific revelation from the past and the active and impelling presence, which is expressed in the performance.

From this perspective the entire worship service is a performative act. All elements contribute to this active presentation of God's salvific action. This is true of both the liturgy and the sermon. Ritual actions do not have more performative "weight" than the sermon. At times this is suggested.[52] A distinction is sometimes made between a ritual and a language-based element of the service. As a result, the sermon may become no more than an explanation, or may receive the label of an instruction on a religious, ethical, or social theme. The sermon thereby loses the force that the Reformation attributed to it: the sermon is robbed of its performative religious power. In the Protestant worship service the sermon, in particular, has a performative character.

Today we pay much attention to the performative function of the spoken word — and rightly so. Here two perspectives converge. First, in the past decennia the philosophy of language has given ample attention to the use of language in the communication between human beings. The basic idea is that language is, in fact, an action. Seen from that angle, the sermon is an utterly dynamic event. Human eloquence and religious impact go hand in hand. The sermon is "language in action"; theology, art, and technique converge.[53] Second, in recent homiletics the role of language has been strengthened through the growing interest in performance studies. This has supported the idea that language not only describes or conveys information but also sets things in motion.[54] The use of language — and this is most certainly the case in the worship service — is much more than a mere linguistic event. It is a social interaction that involves a reciprocity between speaker and hearer. Richard Ward furthers the point: "Performative language is a phrase that arises out of a theory about how language functions in human communication, particularly when the speaker is in her role as pastor, preacher, or liturgist. Based in speech-act theory and performance studies, the theoretical framework that supports the term helps us to understand the power of words."[55]

---

52. Nicol, *Einander ins Bild Setzen*, p. 41.

53. Charles L. Bartow, *God's Human Speech: A Practical Theology of Proclamation* (Grand Rapids: Wm. B. Eerdmans, 1997), p. 3.

54. Richard F. Ward, "Performative Language," in *The New Interpreter's Handbook of Preaching*, ed. Wilson, pp. 234-38.

55. Ward, "Performative Language," p. 234.

Worship as Religious Praxis

Like rhetoric, performance often has a negative image. It is associated with the theater, with the staging of a show. It often carries the sense of something that is not real, not authentic. That, however, is a misunderstanding. For our voices, the acoustics, our posture, and many other factors are certainly important to the way we shape the liturgy. The physical movements of the minister and the congregation are part of the performance — for instance, the entering and the leaving, the sitting and the standing, the folding of the hands and the closing of the eyes. "Performative acts, as distinguished from more casual and spontaneous behaviors," says Charles Bartow, "involve an element of choice, of calculation, of commitment."[56] The performance techniques and the artistic elements are not unimportant. We may expect the implementation of the performance to follow clear criteria. We demand a kind of implementation that befits the genre.

Ministers spend long hours in their study in sermon preparation. Yet, they know that the moment when they give the sermon is decisive. The word "performance" has a deeper meaning than the word "delivery." It is not about simply delivering a text; it concerns a reciprocal event. It is not just a question of implementation but also of "causing to happen." The performance is not successful unless the other is carried along by what happens. At times, ministers have the feeling that what they are saying does not "arrive." Nothing "happens." And the worshippers may also have the sense that what is said passes them by without touching them.

The personality of the minister plays an important role in the performance. By speaking during a public assembly, the speaker presents a message but also presents himself. Performance is always self-performance. In homiletics this is a sensitive topic. For surely the sermon is about the Word of God, not the person of the preacher. Nonetheless, the minister develops his own sermon style, which invariably includes putting real-life experiences into words, and, justifiably, the worshippers attach great value to his integrity, authenticity, and spirituality. And since interpreting God's Word has been entrusted to the minister, the congregation expects him to do so with expertise, honesty, and reliability.

Performance and *performativity* are concepts that help us to better understand the communication process during the worship service. In the literature, this aspect has not received adequate attention, mainly because the focus has too often been exclusively on hermeneutical issues: How can we today understand and give new meaning to texts from the distant

---

56. Bartow, *God's Human Speech*, p. 1.

past?⁵⁷ As a result, less attention has been paid to the communicative processes that are at stake in the performance. How do the worshippers listen to the sermon? How do they interact with what is being said? If listening is an activity of the worshippers, it follows that the processing of what is heard becomes an independent listening act. J. L. Austin charted the totality of the linguistic act and indicated that we discern an *uptake* on the part of the listener.⁵⁸ Therefore, we must deal with this question: What do the words that are spoken bring about? Research has shown that during the sermon, worshippers are existentially and religiously engaged. In the performance, life experiences are brought to the surface, and the life of faith is actualized.⁵⁹

An Interventionist Activity?

Martin Riesebrodt, a sociologist of religion, argues that we will not get an adequate understanding of religious life if we study only the ideas and opinions of people. We must also look at their religious practice. He notes that religion is, in fact, "a complex of religious practices."⁶⁰ In our study of these practices, we encounter an important religious premise: the existence of invisible, personal or impersonal, supernatural powers.⁶¹ What characterizes religious practices, Riesebrodt says, is our concrete interaction with these powers. The fact that people not only believe in the existence of these supernatural powers but interact very concretely with them provides the justification of all religious practices.⁶²

"Religious practices," Riesebrodt adds, "normally consist in using culturally prescribed means to establish contact with these powers or to gain access to them."⁶³ The manner in which this access is realized depends in turn on the religious imagination and the social-cultural concepts that are

---

57. G. D. J. Dingemans, Als hoorder onder de hoorders . . . Een hermeneutische homiletiek (Kampen: Kok, 1991).
58. Theo Pleizier, *Religious Involvement in Hearing Sermons: A Grounded Theory Study in Empirical Theology and Homiletics* (Delft: Eburon, 2010), p. 38.
59. Pleizier, *Religious Involvement in Hearing Sermons*, pp. 246-51.
60. Martin Riesebrodt, *The Promise of Salvation: A Theory of Religion*, trans. Steven Rendall (Chicago: University of Chicago Press, 2010), p. 76.
61. Riesebrodt, *The Promise of Salvation*, pp. 74-75.
62. Riesebrodt, *The Promise of Salvation*, p. 86.
63. Riesebrodt, *The Promise of Salvation*, p. 75.

current. Riesebrodt distinguishes different forms of this interaction with, or access to, these powers: (1) interaction by means of symbolic acts — such as prayer, hymn singing, gestures, pledges, and sacrifices; (2) manipulations, such as the wearing of amulets and "magical acts"; (3) forms of mystical ecstasy or ascetic activity; and (4) activation of dormant potentialities, such as contemplation and enlightenment.

Thus, the participants in religious practices use various methods in approaching the sacred. Riesebrodt refers to these practices as *interventionist*. In some way or another, they presuppose a form of intervention or mediation. Often these practices are referred to with the term "cultus." Riesebrodt, in fact, concludes that ". . . liturgies serve as the ideal-type constructions of the meaning of religious practice."[64]

Are we therefore justified in saying that the Protestant worship service is an interventionist practice? Does the gathering of the congregation serve as an instrument for practicing the interaction with God? When we define the worship service as a performance, what exactly is activated or set in motion? In the Protestant tradition, it is often said that during the worship service the human self is actively involved. This is due to the central role of faith and to the emphasis given to the function of the Holy Spirit (as internal instructor). In the worship service, the human self — the totality of thoughts, considerations, inclinations, intentions, desires, and feelings — gets involved. This includes our human faith and our being part of the world. Worship services have the capacity to channel and regulate emotions and thoughts, frustrations, hopes, and disappointments. The liturgical agenda provides a structure, while the script makes the language available for defining the contradictions of life. But is that what is meant by "interventionist practice"? Could we also say that God actively involves himself in the performance? Does the congregation put God on the stage on Sunday morning? Or is this too dangerous an idea? Protestants — and, particularly, modern Protestants — are extremely reticent at this point. For, surely, God does not allow himself to be manipulated by human techniques.

In this connection it is interesting to note that Riesebrodt mentions two other types of practices — the *discursive* and the *behavior-regulating* practices. In discursive practices, superhuman powers, the access to them, and the common techniques of accessing them are discussed in the form of interpersonal communication. These discursive practices reflect on interventionist practices; they interpret these practices and contribute to their trans-

---

64. Riesebrodt, *The Promise of Salvation*, p. 87.

fer. Theological reflection is one of these discursive practices. The behavior-regulating practices mainly concern the way people live their daily lives: how people interact with each other, what they may or may not eat, at what time and at what place they must perform certain actions, or must avoid certain actions, how they should bury their dead, and so on. Riesebrodt points out, however, that these discursive and behavior-regulating practices are rooted in interventionist practices, which are fundamental: "Only the fact that one not merely 'believes' in the existence of superhuman powers but also communicates with them justifies all the other practices."[65] This means, in fact, that the interventionist practices dramatize and realize the interaction with the divine. "Discursive practices are thus to be accorded a major, albeit derivative, significance," says Riesebrodt; "they are meaningful chiefly in relation to interventionist practices. Only because interventionist practices provide protection against misfortune, and provide blessings and salvation."[66] In short, interventionist practices are the core of religion.

The Suspicion of Modern Protestantism

Protestants have an almost inbred suspicion of institutionalized interventionist practices. As if we, as human beings, are able to effect divine grace and love through our methods and techniques! As if, through our worship services, we are able to bring God himself onto the stage! O. Noordmans puts it like this: the fact that we go to church does not automatically mean that God also goes to church. In other words, Protestants are suspicious of a direct linkage between the worship service as a human performance and God's active presence. It is not the human prerogative to bring God onstage. Moreover, Protestants have an innate suspicion of an overly ecclesiastical, institutional arranging of God's active presence. The golden rule for Protestant worship is that there should not be anything "magic" in our approach of God, and no manipulation in our dealings with fellow human beings.[67]

In the Protestant tradition, this suspicion has led to a thorough disenchantment with church practices. As a result, the worship service can hardly be seen as an interventionist practice. If there is an element of mediation,

---

65. Riesebrodt, *The Promise of Salvation*, p. 86.
66. Riesebrodt, *The Promise of Salvation*, p. 86.
67. Josuttis, *Die Einführung in das Leben*, p. 92.

it is usually localized in the inner life of the human being, or in prayerful receptivity for the Word. But external institutional forms and mediating methods are regarded with suspicion. As a result, the character of worship shifts toward a behavior-regulating or discursive practice. And this, in turn, means that worshippers are instructed in Christian morals (liberal streams) or are taught in the true faith (orthodox-confessional streams).

But in spite of this, the Protestant worship service has not degenerated into a mere human get-together. This is due to the strong emphasis in the Protestant tradition on the Holy Spirit. This emphasis implies that God is indeed working in us. But is this active presence of the Holy Spirit also connected with *the worship service as performance?* Modern Protestantism is inclined to interiorize or spiritualize the activity of the Spirit. As a result, the personal and subjective aspects receive more attention than the external and institutional elements. The church as institution, the authority of the ordained leaders, and the interpersonal communication are not directly linked to the active presence of the Holy Spirit. We find this principle already in Calvin. He emphasizes the role of the Holy Spirit as our internal teacher. Under the influence of the Enlightenment, the emphasis was increasingly placed on the *testimonium internum*. In the nineteenth century this principle fitted well with the emphasis on human subjectivity. In modern Protestantism, the active presence of the Holy Spirit then becomes almost synonymous with the activity of human consciousness. This is clearly evident in the writings of J. H. Scholten, a nineteenth-century Dutch theologian. The truth of religion, Scholten maintains, "is founded on the testimony of the Holy Spirit."[68] He applies this to the working of the Holy Spirit in human beings. He believes this is to be understood not as a supernatural process, but as a natural human capacity, due to the connection between the human mind and God's Spirit. The testimony of the Holy Spirit is "the independent conviction that is not linked to any external authority, . . . which God Himself has awakened in man, and which is strengthened through communion with Christ. . . ."[69] Scholten gives this *testimonium internum* a strongly rationalistic character, the danger being that this religious dimension will disappear behind human reason. Schleiermacher, who also focuses on human subjectivity, puts religious awareness in the domain of feeling. Under the influence of romanticism, this current in modern theology developed the idea that we

---

68. J. H. Scholten, *De leer der Hervormde Kerk in hare grondbeginselen, uit de bronnen voorgesteld en beoordeeld*, vol. 1 (Leiden: P. Engels, 1870), p. 233.

69. Scholten, *De leer der Hervormde Kerk*, p. 217. For his arguments, see pp. 201-33.

may access the sacred through our intuition. Divination is still conceived as a human capacity, but it demonstrates an "overplus" which cannot be defined as theoretical knowledge but comes within our grasp through intuition.[70] Remarkably enough, Rudolf Otto makes a direct connection between this capability of divination and the *testimonium spiritus sancti internum*. He also anchors religious experience in human subjectivity. But he thinks this does not negate the possibility of a direct encounter with "the Holy." This is clear from the following quotation:

> It is one thing to merely believe in a reality beyond the senses and another to have experience of it also. It is one thing to have ideas of "the holy" and another to become consciously aware of it as an operative reality, intervening actively in the phenomenal world. Now it is a fundamental conviction of all religions as such, who may say, that this latter is possible as well as the former. Religion is convinced that not only the holy and sacred is attested by the inward voice of conscience and the religious consciousness, the "still small voice" of the Spirit in the heart by feeling, presentiment, and longing, but also that it may be directly encountered, in particular occurrences and events, self-revealed in persons and displayed in actions, in a word, that beside the inner revelation from the Spirit there is an outward revelation of the divine nature.[71]

Thus, the encounter with the divine is primarily grounded in human subjectivity as an event of feeling. It does, however, correspond to an external revelation, but this can be accessed only through the subject.

We will pause for a moment at the structure of this Protestant way of thinking, taking Schleiermacher as our point of orientation. He sees the worship service as the "exchange of religious interest."[72] The worshippers share in their faith, in their being touched. The only thing the church needs, he says, is a *language* that makes it possible to understand each other and a *space* that makes it possible to be together. The believer is touched in an existential way, and this state of being touched always has a situational, bi-

---

70. Rudolf Otto, *The Idea of the Holy: An Inquiry into the Non-Rational Factor in the Idea of the Divine* (London: Oxford University Press, 1958), p. 150.

71. Otto, *The Idea of the Holy*, p. 147.

72. Albrecht thinks that by giving a central place to the experience of the worshippers, Schleiermacher radically departs from the position of Luther. The worship receives its form by worshippers approaching it as a feast, in full accord with the ideas of romanticism. See Christoph Albrecht, *Schleiermacher's Liturgik* (Göttingen: Vandenhoeck & Ruprecht, 1963), p. 112.

ographical connotation.⁷³ Thereby the religion of daily life, in its personal, subjective shape, takes center stage.

What does this imply for the worship service? What does this mean for the liturgy? In harmony with the culture of the Enlightenment, the religious experience of the individual occupies a central place.⁷⁴ The real location of religion is in our human experience, and there we also find the origin of the worship service. To this two other concepts are added: the idea of assembly (as with Kuyper) and the idea of feasting. If the inner affection of the individual is of a purely personal nature, Schleiermacher asks, how can the expression thereof be communal?⁷⁵ That is possible only if the worship service is perceived in terms of a feast. The worship service becomes a festive, communal expression. "And this festive aspect can be given a concrete format only through the arts."⁷⁶ Therefore, in the execution of our worship we must make use of the arts.⁷⁷ Our human piety is the reason for this feast, and this gives birth to the desire to make it a communal experience, "for every inner experience wants to find outward expression and to demonstrate that it is alive. All instruments that we have to do so are forms of art. . . . The religious principle wants to express itself in a communal way. This is the essence of the cultus."⁷⁸ In this modernist Protestant approach, the worship service becomes primarily a communal, festive expression of religious experiences. In these experiences, something of the sacred becomes manifest. The performative function of the worship service is found in the fact that it is through communal expression that the personal faith experience may be elicited and intensified. If mediation is involved, it is primarily something that occurs between people. When this takes place, there may be some degree of divine presence, but only through the human experiencing of the divine. Insofar as we may speak of worship as an interventionist practice, it is only through the awareness of God on the part of the worshippers.

Could it be that theologians who stand in the tradition of revelation theology are less hesitant to regard the worship service as an interventionist

---

73. Rainer Volp, *Liturgik. Die Kunst Gott zu Feiern*, vol. 2 (Gütersloh: Gütersloher Verlagshaus, 1994), p. 7.

74. Albrecht, *Schleiermacher's Liturgik*, p. 87.

75. Friedrich Schleiermacher, *Die Praktische Theologie nach den Grundsätzen der Evangelischen Kirche im Zusammenhang Dargestellt* (Berlin: Jacob Frerich, 1850; photographic reprint, Berlin/New York: De Gruyter, 1983), p. 737.

76. Schleiermacher, *Die Praktische Theologie*, p. 73.

77. Schleiermacher, *Die Praktische Theologie*, p. 839.

78. Schleiermacher, *Die Praktische Theologie*, p. 737.

practice? In dialectical theology, it is clearly stated that God's active presence for us humans is *unverfügbar* (inaccessible). There is no way in which we humans may give God's active presence a concrete form — not even by means of the sermon, even though the sermon claims to be the ministration of God's Word. This current of Protestantism refers not to the inward nature of human experience but rather to God's freedom. Here the Protestant principle is anchored not in the subjective experience, but in the irreducible divine Word. God's revelation, Karl Barth maintains, is not within our power and therefore not at our command.[79]

In the Dutch context, K. H. Miskotte has expressed this approach in his book *Het waagstuk der prediking*. His *De weg van het gebed* follows the same mode of thinking. Miskotte creates the greatest possible distance between our human speaking and the Word of God:

> Thereby, on the one hand, the preacher is delivered from the stifling illusion that he must speak the Word of God. He stands in this freedom as long as he realizes deep-down that God Himself is the subject of His Word. Thus, he has no other task than to try, as best as he can, to explain and interpret the written Word, and to make it relevant for modern life and to apply it to individual human hearts.... But, always with the critical realization: this, my word, is not in itself the Word of God.... But in the meantime the preacher is charged with another responsibility..., that he should not let his words get in the way of God's Word..., that he will not obscure the message of the Spirit..., and that in a prayerful attitude he will make the Word effective, and thus [will not "administer the Word" but] will serve the Word, that is to say, will offer a service to the impact of the Word.[80]

However, Miskotte does not deny that there is an actual encounter in the sermon. He writes about this in a realistic fashion:

> The word is intended for the creation of a definite sense of communion; it is about naming, invoking, addressing: Thou. For God this speaking is creating; for us this speaking is praising.... We cannot avoid the ques-

---

79. Karl Barth, *Church Dogmatics*, 4 vols., ed. Thomas F. Torrance, trans. Geoffrey W. Bromiley (Edinburgh: T&T Clark, 1936-69), II/I: 69.

80. K. H. Miskotte, *Het waagstuk der prediking* (The Hague: D. A. Daamen, 1941), pp. 43, 44.

tion how the word of God and the word of man relate to each other in the worship service, in particular in its central element: the sermon.... Preaching is: pointing to salvation as a world that has found its destiny, proclaiming peace, giving the assurance of forgiveness, hailing the future, celebrating past blessings. Not an announcement concerning the joy, but a sharing of that joy, and of the participation in the truth and the reality of our eternal destiny.[81]

In his collection of essays *Om het levende woord*, Miskotte expresses himself in even stronger language: "In spite of the religion-historical negative flavor, we cannot find a better word to describe what the Word does than the word 'magical.' The Word happens; on this everything depends."[82]

Worship as True Mediation?

At one time Tillich argued that the Protestant principle is in need of the "Roman Catholic substance." The Protestant principle centers on the spiritual understanding of the justification of the sinner, while the term "Roman Catholic substance" refers to the Eucharistic sacrifice. Tillich noticed that the Protestant worship service can become quite secular:

> Protestantism needs the permanent corrective of Catholicism and the continuous influx of sacral elements from it in order to live.... [Without this,] it becomes cultural activism and moral utopianism. It ceases to be prophetic and becomes political or educational or scientific. It loses its religious character and becomes a secular movement carried on by secular groups. This is the danger of Protestantism....[83]

If the religious character is lost, nothing remains but a secular gathering of people. We already saw that both Rudolf Otto and Miskotte shy away from this secular interpretation. Both of them object to the idea that we can fully grasp our interaction with the divine. It remains hidden, either in the inner human experience or in God's freedom. Otherwise, religion will nullify itself.

---

81. Miskotte, *Het waagstuk der prediking*, pp. 7-12.
82. K. H. Miskotte, *Om het levende woord. Opstellen over de praktijk der exegese* (Kampen: Kok, 1973).
83. Quoted by Carl E. Braaten in *That All May Believe: A Theology of the Gospel and the Mission of the Church* (Grand Rapids: Wm. B. Eerdmans, 2008), p. 68.

Otto realizes that our religious consciousness is aware of *a divine activity*. And Miskotte minces no words when he says that in the worship service, we *participate* in God's grace.

So, according to Miskotte, God's Word does happen. When God manifests his grace, "the Word happens."[84] This may be on rare occasions, but it happens again and again, "when it *pleases* God and when man dares to reach out for it." Miskotte sees the *sermon* as the core element of the worship service. This basic event is more than instruction, more than conversion, more than a clarification of our existence. In an attempt to safeguard this "extra" quality, Tillich enlists the Roman Catholic concept of the sacrament. It seems to me that he refers to the *realism* of the Eucharist. In the celebration of the Eucharist, the bread and the wine explicitly embody the sacrifice of Jesus Christ. It would seem that Tillich sees the sacrament as a kind of guard which ensures that the Christological foundation does not get lost.

The "sacramental element" points to the *true communion* with Christ. This is the permanent correction to which Tillich points. Any worship service in which the focus is not on this true communion with Christ will sooner or later deteriorate into a general human exercise. Modern Protestants run the risk of minimizing the connection with the person and work of Christ. Worship services are, however, Christian events, insofar as the genuine community with Christ is realized. The difference between the Roman Catholic approach and the Protestant approach has to do with the way in which we share in the salvation of Christ. In the Protestant tradition, the emphasis is on the role of the Spirit, who evokes the faith (and connects with our human religious experience), while in the Roman Catholic tradition, the emphasis is on the sacramental act.

The Strong Point of Roman Catholicism: Emphasis on the Eucharist

Let us return for a moment to the Roman Catholic view. When the Christian congregation celebrates the liturgy, the worshippers encounter Christ in his suffering, death, and resurrection, and are thereby renewed. "By the liturgical mystery," J. D. Crichton says, "we are actualizing the past event, making it present so that the saving power of Christ can be made available to the worshipper in the here and now."[85] We are thus dealing with something that

---

84. Miskotte, *Het waagstuk der prediking*, p. 16.
85. J. D. Crichton, "A Theology of Worship," in *The Study of Liturgy*, ed. Cheslyn Jones,

reaches beyond the present, and what happens goes further than the verbal and the psychological. Thus Christ becomes the center of the assembly of that church. "Christ, then, makes effective among men the self-giving of God with all His redeeming power and love." As Paul says, Christ is the mystery that is within us; he is our hope for divine glory (Col. 1:27). Christ makes God's surrender of himself effective for the people.[86]

It is therefore important to note that Christ does not belong to the past, but is an actual reality in the here and now of the worship service. "Just as the paschal mystery was the culmination of Christ's redeeming work, so the Eucharist becomes the culmination and center of Christian worship."[87] In and through the sacramental act, the worshippers share in the saving mystery of Christ.

H. A. J. Wegman describes the Eucharist as follows: "The church remembers in the meal the suffering and death of Jesus, as God's sacrifice for the saving of the world." We are reminded of the words of Malachi 1:11 about a pure sacrifice. According to Wegman, "Sacrifice thus means, on the one hand, a remembering of Christ, who did the will of His Father even unto death, and, on the other hand, the attitude of the congregation, which, guided by the Spirit, follows in the footsteps of the Lord."[88] We are therefore dealing with two modes of time: *then* and *now*. And the foremost question is how the *then* of Christ's suffering and death relates to the *now* in which we find ourselves. In the Roman Catholic liturgy, the connection is made through the sacrifice on the cross and the sacrifice of the mass. Protestants believe that we share in Christ through our faith.

But what we have in common is the conviction that the communion with Christ is all-important. This is the basis of the Protestant principle of the justification of the sinner.[89] The question, however, is whether this aspect is adequately expressed in Protestant worship. Is the communion with Christ truly actualized and made effective in the worship service? In the Roman Catholic Eucharist, the cross and the resurrection are truly part of the service, because Christ is clearly represented through the priest and in the sacrament. Does this also figure in a similar manner in the Protestant worship service?

Geoffrey Wainwright, and Edward Yarnold, S.J. (London: SPCK, 1987), p. 14.

86. Crichton, "A Theology of Worship," p. 11.

87. Crichton, "A Theology of Worship," p. 12.

88. H. A. J. Wegman, *Riten en mythen: Liturgie in de geschiedenis van het christendom* (Kampen: Kok, 1991), p. 88.

89. F. Gerrit Immink, *Faith: A Practical Theological Reflection* (Grand Rapids: Wm. B. Eerdmans, 2005), pp. 73-115.

However that question is answered, the Protestant perspective is different. The cross and the resurrection are directly linked to *faith*, with the result that from the beginning the human subject is crucial for what happens in the service. The effectiveness of the cross and the resurrection is related to our faithful response to the gift of Christ. This means that the work of the Holy Spirit is not primarily (and certainly not exclusively) connected with the acts of the minister, but is rather linked to the personal acceptance in faith. Human subjectivity is part of this process. The suspicion regarding the institutional embellishment of interventionist practices is thus based on the conviction that communion with Christ cannot take place except through our acceptance of him in faith.

The Strong Point of Protestantism: Attention to the Work of the Spirit

The sacrificial work of Jesus Christ is the cornerstone of the Catholic celebration of the Eucharist. Did the Reformers, when they discontinued the sacrifice of the mass, throw out the baby with the bathwater? Was the criticism of the sacrifice of the mass so radical that, as a result, the sacrifice on the cross has been shifted to the margin? That certainly was not and is not the case. In fact, the Reformation stood in defense of the unrepeatability of Christ's suffering and resurrection. It was accomplished then and there, so the thinking was. Protestant worship also knows of the tension between the *unrepeatable* sacrifice on the cross and the *appropriation* of salvation in the present. But the question is, How does this appropriation take place? G. van der Leeuw, a Protestant theologian, thinks that a sacramental approach is justified, on condition that in the Lord's Supper the consecration is replaced by the *epiclesis*.[90] In the final analysis, Van der Leeuw argues, the point of the temporal identification is at issue. God acts historically: a Man was born, and his name was Jesus. He performed miracles, suffered, died, and was buried. In these events the church discovers salvation — not comfort and instruction, but salvation. Therefore, Christ is more than an important figure in the history of thought. If we want to be connected with Christ, these events in some way or another will have to become the historical *perfectum praesens*.[91] In full accordance with the Reformation, Van der Leeuw emphasizes the unrepeatability of the cross and the resurrection: "This is fully historical,

---

90. Van der Leeuw, *Liturgiek*, pp. 231, 232.
91. G. van der Leeuw, *Sacramentstheologie* (Nijkerk: Callenbach, 1949), p. 232.

once and for all." But in the meantime, Christ does not leave his people to themselves: "The reality of the resurrection becomes ours, pneumatically, through the Spirit. The Lord is Spirit. He is here, today. Maranatha."[92] In the administering of the Word and the sacrament, the existential union with Christ is at stake. Protestants believe that this unity is brought about not by an act of a priest (consecration), but through an invocation *(epiclesis)* of the Spirit.

"The reality of the resurrection becomes ours, pneumatically, through the Spirit." Van der Leeuw's statement has a particularly Protestant emphasis. Salvation in Jesus Christ is first of all a salvation-historical reality, and subsequently we are, through the work of the Holy Spirit, participants in the salvific event. With regard to the role of the Spirit, the Reformation primarily emphasizes the Word. Peter Brunner, a Lutheran theologian, states that we can hold on to this salvation only by staying close to the Word, in which the saving act of Christ includes and encloses us. By staying in the Word (this means the constant proclamation of the Word), we remain in communion with the crucified and risen Lord. Keeping our salvation, then, is a continuous actualization of being-in-Christ. It is for this purpose that believers come together — to receive and keep the Word and to keep salvation. "The gathering of the ecclesia is essential," says Brunner, "since there is no other way by which, while on this earth, we can keep our salvation. We must constantly seek the protection of the living Word, in which Christ Himself is present and works for us through His saving acts."[93]

Could Tillich not have found the permanent correction which he considered necessary in the Protestant tradition? In any case, he should have acknowledged that Word and Spirit provide a real mediation with Christ. Apparently, for him the reality of the *communio cum Christo* was so unmistakably present in the Roman Catholic practice of the Eucharist that he considered this a beacon in the sea. But as a liberal Protestant, he might just as well (and more in the spirit of the Reformers) have focused on the role of the *epiclesis* in the worship service and on the connection between the Messiah and the *pneuma*. That would have resulted in a correction on the basis of Reformed theology.

---

92. Van der Leeuw, *Sacramentstheologie*, p. 234.
93. Peter Brunner, "Zur Lehre vom Gottesdienst der im Namen Jesu Versammelten Gemeinde," in *Leiturgia*, vol. 1, ed. Karl Ferdinand Müller and Walter Blankenburg (Kassel: Stauda, 1954), p. 183.

CHAPTER 2

Sharing in Salvation

The worship service is a performative event. The worshippers experience their faith by singing hymns, by offering prayers, by listening to the sermon, and by celebrating the Lord's Supper. The next question we want to address is this: What is the role of salvation history in the worship service? How do the ancient stories of Israel and of Jesus of Nazareth come to life?

This happens through transmission. The apostles proclaimed the gospel, and as a result, it spread around the world. There is an uninterrupted chain of witnesses (the apostolic tradition). Linked to this is the role of an ordained ministry in the worship service. The most important elements of God's history with his people were written down. These texts have been transmitted to us as the *Holy Scriptures* (the Bible). The canonical Scriptures play an important role in Sunday worship, through Scripture readings and proclamation. According to this same tradition, the believers celebrate Holy Communion, an institution established by Jesus himself. The congregation assembles around the Scriptures and around the table as a *confessing* community. Through the centuries the church has confessed its faith, and this faith has been kept alive in the worship service (Apostolicum).

But more is happening than just the transmission and the creation of a tradition. In their speaking and acting, worshippers become so involved with God's saving work that they experience this as an active reality. "In the worship service," Manfred Josuttis states, "The sacred becomes present, and a sphere of influence is discernible. The depth of the Godhead opens itself. The experience of the sacred is poured out on the participants. The fullness of Christ touches the people."[1] The worship service is an event in which

---

1. Manfred Josuttis, *Die Einführung in das Leben. Pastoraltheologie zwischen Phänomenologie und Spiritualität* (Gütersloh: Kaiser Verlag, 1996), p. 97.

Sharing in Salvation

worshippers experience an inspiring and active power. The sacred touches the human. In that sense the performance goes beyond a "making present." The Spirit not only ensures that Christ is present, but also connects with worshippers and is the agent in their sharing in the event. As a result, there is a reciprocal movement: the actual presence of Christ touches the human self (including his/her subjective inner life), and at the same time the activated human self discovers Christ as a living reality. This personal encounter with the living Christ in the community of believers is a crucial factor in Christian worship. The performance in the worship service is not primarily a matter of facts that are communicated to us — however important they may be in themselves. Worshippers place their trust in Jesus Christ as a living person whom they follow and in whose name they approach the Father. The Christ in whom they believe is the living Lord. Theology has the task of studying the essence of worship from the perspective of the mystery of faith.

Salvific Facts and Spiritual Participation

Theologians often refer to *salvific facts* — the facts of salvation. Yet, this combination of historical facts and their salvific meaning is not without its problems. For what exactly is the factual character of these events? A. A. van Ruler states that Christ's resurrection is a salvific fact: "It has the characteristics of a fact. It happened in history. It happened just once, on a particular day, at a particular moment." Van Ruler thus emphasizes the unrepeatability and the factuality of the event. But then he hastens to add, "It is the victory over death, the redemption from the very essence of destruction, the emergence of the eternal, that is, of a life of salvation. And that is a totally incomparable reality. It is more unique than any other unrepeatable or incomparable historical event."[2] This clearly describes salvific meaning. A salvific event is not like any other event, for it is a breaking through of eternal, redeemed life. It is something eschatological: the time of salvation has come.

The Reformation has always emphasized the *unique* and *decisive* character of the cross and the resurrection. It was then and there — in the life, suffering, death, and resurrection of Jesus of Nazareth — that the atonement between God and man became reality. He is the Christ. There cannot be any liturgical repetition in the sacrifice of the mass. In the middle of the twentieth century we notice a renewed attention on the unrepeatability of

---

2. A. A. van Ruler, *Ik geloof* (Nijkerk: Callenbach, 1971), pp. 102, 103.

the Christ event. This was under the influence of the salvation-historical approach towards the Bible. Oscar Cullmann provides a striking example. He speaks of "die Einmaligkeit der Christustat in der Mitte" ("the uniqueness of the act of Christ in the midst of time"), while referring to such texts as Romans 6:10: "The death he died he died to sin, once for all, but the life he lives he lives to God." Cullman also refers to the letter to the Hebrews, which deals with the sacrifice of the high priest. There it is stated of Christ that he himself was sacrificed, once and for all (Heb. 7:27). The theological framework in which this thought was developed was to a large extent determined by notions such as *election* and *vicariousness*. Israel was chosen by God for the sake of the salvation of the world. As salvation history progresses through the Old Testament, the idea of the *remnant* becomes prominent: a small group takes the place of the entire people. Eventually the idea of the remnant culminates in one person, who takes the place of all Israel: the Servant of the Lord in Deutero-Isaiah. The Son of Man theme of Daniel also plays a role. This chosen man, who ultimately is presented as the one who takes the place of Israel (and of the world), is Jesus of Nazareth, who, Cullman notes, continues the "mission of the Suffering Servant of God and that of the Danielic Son of Man; by his vicarious death he first completes that for which God had chosen the people of Israel."[3] This salvation-historical approach stresses the unrepeatability of the Christ event to the extent that the actualization of this salvation in our present existence and in the *eschaton* tends to disappear into the background. Likewise, questions about the salvation order — that is, about the actualization of salvation in our daily life in the present, through faith and renewal — move to the background. Nonetheless, the Protestant faith practice also wants to express how the redemption through Christ has a positive influence on our present existence.

Using one of his sermons on the resurrection, I want to illustrate how Luther makes a connection with the worshipper. Here is how he begins:

> First, we want to tell the story of how it happened, as every Christian ought to know, and then we want to preach about the importance and the power of the resurrection of Christ. The four evangelists did not make any effort to relate the events in the right order; everything is juggled around; the one refers to something quite early on, while the other refers to it later. They are primarily concerned that the fact itself is described, without

---

3. Oscar Cullmann, *Christ and Time: The Primitive Christian Conception of Time and History* (London: SCM Press, 1951), p. 116.

worrying about the time aspect and sequence. It is like it always is: when something important happens, everybody talks about it, but one tells it in this way, and the other in a different way. And it is a truly important story when someone rises from the dead. The evangelists all describe the same event, but not in the same order, nor in identical words.[4]

Luther tells the story in a way that underscores most of all the surprising and unexpected character of the resurrection. The women are overwhelmed by grief as they go to the tomb. They have no idea that the stone has been rolled away. When they went to the tomb the first time, they found nothing. They believed that guards had taken the body away.

> They did not think for a moment that He could have risen. They walked around the tomb, and looked closely, and looked again, as the evangelist says. After having gone back and forth in their search, the angels return.... The angel says: He has not been taken away or stolen, but He has risen. This message sounds strange in their ears. They understand the words, but they do not believe what they hear and are afraid. But they were commanded to tell it to the disciples and Peter. That was their first visit to the tomb.[5]

The disciples, likewise, thought that the resurrection story was nonsense; they did not believe it. When John sees the linen shrouds, he believes — that is, he assumes that the body has been taken away — but he still does not yet believe that Jesus has been raised from the dead. The others also go to have a look; they wonder what has happened, but they do not believe that Jesus has been resurrected. It is only when Christ himself says "Mary" that faith breaks through. But even then the disciples do not believe what she says.

That is the first part of the sermon. But, Luther argues, this is not sufficient. "Therefore, listen and open your ears! It is not enough, I tell you, to know that he has escaped from the tomb in the rock, before the stone was taken away, and so on":

> You have to come further, so that you will understand the fruit and the effect of the resurrection. For that reason the apostles did not worry about

---

4. Martin Luther, *Predigten über die Christusbotschaft* (Gütersloh: Gütersloher Verlagshaus Mohn, 1979), p. 175.

5. Luther, *Predigten über die Christusbotschaft*, p. 176.

the order of the events and the historical sequence in the resurrection story, but they emphasize the power and the purpose of the resurrection. However, the people are least interested in this. Our natural curiosity makes us more astonished about the story than about the effect of the resurrection. The evangelists, however, did not overly concern themselves with the sequence of events and the history as such, but much more with the question [of] why the resurrection is important and how it can profit us. Many have preached about this resurrection and used many words to describe the manner in which He might have risen. But make sure that you know why the resurrection took place, and that you do not just hear and see how the story is told — as we would become excited about the arrival of a king — but that you are included in this resurrection, and that the resurrection is in you *(sondern damit du in dieser Auferstehung drin bist und sie in dir).*[6]

Then Luther points to 1 Corinthians 15 and states that if Christ is not resurrected, we are still in our sins. He also refers to Romans 4:25, where we are told that Christ died for our sins and was resurrected to provide for our righteousness. For Paul does not simply say, "Christ died and he rose." No. He died — but why? Because of our sins. He died — but why? To provide for our righteousness. According to Paul, this passage of Scripture includes everything that a preacher can say about Christ. And thus the emphasis is placed on the saving effect of Jesus' death and resurrection.[7]

Effects in the Present

The fact that the Reformation underscores the unrepeatability of the sacrifice of Christ does not take away from the effectiveness of this sacrifice in the present. The crucial issue in the debate with Rome is that the actualization of salvation centers on the faith relationship with Christ. This salvation is not the result of a liturgical act, but the result of the spiritual union with Christ in faith. On this point the Reformation follows the core of Pauline theology. This is in essence a Christological soteriology and a pneumatological concept of salvation. In the historical revelation in Jesus Christ, God's righteousness has been revealed, and this new righteousness is actualized by the Spirit in

---

6. Luther, *Predigten über die Christusbotschaft*, p. 177.
7. Luther, *Predigten über die Christusbotschaft*, p. 178.

Sharing in Salvation

the life of human beings and of the world. Supported by Paul, Luther regards the suffering and death of Jesus as an all-encompassing event. He is the second Adam: "For if many died through one man's trespass, much more have the grace of God and the free gift in the grace of that one man Jesus Christ abounded for many" (Rom. 5:15). Through the resurrection of Christ and the work of the Holy Spirit, the gospel of Christ has an impact in the here and now: "It is no longer I who live, but Christ who lives in me" (Gal. 2:20).[8]

Within Protestantism, Reformed theology in particular focuses on the actualization of salvation in everyday life. The key thought is that this salvation becomes a concrete reality *in* the human person, *in* everyday life, *in* the ups and downs in the world. Salvation is not only an eschatological reality; it also penetrates our lives through the working of the Holy Spirit. This idea is supported by Paul's prayer: ". . . that according to the riches of his glory he may grant you to be strengthened with might through his Spirit in the inner man . . ." (Eph. 3:16). This means — precisely because of the emphasis on faith — that the human person and his/her spiritual functioning are important links in the actualization and realization of salvation. Calvin has further elaborated this in Book III of his *Institutes,* where he explains how the Holy Spirit forms the bond between us and Christ: "First, we must understand that as long as Christ remains outside of us, and as long as we are separated from Him, all that He has suffered and done for the salvation of the human race remains useless and of no value for us. Therefore, to share with us what He has received from the Father, He had to become ours and to dwell within us."[9] The Reformed orthodoxy further enlarged upon this theme by distinguishing between the merit and the effects of Christ's work. Christ allows us to share in the merits of his work by his present ministry in us.[10] Therefore, Christ's priestly ministry exists not only in the sacrifice that he made once and for all, but also in his advocacy for us in the heavenly sanctuary. These are not merely distinctions from theological manuals; these were also patterns that developed in the praxis of faith. We find a striking example of this in the manner in which the Heidelberg Catechism speaks of the resurrection. In a simple way, it connects the three temporal aspects of past, present, and future:

---

8. For Paul's anthropology, see George H. van Kooten, *Paul's Anthropology in Context* (Tübingen: Mohr Siebeck, 2008), pp. 340-92.

9. John Calvin, *Institutes of the Christian Religion,* Book III, 1.1 (London: SCM Press, 1961), p. 537.

10. Heinrich Heppe and Ernst Bizer, *Reformed Dogmatics* (London: George Allen & Unwin Ltd., 1958), p. 356.

Q. 45. What doth the resurrection of Christ profit us?

A. First, by his resurrection he has overcome death, that he might make us partakers of that righteousness which he had purchased for us by his death; secondly, we are also by his power raised up to a new life; and lastly, the resurrection of Christ is a sure pledge of our blessed resurrection.[11]

According to the catechism, our salvation is anchored in the cross and the resurrection. The life, death, and resurrection of Jesus Christ is confessed as the decisive turning point in history. Then and there this particular human being atoned for sin and conquered death. That is what we mean when we use the term "salvific fact." In the life of Christ, God was fully and decisively acting on behalf of his creation and his people. On the day of the resurrection, this new, redeemed life breaks through. The conviction that this new eschatological fact becomes reality in Jesus Christ, the certainty that he is the Messiah — this is the core of the Christian faith. But this salvific fact is not an isolated event. It has its saving impact in the *here and now*. The catechism derives this second aspect from Paul's theology. For Paul states that the last Adam is a "life-giving spirit" (1 Cor. 15:45). The Messiah does not work in isolation but becomes operative in us through the divine Spirit *(pneuma)*. This unique and special revelation in Jesus Christ brings us a new way of life. Believers in Jesus Christ enter a new dimension. Everyday life is impacted by the Messiah and the *pneuma*. The Heidelberg Catechism expresses this new dynamic by employing three temporal modes: Christ *has conquered* death; we are *now* enabled to lead a new life; and we *expect* the glorious resurrection. So, the salvific facts are comprised within the framework of the work of the *pneuma*. The life-giving Spirit fulfills his assignment between the creation and the *eschaton*. Paul is a key witness: "If the Spirit of him who raised Jesus from the dead dwells in you, he who raised Christ Jesus from the dead will give life to your mortal bodies also through his Spirit which dwells in you" (Rom. 8:11).

Non-Dogmatic Christendom?

The Reformed tradition leans strongly on Pauline theology and remains loyal to the confession of the church by, on the one hand, its emphasis on the de-

---

11. In "The Catechism, or Method of Instruction in the Christian Religion," in *The Psalter: With Doctrinal Standards, Liturgy, Church Order, and Added Chorale Section* (Grand Rapids: Wm. B. Eerdmans, 1984), p. 6.

cisive revelation of God in Jesus Christ (cross and resurrection), and, on the other hand, its stress on the actualization of this event in the present through the working of the *pneuma*. Its difference with the Roman Catholic tradition is primarily its different view of the working of the *pneuma* in the present. But both traditions maintain that atonement and redemption are effected by God himself, through the suffering and resurrection of Jesus Christ.

Among Protestants in the eighteenth and nineteenth centuries, in particular, we notice a resistance against this classical Christology. To a large extent, this was connected with the emergence of the critical-historical approach to the Bible. Scholars in biblical criticism embarked on a search for the so-called real, historical Jesus, and concluded that the original historical Jesus must have differed significantly from the Jesus whom we find in the tradition of the early church. Is this Christ of the ecclesial tradition a "dogmatic Christ"? Is he a product of the early church? And does this dogmatic construct in fact correspond with the historical Jesus whom we can reconstruct from the sources? The "true" Jesus — so the argument goes — is rather a religious personality who was filled with the Messianic expectation of the reign of God. These expectations were completely colored by the apocalyptic expectations of his day. As a result, we get a picture of the historical Jesus possessing the traits of a religious and moral personality. Adolf von Harnack played an important role in this process of differentiating between the historical Jesus and the kerygmatic Christ of Christian orthodoxy. Cross and resurrection formed the basis for a theology of atonement, grounded in the dogmas of the church, and these, in turn, were supported by the hierarchically structured church — this was truly something different from what the historical Jesus envisioned. This liberal Protestantism was characterized by strong anti–Roman Catholic sentiments. The early ecclesiastical developments of doctrine and clergy are — so it is argued — to be regarded as a *decline* of Christendom that dates from the very beginning.

This idea of decline has exerted a strong influence on modern Protestantism. The idea is that Jesus was an ethical-religious personality whose life and teachings represented a major advance over the thinking of the Old Testament. But soon the decline set in, mainly due to the impact of Greek philosophy on the original gospel. This Hellenization of Christianity, it was suggested, was caused by Gnostic influences and by adaptation to Greco-Roman culture. This trend was already noticeable in the later writings of the Old Testament. The process continued in the early church when church doctrines were formulated with the use of philosophical concepts, and when the sacrament absorbed magical, ritual elements. Reform movements have consistently tried to turn this decline around. The Reformation of the sixteenth century was one such movement that tried to restore the original faith.

Geurt Henk van Kooten points out that New Testament scholars no longer universally accept Harnack's approach to history. Van Kooten thinks that the Hellenization was not a later development but that, from its very beginning, early Christendom interpreted its ideas within the context of Greco-Roman culture. As early as the third century B.C., the Mediterranean region became Hellenized. "According to recent views of history," says van Kooten, "the various currents of Greco-Roman Judaism and early Christianity were in the same position, since both were *within* the sphere of influence of Greco-Roman culture." From this he concludes that there is no divide between Pauline Christianity and the early church: "Already with Paul and his disciples we find that Christianity is a synthesis between Jewish and Greco-Roman thought.... During their weekly assemblies they read from the available Scriptures and discussed their convictions, in particular during their conversations after the evening meal."[12]

In the twentieth century, Karl Barth and Rudolf Bultmann were foremost in opposing the view of Harnack — not by promoting a particular view of history, but by emphasizing the central meaning of cross and resurrection. We often refer to these two men as kerygmatic theologians, since they gave a central place to the *kerygma* (the message) of cross and resurrection. Fully in line with Luther and Calvin, their main concern was with the decisive significance of the salvific event in Jesus Christ and its relevance for the present.

The question is this: How does this event of salvation that is revealed in Jesus Christ come alive in the worship service? The Reformation emphasizes that the historical revelation in Jesus Christ has a decisive character. It is a *salvific* fact. And precisely because it is a salvific fact, it has power and meaning for the here and now! We who are presently living share in Christ's salvation through the effect of the *pneuma* — not through a sacramental, dramatic repetition in the sacrifice of the mass, but through a spiritual union with Christ through faith. What role does worship play in this? A less direct role than in the Roman Catholic Church, for the benefits that Christ provided are not mediated through clerical, ecclesiastical rites. Nonetheless, in the Protestant faith practice the worship service also has a crucial role. The worship service facilitates a sharing in the salvation that Christ provided. *How* this happens we will perceive only if we understand the central role that

---

12. Geurt Henk van Kooten, *Paulus en de kosmos. Het vroege christendom temidden van de andere Grieks-Romeinse filosofieën* (Zoetermeer: Boekencentrum, 2002), p. 236.

Sharing in Salvation

is attributed to the Holy Spirit. In Protestant worship, in particular in the Reformed tradition, the prayer for the presence of the Holy Spirit *(epiclesis)* is the pivotal element in the service. I will elaborate on this point later in the book.

This emphasis on the role of the Holy Spirit relativizes the church as an institution. The Protestant tradition connects the Holy Spirit with people, and with the inner life, rather than with institutions. In the past this has led to considerable flexibility with regard to the Christian Year. In the Reformed Reformation, in particular, the stringent order of the ecclesial calendar was not enforced. The order of the Scripture readings was replaced by a continuous reading of the entire Bible. The calendar of feasts was also severely curtailed. Only the central salvific events remained, and the (days of the) saints disappeared from the stage. The Reformers in Geneva, especially, drastically shortened the list of feast days and holy days. This may be illustrated by the fact that Calvin once preached on Christmas Day (a Wednesday) in 1555 about Deuteronomy 21:10-14. He did not choose the Christmas story but simply continued with the series of midweek sermons on the book of Deuteronomy. It should be noted, however, that Calvin did preach on the Sundays before and after Christmas about the Christmas gospel.

Before I deal any further with the prayer for the presence of the Holy Spirit in the worship service, I want to pay attention to some of the main aspects of the Christian Year and the Christian feasts. For, after all, the Christian Year shows us the richness of the Christ event, and in celebrating the Christian feasts we share in the salvation of Jesus Christ.

The Christian Year

The Christian Year developed over the centuries.[13] It is based on two older institutions: the weekly celebration of Sunday and the annual celebration of Easter. Without these two festive events, it would be difficult to understand the origin of the Christian Year. Therefore, I will first address the topic of Sunday. The Christian church keeps Sunday as the day of Christ's resurrection. From the very beginning, specific references to time play an important

---

13. Karl-Heinz Bieritz offers a good survey of the Christian Year. See his *Das Kirchenjahr. Feste, Gedenk- und Feiertage in Geschichte und Gegenwart* (Munich: C. H. Beck, 1991), p. 3; see also Dirk Monshouwer, "Pasen en de andere feesten," in *De weg van de liturgie. Tradities, achtergronden, praktijk*, ed. M. Barnard and F. G. Immink (Zoetermeer: Meinema, 2008), pp. 108-23.

role in the stories of the resurrection. In Mark 16:2 we read, "And very early on the first day of the week they went to the tomb when the sun had risen." This time reference is based on the Jewish calendar: the day after the Sabbath. The New Testament provides a few other examples of meetings on the first day of the week. First Corinthians 16:2 points to a collection: "On the first day of every week, each of you is to put something aside and store it up, as he may prosper, so that contributions need not be made when I come." In Acts 20:7 we read, "On the first day of the week, when we were gathered together to break bread, Paul talked with them . . . ; and he prolonged his speech until midnight." And in Revelation 1:10 we read, "I was in the Spirit on the Lord's day." Most likely, the expression "the day of the Lord" or "the Lord's day" was common in the Greek-speaking churches.[14]

In the early church, the day of the resurrection was known as the first day of the week. From early on we hear in this term the eschatological dimensions. The expression "the first day of the week" reminds us of creation. But now the first day of the week is the day of the resurrection, the day on which God creates a new world. This day reflects the world to come: it offers a glimpse of the eternal rest. Justin Martyr elaborates: "We all hold this common gathering on Sunday, since it is the first day, on which God, transforming darkness and matter, made the universe, and Jesus Christ our Savior rose from the dead on the same day. For they crucified him on the day before Saturday, and on the day after Saturday, he appeared to his apostles and disciples and taught them these things which I have passed on to you also for your serious consideration."[15]

In 321, Emperor Constantine decreed that Sunday would become an official day of rest: "On the venerable Day of the Sun let the magistrates and people residing in cities rest, and let all workshops be closed. In the country, however, persons engaged in agriculture may freely and lawfully continue their pursuits, for often this is the most suitable day to sow grain and plant vines, in order that the right moment, provided by divine providence, not be lost, for the suitable season is but of short duration."[16]

The Christian Year gradually grew out of the weekly celebration of Sunday. The more elaborate annual cycle emerged in the latter part of the second

---

14. Peter G. Cobb, "The History of the Christian Year," in *The Study of Liturgy*, ed. Cheslyn Jones, Geoffrey Wainwright, and Edward Yarnold, S.J. (London: Oxford University Press, 1987), p. 40.

15. Quoted in James F. White, *Documents of Christian Worship: Descriptive and Interpretive Sources* (Louisville: Westminster John Knox Press, 1992), p. 19.

16. Quoted in White, *Documents of Christian Worship*, p. 19.

Sharing in Salvation

century. The point of departure was Easter Sunday. "Originally, when this Feast of Feasts emerges into the light of history in the second century, it is a unitive commemoration of the death and resurrection of our Lord, a nocturnal celebration of a single night, constituting the Christian Passover. It was also, or soon became, the normal occasion for converts to be initiated into the Christian Mystery."[17]

It should be noted that there is a link between the Christian feasts and the Jewish calendar. The cross and the resurrection, for example, must be seen against the background of the Jewish Pesach (Passover).[18] It is clear that the Christian church did not separate God's saving activity from God's involvement with Israel. And the connection with the Old Testament feasts shows yet another aspect. Israel's religious festivals were clearly connected with the order of the seasons. Indeed, they were originally agricultural feasts that gradually received a new meaning as they became connected with the saving acts of God: "In early Israel the rhythm of the important feasts was still linked with the course of the seasons. But soon the feasts were connected with events in the history of the people. The feasts owed their existence to those events and were experienced as saving acts of God."[19] We may conclude that the idea of a cyclic repetition is not fully absent in the Christian Year.

Over time the Christian Year developed within the framework of the feasts, with Easter in the center. The Old Testament backgrounds also played a role. For instance, Paul hinted at the Jewish feast of Pesach when he addressed a heinous sin in the church: "Cleanse out the old leaven that you may be a new lump, as you really are unleavened. For Christ, our paschal lamb, has been sacrificed. Let us, therefore, celebrate the festival, not with the old leaven, the leaven of malice and evil, but with the unleavened bread of sincerity and truth" (1 Cor. 5:7-8). Paul thus connected the Jewish Passover feast with the Christ event. When the Jewish Passover feast was instituted (Exod. 12), a Passover lamb was slain, and its blood was applied to the doorposts. Christ, Paul said, is our Passover lamb.

The history of the development of the Christian Year is very complex. In the New Testament we notice Paul's remark about "our Passover lamb" that we just mentioned. He sees how the Christian's new manner of life is prefigured in the Jewish custom of removing all old leaven at the time of

---

17. Peter G. Cobb, "The Calendar," in *The Study of Liturgy*, ed. Jones et al., p. 407.
18. R. Boon, *De joodse wortels van de christelijke eredienst* (Amsterdam: Dr. Van der Leeuw Stichting, 1973).
19. Bieritz, *Das Kirchenjahr*, p. 25.

the Passover. But this does not yet constitute firm evidence of an Easter celebration. We do not encounter any real evidence for this until the second century. We find that a controversy had erupted in Asia Minor about the exact date of Easter. Some congregations believed they should celebrate the feast on the very same day that the Jews sacrificed the Paschal lamb — which might be on any day of the week. Others were convinced that the Christian Easter celebration ought to be on a Sunday, the day of the resurrection.[20] Clearly, Easter was being celebrated, though there was disagreement about the correct date. After the Council of Nicaea (325) Easter was celebrated on the Sunday after the first full moon in the spring.

At this point I am interested not so much in this discussion as in the fact that Easter is the oldest Christian feast. Most likely, it was celebrated in the night before Easter Sunday in memory of the death and resurrection of Christ. Shortly thereafter it also was the time when new converts were baptized. "Thus it combined the commemoration of both the death and the resurrection of Christ and the celebration of both baptism and the Eucharist."[21]

While at first it was one, undivided feast, in the sense that it was in memory of the death and the resurrection of Christ, gradually it developed into three separate holy days (in the fourth century): On Friday, the suffering and death of Christ were remembered; then followed Holy Saturday; and on Easter Sunday, Christ's resurrection was celebrated. In this *Triduum sacrum* the church followed, as it were, the historic order of the Christ event. Eventually this was expanded and became the "holy week" before Easter. The Easter cycle as we now know it consists of a time of penance (Lent, or the Forty Days) which, during Holy Week, is concluded with Maundy Thursday, Good Friday, and Holy Saturday; Easter Sunday is the culmination. Ascension Day then follows on the fortieth day after Easter, with Pentecost (the outpouring of the Holy Spirit) on the fiftieth day; the cycle ends with Trinity Sunday.

The Easter cycle explicitly reminds the church of the Christ event. During Lent it reminds the church of the suffering and death of Christ; on Easter, of his resurrection; and on Pentecost, of the *modus* of Christ's presence among us: it is spiritual rather than physical. Pentecost is not an extension of Easter, or an appendix; it marks the new way in which the church meets Christ: in spirit and in truth. When Christ appears in our midst, it is in the form of spirit and truth, in our hymns and prayers, in the

---

20. Wegman, *Riten en mythen: Liturgie in de geschiedenis van het christendom* (Kampen: Kok, 1991), pp. 74-75.

21. Cobb, "The Calendar," in *The Study of Liturgy*, ed. Jones et al., p. 407.

emblems of bread and wine. O. Noordmans accentuates the new situation after Pentecost by suggesting that Peter is the departing man and Paul the coming man. Peter knew Jesus "in the flesh," while Paul did not. On the road to Damascus he was called by a voice from heaven. "The appearance to Paul differs from Christ's appearance to the disciples. . . ," says Noordmans. "It is noticeable that the Holy Spirit has been poured out. Jesus no longer shows His hands and feet, no flesh and bones (Luke 24:36ff.), and does not point to His wounds. There is only a light and a voice, and the men who accompanied Paul did not even see the light, though they heard the voice (v. 7). The word has become the key element, more than the actual appearance."[22] The feast of Pentecost — as part of the Easter cycle — emphasizes that Christ is henceforth present in the person of the Spirit.

The Easter cycle offers a wide array of emphases. By stressing Christ's suffering and death on the cross, we evoke the picture of Jesus as the high priest and point to the atonement of sin and guilt. The cultic language of the Old and the New Testaments, in which sacrificial terminology holds a central place, reminds us of the atoning significance of the death of Christ, "whom God put forward as an expiation . . ." (Rom. 3:25). In the Reformed form for the Lord's Supper, this is very clear in the section that reminds us of Christ: ". . . as He was bound so that He would release us from our bonds. . . ." These words direct our thoughts to Isaiah 53 and to the letter to the Hebrews. In the Protestant ecumenical tradition, as it is presented in the new *Dienstboek* (Worship Manual) of 1998, the emphasis is on Easter. It is significant that in this approach the Easter vigil is the heart of the Christian Year. Although a nightly vigil has not been introduced in many congregations, the Easter candle is now present in many churches. In the Protestant ecumenical tradition, the theological emphasis is on the resurrection. Communion is a feast, a festive meal, the breaking of bread on Easter morning — inspired by the encounter of the men from Emmaus. The eschatological perspective is also more clearly present. The Lord's Supper is in memory of the death of Christ, but it also expresses another dimension. For the bread and the cup are accompanied by the words "For as often as you eat this bread and drink the cup, you proclaim the Lord's death until he comes" (1 Cor. 11:26). In the Gospel of Mark the wording is even stronger: ". . . I shall not drink again of the fruit of the vine until that day when I drink it new in the kingdom of God" (Mark 14:25). The elements of resurrection, victory, and eschatological banquet are more forcefully accentuated.

22. O. Noordmans, *Verzamelde werken*, vol. 8 (Kampen: Kok, 1980), p. 378.

The Easter cycle forms a diptych of cross and resurrection. In his encounter with the men on the road to Emmaus, Christ himself said that he *had* to undergo this suffering in order to enter into his glory. For Paul, the connection between cross and resurrection is a recurring central motif. Jesus "... was put to death for our trespasses and raised for our justification" (Rom. 4:25). Christ Jesus "emptied" himself when taking the form of a servant; for that reason, "God has highly exalted him and bestowed on him the name which is above every name" (Phil. 2:7-9). The cross calls us to repentance and remorse; the resurrection brings hope and joy. The death on the cross makes us focus on the *atonement,* the resurrection on the *redemption.*

The early Christians were convinced that this crucified Jesus was in fact the glorified Lord. The victory motif of Christ sitting at the right hand of the Father became very prominent. Through their non-narrative character, the letters in particular gave a great prominence to the Christ event. The gospel message consistently underscored that Christ died and was raised for us. As Paul writes in 2 Corinthians 5:15, "And he died for all, that those who live might live no longer for themselves but for him who for their sake died and was raised." Noordmans points to this early emphasis on the Christ event: "The letters of Paul constitute the oldest section of the New Testament. These letters were already being read when the gospels had not yet been written.... The foreign Jews and the Gentiles, who had not known Jesus in the flesh, and who only gradually received the gospel tradition, accepted Him on the basis of a sermon and a letter."[23] The discourse about Jesus, Noordmans says, was not historical in nature, but spiritual: "The early Christians did not have the opportunity to quietly learn about the facts that must have taken place in Palestine.... No, in a sermon or a letter they had an immediate encounter with the Holy Spirit."[24]

The Prayer for the Presence of the Holy Spirit *(Epiclesis)*

J. J. von Allmen states that we cannot force Christ to be present; we can only plead for that presence.[25] The early church did so with the exclamation *Maranatha!* This term points us to the core of Christian worship: the issue of

---

23. Noordmans, *Verzamelde werken*, vol. 8, p. 427.
24. Noordmans, *Verzamelde werken*, vol. 8, p. 428.
25. J. J. von Allmen, *Worship: Its Theology and Practice* (London: Oxford University Press, 1965), p. 28.

the *epiclesis*. Christ is expected, but he is not at our command. The worship leaders are servants, not religious magicians. This is what the *epiclesis* is: the calling for and invocation of the Holy Spirit. This invocative character is a crucial element in the worship service.

In this prayer for the presence of the Holy Spirit, the congregation expresses its trust that God himself will be actively involved in the gathering of the church. This happens in such a way that the Word becomes a living reality for worshippers. It means that hearts will be opened and minds will be enlightened. In this prayer for the presence of the Spirit, worshippers therefore also ask for accessibility and receptivity on their part. The preaching of the Word and the celebration of the Lord's Supper are not accidental customs but spiritual exercises in which God's saving work is considered and experienced.

In the Reformed orders of worship we find two specific moments when this *epiclesis* receives an explicit form: at the beginning of the ministry of the Word and in the celebration of the Lord's Supper. In the liturgy that was proposed by Marten Micron for the congregation of Dutch fugitives in London — one of the earliest liturgies in the Dutch language — the ministry of the Word is at the very beginning of the meeting, even before the confession. Micron opens with the remark "that we never hold any church gathering in which there is no instruction from the Word of God, aimed at edification, admonition, and comforting" (with reference to 1 Cor. 14). When the congregation meets, we are told, the servant ascends to the pulpit to "teach your souls salvation" from the Word of God: "So let us first call upon the Lord to ask for his divine grace (without which we cannot do anything), in order that I will not utter anything but the pure teaching of the divine Word, and that you may hear this for the furtherance of your salvation." Then there is a prayer that introduces the sermon, which is followed by the Lord's Prayer. It is clearly a prayer for illumination by the Holy Spirit:

> O heavenly Father, whose law is perfect and converts the soul, a true testimony which gives wisdom to the simple people, and gives light to the eyes: we humbly pray You, that through Your infinite goodness You will enlighten our spiritual blindness by Your holy Spirit: so that we may be able to rightly understand and confess Your law, and may live accordingly.

Following the prayer, a psalm is sung, and then the minister continues with the text (the Scriptures) at the point where he was at the end of the previous sermon. In other words: *lectio continua*. Immediately after the sermon another prayer is offered:

> Most merciful Father, Your dear son Christ Jesus has taught us that those who hear and keep Your Word are blessed. But because we cannot keep it, unless You write it with Your Spirit in our hearts, we pray You from the bottom of our hearts that You will keep the Satan away from us, so that he will not take Your Word (that we have heard) from us. Please, remove also our hearts of stone, so that the fruits that have newly sprouted will not wither. And we ask You also to take the cares of this world from our hearts. Make us into a fertile soil, in order that what has been sown in it may bear fruit in abundance, for the sake of Your holy name, through Your own son, our Lord Jesus Christ. Amen.[26]

These passages clearly indicate that the reading of the Bible and preaching owe their effectiveness to the active presence of the Holy Spirit. With the use of the biblical metaphors of the parable of the sower, the path of the Word to the heart and life of the worshipper is pictured. This pneumatological approach is typical of the Reformed Reformation. Without the illumination by the Holy Spirit, the Word is fully ineffective, Calvin maintains. He thereby refers not only to the illumination of the mind, but also to the impact on the heart. The Word that generates faith is a special gift of God, "with respect to the fact that it cleanses us human beings, so that we may taste God's truth, and with regard to the fact that the heart is confirmed in that truth." The Word of God is indeed like a sun that sheds its rays on us, but it cannot penetrate into our hearts, "unless the internal teacher, the Spirit, prepares the access through His illumination."[27]

The *epiclesis* also plays an important role in the classical Reformed form for the Lord's Supper:

> O most merciful God and Father, we beseech Thee, that Thou wilt be pleased in this Supper (in which we celebrate the glorious remembrance of the bitter death of Thy beloved Son Jesus Christ) to work in our hearts through the Holy Spirit, that we may daily more and more, with true confidence, give ourselves up unto Thy Son Jesus Christ, that our afflicted and contrite hearts, through the power of the Holy Ghost, may be fed and comforted with His true body and blood. . . .[28]

---

26. Marten Micron, *De Christlicke Ordinancien der Nederlantscher Ghemeinten te Londen (1554)*, re-edited by Dr. W. F. Dankbaar (The Hague: M. Nijhof, 1956), p. 59.

27. Calvin, *Institutes of the Christian Religion*, Book III, 2.33.

28. "Form for the Administration of the Lord's Supper," in *The Psalter: With Doctrinal*

Sharing in Salvation

The Holy Spirit, it is believed, facilitates the communion between Christ and the believers. In the communion the Spirit feeds them with the heavenly bread. This is also clear from the wording of the *Sursum Corda*, which is spoken of just prior to the communion:

> ... but we shall as certainly be fed and refreshed in our souls through the working of the Holy Ghost.

The celebration takes place in the expectation that the communion will have a spiritual impact.

In this context I will give a brief survey of the importance that G. van der Leeuw assigns to the *epiclesis* in the liturgy of the Lord's Supper. He believes that quite soon the early church embarked on the wrong road, when the *epiclesis* began to change into consecration. That process has been determinative in the further development of the Roman Catholic Eucharist. The prayer asked for the coming of the Holy Spirit, so that the bread would become the body and the wine would become the blood of Christ. The idea that the emblems would actually be changed through the *epiclesis* was, according to Van der Leeuw, originally absent. "The Holy Spirit," he continues, "transforms them, of course, into something else than simply bread and wine, but He also does this with us, the church. In other words, the Holy Spirit changes the entire act with its object and subject into a sacrament, that is to say: into a divine activity. Moreover, He does not do this automatically, but in answer to the plea of the church. He is called upon, invoked." Van der Leeuw says that the *epiclesis* was still clearly present in the Gallican liturgies. The Gregorian revision eliminated it and replaced it with the consecration. This happened in the fifth century, and as a result the *epiclesis* was pushed aside by the consecration. This consecration — it was thought — occurred when the words that instituted the Lord's Supper were recited in the prayer at the altar.[29]

In the Protestant celebration of the Lord's Supper, the *epiclesis* has an important function. See, for example, the Worship Manual of the United Protestant Church of the Netherlands of 1998. The *epiclesis* is a prescribed part of the prayer at the communion table. The words indicate that the emphasis is on the congregation that celebrates the communion and not on the emblems of bread and wine:

Standards, Liturgy, Church Order, and Added Chorale Section, rev. ed. (Grand Rapids: Wm. B. Eerdmans, 1947/1984), p. 63.

29. G. van der Leeuw, *Liturgiek* (Nijkerk: Callenbach, 1946), p. 231.

> Merciful God and Father,
> we ask You:
> Cover us with Your Holy Spirit,
> so that in bread and wine
> we may share in our Lord Jesus Christ.
> Unify us through Your Spirit
> with Him who has given Himself for us,
> and connect us to each other
> as living members of His body,
> to the honor and glory of Your name.

The community rather than the individual holds center stage. The Spirit engenders the formation of a community. As to the order of this Table Prayer, the *epiclesis* follows the words that remind us of Christ:

> ... Remember the sacrifice of the Son of Your love
> and accept our token of praise and thanksgiving.
> Send Your Spirit upon us ...
> the Spirit who gives life. ...
>
> Send Your Spirit in our midst
> and join us all together
> unto a living community. ...

We do, however, find some occasional statements in the *Dienstboek* in which the Spirit is invoked over the gifts of bread and wine:

> And so, our great God, we remember
> the mystery of the Crucified One,
> Jesus Christ, the Righteous One,
> Whom You have raised from the dead.
> Send, we pray, Your Holy Spirit
> over these gifts of bread and wine;
> and also pour out Your Spirit over us. ....[30]

---

30. *Dienstboek een proeve: Schrift, maaltijd, gebed* (Zoetermeer: Boekencentrum, 1998), pp. 178, 209, 218, 257.

The Participation

The prayer for the Holy Spirit implies the trust that God himself will be actively present in the assembly of the church. In the Protestant tradition, this active presence is not primarily located in the ecclesiastical ritual as such. Protestants believe that God will involve himself with the gathered community, with the worshippers. The central idea is that the congregation communes with God *in faith*. With regard to the worship service, this means that the *human self* and *interpersonal communication* belong to the domain of the Holy Spirit's activity. It implies that the Spirit engages all our physical, mental, and spiritual qualities.[31] In Reformed theology, with Calvin as the primary champion, the faith dimension receives full attention, while the underlying psychological and mental processes are hardly mentioned. This is not so strange when we recognize that there was the constant fear — especially in view of the development of liberal Protestantism in the nineteenth century — that the specifically religious dimension would be dissolved into psychological and ethical processes.[32] A. A. van Ruler makes a passionate plea for the interpretation of the work of the Holy Spirit as a unique divine action. Taking his cue from Reformed theology, he attributes an important place to the idea of the indwelling. Van Ruler does indeed arrive at a revaluation of the role of the human being in the salvific process, but gets caught up too much in doctrinal terminology.[33] He does not pursue the interaction between God's Spirit and the human spirit.

Could something be said about the way in which the congregation shares in the salvation provided by Christ? In this paragraph I want to explore that question. Let me begin by saying that the prayer for the presence of the Holy Spirit in the worship service underscores that the church acts in *receptivity*. The performance of the church is a human activity, but it is executed in the awareness that grace and love do, ultimately, come from God. And, thereby, *in our worship we are touched by the sacred*. This means that worshippers are impacted by what God does during the service. It happens this way: God is believed upon his Word; worshippers experience comfort and encouragement; and faith, hope, and love come alive. As a result, the service has an *evocative* power. The human imagination is

---

31. F. Gerrit Immink, *Faith: A Practical Theological Reflection* (Grand Rapids: Wm. B. Eerdmans, 2005), pp. 21-28.

32. G. J. Heering, *Geloof en openbaring*, 2 vols. (Arnhem: Van Lochum Slaterus, 1935-1937).

33. A. A. van Ruler, "Structuurverschillen tussen het christologisch en het pneumatologisch gezichtspunt," in *Theologisch werk*, vol. 1 (Nijkerk: Callenbach, 1969), pp. 175-90.

activated, and the mystery of God is revealed. God's holiness is actualized. The Holy Spirit inspires and activates the human self. There is, indeed, *a touch of the sacred*.

The active presence of the Holy Spirit is expressed in different ways.[34] Some theological traditions strongly emphasize the aspect of human feeling and locate the activity of the Spirit in our feelings. According to Rudolf Otto, the presence of the Spirit is an energetic event in which "the holy" makes itself available and is active, and thus evokes a passion in believers. Subjective, inner experiences are underscored, although they are not detached from the impact that comes from external sources.[35] In his liturgical studies, Romano Guardini tries to keep the objective and the subjective elements together. He appreciates the existential role of our feelings, but he also sees their limitations. He believes that the liturgy is, in fact, able to express the objective aspect. The objective element is not just an ecclesiastical form; it is linked to the discovery of ultimate *Wirklichkeiten, Wahrheiten, Wesenheiten* (realities, truths, essentials).[36] In the worship service, the congregation encounters the *Gegenständlichkeit* (objective reality) of God as a living personality. Guardini places a high value on our inner life, our feelings, but, in addition, emphasizes that our *thoughts* are also crucial in our communion with God.[37] He refers to the rational aspect of faith, including its doctrinal content. The worship service is about *something*.

The Holy Spirit and the Human Self

The worship service is an existential event in which worshippers are actively involved. During the service they are occupied with various things that relate to their faith and life. In the prayer for the illumination by the Holy Spirit, the church asks that the performance have an existential-religious impact. Worshippers pray that this concrete gathering will evoke and strengthen faith, that the gospel may develop roots and bear fruit. Worshippers trust that the existential-religious impact will come from their singing and praying, and from the administering of the sacraments. In doing these things,

---

34. Immink, *Faith*, pp. 30-42.

35. Rudolf Otto, *The Idea of the Holy: An Inquiry into the Non-Rational Factor in the Idea of the Divine* (London: Oxford University Press, 1958).

36. Romano Guardini, *Liturgie und Liturgische Bildung* (Mainz/Paderborn: Matthias-Grünewald-Verlag, 1992), p. 2.

37. Romano Guardini, *De geest der liturgie* (Turnhout: Brepols, 1944), p. 95.

Sharing in Salvation

the church communes with God and experiences his grace and love. The prayer for the Spirit does not relativize the concrete human acts. On the contrary: the prayers dedicate all human activity to God. Thus, human words and activities are sanctified. Not in the sense that human shortcomings and human failings are sanctioned. The plea is rather that the spiritual lives of the worshippers will be at their best, and that their interpersonal communication will be meaningful. A praying church will endeavor to execute its worship in a manner that is carefully thought out and will have style. In its prayer the congregation expresses its trust that the human performance will function as an instrument of God's Spirit.

The prayer for the active presence of the Holy Spirit presupposes that the human self — which includes the passions and emotions, the knowing and willing, the desire and the longing — will be activated by the Spirit. The Reformed tradition has always paid attention to this dimension of the Holy Spirit's work — the *testimonium internum*. The Spirit is invoked in order that the worship service may be executed in such a way that something real will happen between God and the worshipper — that there will not be any hindrances, that the human spirit may not be darkened, that the heart will not turn to stone, but will open itself to the new and unexpected. This will allow the situational, the contextual, and the subjective to come alive. This will include the daily joys and sorrows of human existence — the brokenness of life, sickness and sin, the misery and sorrow. And, likewise, the surrender in faith, the obedience, the life that is inspired by the promise and the Commandments. The prayers for the active presence of the Holy Spirit give expression to the idea that the service is more than Christological. This Christological character is an aspect of the Christian Year and of the celebration of Sunday as a day of the resurrection. But, in addition, the worship service has a pneumatological-anthropological structure which centers on the connection with actual life in the here and now. The Holy Spirit prepares the place where Christ may dwell in the life of people, in their social and relational networks. And thus, everyday life becomes part of the picture. Worshippers live with health and illness, with joyful experiences and threats of disaster, with love and violence, with life and death. The worship service offers the possibility of putting all these aspects of human life in the spotlight. They are addressed in our praise and in our humbling before God, in our complaints and in our victories — in the light of the revelation of Jesus Christ. By going to church, a person runs the risk of becoming existentially involved. This may happen in different ways, and the degree of involvement may vary considerably. Numerous factors can play a role: the worshipper's familiarity with the liturgy, the situation in which the worshipper finds himself, the wider context of the service, the personality of the minister, and so on. During the service the concentration of the people may vary. One may be struck by a hymn, or, at another moment, by the words of a prayer, or a part of the sermon. Few worshippers are totally involved from beginning to end. Worship is a cumulative event. By weekly attendance, people accumulate experiences, building up a faith disposition and acquiring new insights along the way.

Theo Pleizier's research has shown that some worshippers experience the service in a very *direct* manner, while others participate in a more *reflective* way.[38] With regard to the first response, we note that worship concerns things that touch worshippers in a direct way. These things are immediately evident, and there is instantaneous recognition. With regard to the second response, we note that worshippers reflect on what they hear and see. They claim more space for themselves and can, at some distance, arrive at their own considerations and conclusions. Both responses may, however, be experienced by the same individual in the course of a single worship service.

At moments when worshippers pay attention and are concentrating, their religious involvement is also at stake. At times they must make a real effort to stay focused. This may be caused by their state of mind, but also by the way in which something is presented. Does it interest me? Does it speak to my imagination? Is it relevant for my own life? Usually the here and now in worshippers' lives predominates. Even during the worship service the issues of everyday life can be present in our consciousness with an all-encompassing intensity. However, things that have been deeply hidden in our inner recesses may suddenly emerge. At times, just one word or line in a hymn, a prayer, or a sermon connects with us, and we develop our own train of thought from this fragment. Ministers are sometimes surprised to hear that certain incidental remarks in a sermon had so much effect.

Our attention during the service is tied to the focus and concentration of our consciousness. When we are able to shut out certain things and to consciously direct our thoughts to the service, we experience mental clarity, a focused heart, or an impetus to act. Sometimes we find it extremely difficult to stay alert, while at other times it happens automatically. Wor-

---

38. Theo Pleizier, *Religious Involvement in Hearing Sermons: A Grounded Theory Study in Empirical Theology and Homiletics* (Delft: Eburon, 2010), pp. 191-207.

shippers sometimes talk about their joy in listening, the pleasure of being carried along by something that inspires or fascinates. New worlds may open themselves. But worshippers often also tend to listen selectively; they may be able to use what they hear to benefit their own situation. To summarize: the worship service generates *spiritual attention*.

Does this imply that the work of the Holy Spirit is absorbed into the effectiveness of the human performance and the keenness of our spiritual abilities? That would be a reduction of the work of the Holy Spirit. However, when the Holy Spirit brings the salvation of Jesus Christ to the people, this also means that the Spirit has a role in the sphere of this performance and this human receptivity. How would believers make this salvation their own, and how would they be able to live in communion with Christ, if these things were not anchored in the human self? If the Holy Spirit is indeed the internal teacher, he must also be active in the human spirit by creating a space for faith. And if this faith is truly appropriated, this faith will somehow be part of the manner in which we function as humans. So, in addition to the Christological exterity of God's saving work (its being anchored in God's salvific activity), we must also recognize a pneumatological-anthropological anchoring. If the Spirit brings the richness of Christ into our hearts, it brings us something real. The Holy Spirit then lives within us. That indwelling is not to be understood as a merger of God's Spirit with our spirit.[39] But our spirit and our performance are the domains where the Spirit is at work. In praying for the active presence of the Holy Spirit, we must take with utter seriousness these domains for the practical implementation of his presence.

The State of Mind of the Worshippers

Extensive research in the United States has shown that worshippers experience worship with a variety of *states of mind*.[40] This research is based on some important concepts in rhetoric. In the ancient world it was agreed that a speaker could employ various structures. *Logos,* it was thought, points to

39. Immink, *Faith,* pp. 84-115.
40. *Listening to Listeners: Homiletical Case Studies,* ed. John S. McClure and Ronald J. Allen (St. Louis: Chalice Press, 2004); Ronald J. Allen, *Hearing the Sermon: Relationship/Content/Feeling* (St. Louis: Chalice Press, 2004); *Believing in Preaching: What Listeners Hear in Sermons,* ed. Mary Alice Mulligan, Diane Turner-Sharazz, Dawn Ottoni Wilhelm, and Ronald J. Allen (St. Louis: Chalice Press, 2005).

the order in the speech as well as to the content. But that is not the only concern when someone gives a speech; *pathos* is also an important element. The speaker wants to touch the emotions. In addition, the speaker is not just someone who provides technical information; to be believed, he must be ethical — trustworthy and honest. This is referred to as *ethos*.

These distinctions in classical rhetoric were used as the point of departure when worshippers were questioned about their involvement in the worship service. The study indicated that these various categories may also be applied to worship participation. The worshippers indicated that the character and personality of the minister greatly influenced their involvement in the service.[41]

The manner in which minister and congregation interact has a direct influence on the listening process; *logos* and *pathos* also affect that process. It is not true, however, that worshippers use just one listening pattern throughout the service. Usually there is a mix of patterns, though often one is dominant. Listeners with a dominant focus on the *logos* will be more interested in the content than in (the relationship with) the minister. They like to be challenged to think in order to better understand, and they regard their feelings as being on a secondary level that cannot always be relied on. But for listeners who are more sensitive to the *pathos*, feeling is fundamental in their act of participation. They value particular concepts as these allow them to define diffuse emotions, but for them an intellectual understanding is not enough. They want to be touched on the inside. And it should be noted that these listeners are less worried about a plurality of meaning or vagueness.

Worshippers for whom the *ethos* is most important attach great value to their relationship with the minister and to her personality. She must come across as a person of integrity, as authentic and trustworthy, and this must permeate her prayers and her sermon. The minister must demonstrate in her life, and must radiate, what she proclaims to others. A guest preacher whom worshippers do not know is not likely to impress them. Ronald Allen comments, "Everything we do has to do with personal relationships. Therefore, as concerns the preacher, it's not just a matter of preaching but of having the right personal relationship with the people. . . . The pastor has to be caring, . . . must be able to communicate, and have a relationship with the people."[42]

---

41. Pleizier's research confirms this. See Pleizier, *Religious Involvement in Hearing Sermons*, pp. 242-46.

42. Allen, *Hearing the Sermon*, p. 27.

Worshippers for whom the *logos* is most important present another picture. Even though they also appreciate a lively use of language, well-chosen illustrations, and an affective delivery, they demand above all an interesting or important thought that is carefully developed. Lucy Lind Hogan and Robert Reid quote a *logos*-dominant listener on this point: "For me the sermon is an opportunity to learn something. I am open to hear something new, something I did not know before. I am prepared to change my opinion on certain things." Hogan and Reid believe that listeners who prize the *logos* element in rhetoric want to actively think about and consciously reflect on situations.[43] Worshippers in this category are mostly interested in well-defined content and operate with a conceptual framework. Clarity, consistency, and credibility are essential criteria. A quote from Ronald Allen makes the point: "Give me the one thing I demand out of sermons. It would be content. The sermon is the time to make sure we keep learning new things from the Bible and keep connecting our faith with the real world."[44] It is not so much information that they want; they are looking for a continuous learning process that will enrich their lives. Worshippers with this listening pattern strongly emphasize their own responsibility; another quotation from Allen underscores this: "I think you have to have somebody up there that is trying to get your thoughts provoked, getting you to think for yourself."[45]

Worshippers for whom *pathos* is most important, however, stress the inner life of feeling and emotion; one of them says, "There are moments when you can feel that the hearts of the congregation have been moved."[46] This feeling is described as a way of knowing. It is an experience that is mostly intuitive in nature and is at times difficult to describe in conventional language. Words cannot always express the complexity of faith, says one worshipper. The entire person is involved: the mind, the senses, including the sense of smell, the ears, the eyes, and the voice. In addition, our feelings are accessible in ways that may escape our consciousness. At times something is hidden in our subconscious. This underlying network of emotions and associations explains why worshippers may react quite differently from the way the minister expects. Ronald Allen points out that when worshippers feel sudden emotion, this may often be the signal to them to start listening attentively. It is this tapping into emotions that explains why worshippers

---

43. Lucy Lind Hogan and Robert Reid, *Connecting with the Congregation: Rhetoric and the Art of Preaching* (Nashville: Abingdon Press, 1999), p. 91.
44. Allen, *Hearing the Sermon*, p. 45.
45. Allen, *Hearing the Sermon*, p. 49.
46. Allen, *Hearing the Sermon*, p. 61.

may tell the minister that they find the worship services inspiring without being able to say why. "Maybe the sermon was not very effective as far as the words were concerned," says Allen, "but the Spirit was clearly present and His power could be felt. The people were revived by the sermon, and the message had a tremendous impact on the congregation."[47]

It should be noted that, through the centuries, the Christian tradition has placed different emphases on different elements. In confessional orthodox circles, the emphasis was often on the intellectual aspect of faith, and on understanding. In pietistic, evangelical currents, inner experiences and emotions were crucial. In certain "modern" circles today, rationality as well as aesthetics may be most significant. In this context it is important to note that in the last century our culture has increasingly emphasized entertainment, giving a central place to amusement and emotion. Attention is often focused on the immediate, intense experience. It is all about excitement, the drawing of attention, the kick of the moment. After the performance, the show is over. Entertainment looks for instant fun and excites people — its intensity pulls them in. Entertainment can also be amusing and flattering. It is more focused on the immediate emotion than on deeper feelings and the inner life.

Nevertheless, we must admit that emotions do play an important role in religious expression. This is to be expected, since faith and religion are accompanied by stimuli of the senses. Under certain conditions our emotions are activated during a worship service, and emotions often affect our state of mind. Singing a particular hymn, hearing certain words in a prayer, seeing a baptism, participating in the celebration of the Lord's Supper — at such moments our emotions, our state of mind, and our thoughts may reinforce each other and lead to a very intense experience. Because the worship service has a performative impact, the human self is addressed at a profound level.

Communion with God is an intense event of encounter. The history of God with his people Israel and his revelation in Jesus Christ have an immense impact on this encounter. Clearly, God is an inexhaustible source of life and love. In singing hymns and saying prayers, in reading Scripture and hearing the sermon, in celebrating the Lord's Supper, the church continues to sense the richness of this communion with God. This communion, which takes a particular form in the worship service, touches the human mind and activates the human spirit.

---

47. Allen, *Hearing the Sermon*, p. 91.

Sharing in Salvation

Imagination and Mystery

Faith and religion are anchored in the human self. As a result, religious language always has an *expressive* character; in our speaking we try to express what touches us and moves us. Nonetheless, we find it hard to put into words what we feel. "I can't put my finger on it," we say, or "It's truly beyond me." Metaphors or poetic language may help. In fact, this should not surprise us, for our inner being has a *transcendent* dimension. That is why we speak of the hidden work of the Spirit in our hearts; it cannot always be fully traced. Our understanding remains partial and fragmentary. We do not always succeed in placing our various experiences in a meaningful framework, because so much is intuitive in nature. We are seeking to find the words for a reality that appears to escape us.

Language serves as *self-disclosure,* but it also has a *referential* function. We use language to express our involvement with the reality that surrounds us. This applies not only to the natural, physical environment but also to the social and cultural world in which we live. We approach life and the world around us in a particular way, and this becomes clear in our language, our speech. In the worship service we speak about the world in the light of God's kingdom. We connect the name of God with the world in which we live. God is referred to in words, images, and concepts that are derived from the Christian tradition. Regular worshippers are familiar with these. In our secularized culture, however, this kind of language hardly finds any echo. And this has an impact on the way we speak about God in our worship. Many worshippers are accustomed to a secular way of life and often find it hard to understand references from a religious worldview. A communal invocation and a communal way of addressing God in the liturgy are less and less evident in today's world.

Still, we should not underestimate the evocative power of the language of the Bible. Through the use of paradoxes and metaphors, new worlds become accessible.[48] Biblical images and metaphors stimulate the imagination, and the power of imagination remains an important resource for the human spirit.[49] Eberhard Jüngel says that the Christian faith points us beyond everyday reality — not so that we may become otherworldly, but so that we may arrive at a more profound understanding of life itself. The truth of faith

---

48. David Buttrick, *Homiletic: Moves and Structures* (Philadelphia: Fortress Press, 1987), p. 183.

49. Thomas Troeger, *Imagining the Sermon* (Nashville: Abingdon Press, 1990).

is, in fact, that religious language refers to a world that is not identical with the empirically verifiable.[50]

Metaphors place reality in a new light. Metaphorical language is not necessarily non-literal or purely emotive. That would reduce metaphorical language to something non-referential. It should be recognized, however, that metaphorical language can make it more difficult to determine exactly what the speaker intends to say. It is "deviant discourse." But it is not simply incomprehensible, for that would mean that there is no disclosure of meaning. And little could be said about God if there were no metaphorical language at all.

Cas Vos says that metaphors are sparks of the imagination. "The meaning of metaphors is not set in concrete, and their effect cannot be predicted in detail. A metaphor tends to be defined as a word or expression within an unusual context. Metaphors may therefore be compared to some kind of dynamite that shocks people toward new insights, and gives rise to new worlds."[51] A metaphor helps us discover the unknown in terms of the known. It evokes a linguistic tension that contains both similarities and differences. In Psalm 18, for instance, an imaginative connection is made between God and a rock. The metaphor indicates that God is like a rock — something solid and strong, a place of refuge. This conceptual framework enables the hearer to associate the metaphor "God is a rock" with certainty, strength, and safety. Thus a new perspective is offered on God and our experience with God.[52] Metaphorical language also permits us to connect two realities to the divine, as in "The LORD God is a sun and a shield" (Ps. 84:11).

Metaphorical language is not the same as flowery language. Certainly, the use of images is an indirect use of language, but its intention is to strike at the heart of the matter. Its intention is not to find more complex, beautiful words for something that could also have been expressed in simple words; nor is it to clarify what is meant for less intellectual people. The metaphorical use of language is most essential when it helps us to more effectively communicate the meaning of particular things, at times with an unexpected immediacy. Metaphors are linguistic signals towards a reality that deeply concerns us, that involves us, but these signals tend to be outside the sphere

50. See Albrecht Grözinger, *Homiletik* (Gütersloh: Gütersloher Verlagshaus, 2008), p. 224. See also J. Muis, "The Truth of Metaphorical God-Talk," *Scottish Journal of Theology* 63 (2010): 142-62.

51. Cas Vos, "Liturgische taal als metaforische taal," in *Nieuwe wegen in de liturgie*, ed. Marcel Barnard and N. A. Schuman (Zoetermeer: Meinema, 2002), p. 84.

52. Vos, "Liturgische taal als metaforische taal," p. 87.

Sharing in Salvation

of interest of the modern generation, because they are "hidden" and cannot in any way be empirically verified.[53]

We often enlist the help of biblical metaphors and stories in our prayers and sermons, since they may disclose a symbolic dimension in which people recognize something of their own lives. The following few paragraphs from a sermon illustrate this usage:

> The story about Peter who is about to drown
> is about our despair, about how we live
> between anxiety and faith, between hope and fear.
> It begins late in the evening, when the night falls,
> and it ends early in the morning when the light breaks through.
> . . .
> Then we see the disciples in a boat.
> The ship, the age-old symbol
> of our journey through life.
> . . .
> At times the waves are sky high,
> and everything is against us. Then there is only fear.
> Our only thought is: I am not going to make it,
> with regard to my health, my work,
> my marriage, and my children.[54]

In the Kyrie prayer we find this same kind of metaphorical language:

> God, we call upon You,
> on behalf of the people who live in the night,
> estranged from their own selves,
> lost to each other. . . .
> Therefore we beseech You: Have mercy on us.

---

53. Ad den Besten, "Over beeldtaal van het geestelijk lied," in *Jaarboek voor de eredienst*, 1967-1968 (The Hague: Boekencentrum, 1968), p. 47.

54. From a sermon by Dr. P. Oskamp, 18 November 2007.

CHAPTER 3

The Mystery of Christ

The Resurrection of Christ

The emergence of modern theology and of critical biblical scholarship have put the unity of the cross and the resurrection as salvific history under further pressure. H. J. de Jonge says that the idea of a unique, salvific fact is unacceptable for any exegete who favors a historical-critical approach. On principle, a strict historian cannot regard as credible the stories about a dead person who returns to life and leaves his tomb. A resurrection would be totally unique, since it is at odds with the order of things as we know it. The historian can no longer take the stories about the empty tomb as a credible argument for Jesus' resurrection, de Jonge says. At the same time, as a New Testament theologian, he points out that, for the early Christians, *faith* in Jesus' resurrection belonged to the core of their convictions.[1] How can we bridge the tension between the *historical fact* and the *faith* of the Christian church?

An Eschatological Event

Rudolf Bultmann describes this complex matter in a rather insightful way. He suggests that the Christian faith has a paradoxical element, which is that a historical event is also an eschatological event: Jesus' coming and departing — his cross![2] What does Bultmann mean by this? That while we may regard the crucifixion of Jesus as a historical occurrence, we can at the same

---

1. H. J. de Jonge, "Ontstaan en ontwikkeling van het geloof in Jezus' opstanding," in *Waarlijk opgestaan! Een discussie over de opstanding van Jezus Christus*, ed. F. O. van Gennep and R. Zuurmond (Baarn: Ten Have, 1989), p. 32.
2. Rudolf Bultmann, *Glauben und Verstehen* (Tübingen: J. C. B. Mohr, 1960), pp. 197-212.

The Mystery of Christ

time recognize that the events which surround Jesus have an eschatological character. For lack of space here, we cannot discuss at length what Bultmann means by an *eschatological* event; a brief exploration will have to do.

Martin Hengel points out that in the first half of the twentieth century, Barth and Bultmann gave the concept of eschatology a totally new understanding which differed from the dominant liberal understanding.[3] Because of them, eschatology acquires a revelatory dimension: our future redemption appears in the present. In God's revelation as an eschatological event, the radically new appears. "Eschatology" thus refers to the salvation from God that is revealed within time. Bultmann underscores that we should acknowledge that this eschatological event is described against the background of the mythical worldview of the New Testament. The underlying idea is that the end of time (hence the term "eschatology") has been revealed in the resurrection of Christ. The resurrection thereby becomes the beginning of a new world in which death no longer rules. When a person is connected with Christ through faith (that is the existential dimension), he already shares in this new reality. Bultmann believes that this eschatological salvific event is linked to the historic person of Christ. His cross is a salvific fact. But can we also say that his resurrection is a historical event? No, Bultmann affirms, because his resurrection is not an event in history. According to Bultmann, with regard to salvation history, we can recognize that there are certain historical facts about Jesus (the so-called historical Jesus), but this does not apply to the resurrection. In the strict sense of the term, the resurrection is not a historical event. But what may be considered a historical reality is the *faith* of the first disciples and of the early church in the resurrection: "To the extent that, together with the cross, the Easter event may be called a historical event, it is nothing but the genesis of faith in the Risen One, in whom the proclamation finds its origin. The Easter event as the resurrection of Christ is not a historical event. Only the Easter faith of the early disciples was a concrete fact as a historical event." For the historian, the Easter event may be reduced to "visionary experiences of the first disciples."[4]

Here my primary concern is not whether Bultmann's position is theologically defensible. My primary interest in his position comes from the fact that it provides us with a useful point of departure for charting the discussion of the nineteenth and twentieth centuries about the cross and the resurrection.

---

3. Martin Hengel, *Paulus und Jakobus. Kleine Schriften* iii, Wissenschaftliche Untersuchungen zum Neuen Testament (Tübingen: Mohr Siebeck, 2002), pp. 312-17.

4. Bultmann, *Glauben und Verstehen*, pp. 197-212.

Bultmann discusses the resurrection against the background of the *faith* of the disciples and the early church. He does not think that the resurrection can be regarded as a fact that is historically verifiable. Whether or not we may speak of a salvific event on the edge of time and space is beyond our horizon. But *faith in the resurrection* is within the boundaries of time and space and is thus open for historical research. The historian and the exegete can study the development of this faith and the sources and parallels that exist. Whether these are based on experiences or whether these experiences may be viewed *as experiences of an event* is beyond the limits of strict scientific discourse.

However, this does not imply that one can no longer preach about the resurrection within this framework. Critical scholarship and modernity may have caused severe damage to the confession of the church, but, even so, contemporary faith communities continue to proclaim the message of Easter. However, emphases have shifted. Now attention is particularly focused on the *faith* of the disciples and of the early church. I found a good example of this in a sermon by Friedrich Heiler:

> What, however, is this strange resurrection of Christ? It is the breaking through of the eternal divine mystery of life in this terrestrial world that is subject to the laws of death and decay. Only such a breakthrough can explain the radical change in the hearts of the disciples after Jesus' death. . . . There must have been some event that was intense, incomparable, and decisive. For, how else could faith in the resurrection have arisen in these simple people? However, all of this is and remains a mystery to us. Yes, the disciples themselves could only stammer about this mystery. . . . The resurrection stories are but feeble attempts to speak about the unspeakable, to put into words the mystery of life that triumphs over death. One thing was absolutely certain for these simple Galileans: they not only hoped to see their master again in a different world, or in a new dimension of time, but they saw and heard Him on this earth and in this present time. They lived with Him; they encountered Him time and again in their religious assemblies, where He spoke to them through the mouth of inspiring prophets and where, as their host, He broke the bread with them during the holy meal. . . .
>
> The true and genuine faith in the resurrection is a faith in the present. For the mature Christian, salvation is not just a matter of hope, but a blessing that is theirs in faith.[5]

---

5. Friedrich Heiler, *Mysterium Caritatis. Predigten für das Ganze Kirchenjahr* (Munich: E. Reinhardt, 1949), p. 190.

The Mystery of Christ

In itself, this approach to the resurrection fits within the Protestant faith tradition. It is, however, a radicalization of this tradition. The sole focus is the effect of Christ's work. The resurrection of Christ is totally embedded in human faith, and this faith apparently needs no support from beyond itself, not even from history.

This perspective on faith in the resurrection and on human imagination is not something that comes from the past alone. In a recent sermon, Carel ter Linden speaks in a similar fashion about the cross and the resurrection. If we travel with Jesus, he says, we will see that the cross is not God's final word. Ter Linden begins his sermon with a short explanation of a painting in the State Museum for Religious Art in Utrecht (Catharijne Convent). In this painting, entitled *The Man of Sorrows*, Geertgen tot Sint Jans, a painter from Haarlem, depicts Jesus with his cross on his back and with a crown of thorns on his head. But if one looks carefully, one may already see the bloody wounds in his hands, as if the crucifixion has already taken place. And then one sees the women kneeling beside the tomb — but the tomb is open, and the Crucified One is standing. Ter Linden continues: "It seems as if the painter tells us: your eyes should not remain fixed on the cross; you must look beyond it. When it comes to this dead person, the cross does not have the final word. . . . We will continue to hear of Him. This dead person is alive!"[6]

It is remarkable how Ter Linden deals with the resurrection event through his narrative way of preaching, as this excerpt shows:

> This dead person is alive. But the crucified victim could not see that Himself. His followers, however, came to the realization that His word was true: through this man God Himself had spoken to His people and — as became clear later — to the world. And therefore, it was impossible to think that He was finished. Gradually they came to believe that God had been with this man, and, yes, had drawn Him into His glory. The disciples experience His presence in their midst; they experience His presence in visions. Later again, a story emerges that He had died and was buried, but that God had delivered Him from His tomb, and that He had appeared to His disciples. As the years go by, the story grows and each writer adds new details. But, as is typical for the mythic story-telling of those days, they all testify with one voice in audacious metaphors: God has taken the life of this man in His care and has delivered Him from death, so that His

---

6. Carel ter Linden et al., *Haghepreken* (Zoetermeer: Meinema, 1999), pp. 89-96.

people, even all the peoples in the world, would hear His voice and would live, and live together, in His spirit.[7]

Ter Linden also places the emphasis on the faith in the resurrection that gradually developed through the narrative character of the writings that emerged. While Heiler connects the faith with the experience of an event, Ter Linden gives the impression that a certain *perception* gradually emerged: "Gradually they came to believe that God had been with this man, and, yes, had drawn Him into His glory." This comes quite close to the thinking of H. J. de Jonge, the New Testament scholar mentioned earlier, who believes that the image of the "suffering righteous man" had an impact on the way in which the disciples interpreted the end of Jesus' life. The disciples took the story of the heavenly resurrection of the Jewish martyr (2 Maccabees) and applied it to Jesus. The central idea was that immediately upon his death a martyr was permitted into heaven. That would be in line with the words Jesus spoke on the cross to one of the men who were crucified with him: "Truly, I say to you, today you will be with me in Paradise" (Luke 23:43).

State of Mind and the Object-Aspect

Clearly there are differences between the sermon of Heiler and that of Ter Linden. Heiler stresses how the divine mystery breaks through into our earthly reality. He speaks about a mysterious occurrence that touches us in a certain way and moves us. Even though we cannot come to grips with it rationally and conceptually, it touches our experience and our existence. It fits well with the philosophical concept of religion of Rudolf Otto — the tradition in which Heiler feels at home. The accent is indeed on religious experience and human subjectivity, but this does not exclude the powerful presence of a mysterious event. Faith in the resurrection is not reduced to a *state of mind*. This faith encompasses more, and the subjective experience of the disciples stems from the resurrection event. Ter Linden, however, believes that this faith is indeed a *state of mind*, an attitudinal belief that slowly developed as the narratives took shape. In accordance with De Jonge, Ter Linden suggests that the *idea* of the rehabilitation of the righteous martyr provided the basis upon which faith in the resurrection

---

7. Ter Linden et al., *Haghepreken*, pp. 89-96.

could develop. This agrees with older theories about the historical Jesus, in which the "divinization" of Jesus was seen as a later development. It should be noted, however, that this approach no longer dominates New Testament scholarship.[8]

At this point I want to make two preliminary remarks. First, there is a conceptual aspect involved here. When people arrive at some awareness of God, it involves human subjectivity and intentionality. It has to do with becoming aware of something through experience and observation. This is connected to a state of mind, with spiritual, psychological, and physiological processes. This does not, however, mean that these experiences or observations refer solely to a spiritual condition. They may well be experiences or observations of an (external) event, of a person, or of a certain state of affairs.[9] When we are getting involved with something, this implies *intentional* involvement. That is to say, our spiritual capacities and our emotions are involved. These factors, of course, also play a role in the Christian faith. Faith in Christ is an "attitudinal *belief.*" But it is more than that. We note that "religious belief" may also touch on the dimension of content — for instance, on an "article of faith" — or on the psychological dimension — for instance, the love for one's faith, argues philosopher Robert Audi.[10] The content of our faith has two aspects. First, there is the *propositional* element: we make statements about *who* Christ is. Second, there is the *object*-aspect: we believe that Christ is a person, and we ascribe certain characteristics to him. In other words, religious belief concerns not only the "subject-side" of the believer, but also the "object-side": the person of Christ. However, in addition to the subjective-psychological and objective dimensions, we must consider a third dimension: the active and effective presence of the object. In the stories of the resurrection and of the appearances of Christ, he himself is present, acting and speaking. He makes himself present and identifies himself. Thus, the human state of mind and attitude develop through the encounter with Christ. This demonstrates the complexity of religious faith. Numerous factors and dimensions play a role. Since an appearance of Christ is also hermeneutically rather ambivalent and demands certain skills to define and describe, it is

---

8. Larry W. Hurtado, *Lord Jesus Christ: Devotion to Jesus in Earliest Christianity* (Grand Rapids: Wm. B. Eerdmans, 2003). Geurt Henk van Kooten alerted me to this study.

9. F. Gerrit Immink, "Theological Concepts in Empirical Research," in *Dreaming the Land: Theologies of Resistance and Hope*, ed. Hans-Georg Ziebertz and Friedrich Schweitzer (Berlin: LIT Verlag, 2007), pp. 190-98.

10. Robert Audi, "Belief, Faith, and Acceptance," *International Journal of Philosophy of Religion* 63 (2008): 89.

important not to lose sight of these various dimensions and not to attribute everything to the state of mind of the believer.

Second, besides these conceptual considerations, we must also keep in mind that exegetical and theological aspects come into play. If we take recent studies on Saint Paul seriously, we must conclude that "high Christology" is not a later development under the influence of the Hellenization of Christendom. We may already discern this emphasis on Christ's divinity in the studies of the Gospels. With regard to homiletics, it appears that the narrative shift has placed a disproportionate emphasis on the Gospel stories, at the expense of Paul. James W. Thompson thinks that the "Pauline texts do not fit easily with the postmodern fascination with story."[11] However, Richard Lischer, an American homiletics scholar, maintains that the New Testament witness has a non-narrative core. The message of the angel is "He is risen!" That is not a story, but an announcement about a state of affairs. That is how things are — with God, with you, and with the world.[12]

Historical Interest in Human Perception

It is clear that the early Christians used some well-established formulas with regard to the resurrection. We notice this in Paul's letters: "We believe that Jesus died and rose again . . ." (1 Thess. 4:14); "If you confess with your lips that Jesus is Lord and believe in your heart that God raised him from the dead, you will be saved" (Rom. 10:9). Historical-critical exegesis devotes much attention to the emergence and further development of faith in the resurrection. This leads to an important question: Where did this faith originate, and how did it develop? De Jonge points out that many Jews in those days believed that a highly valued person would be granted an afterlife in heaven. In the end, God would rehabilitate the righteous ones who had suffered. This idea was quite current. It should be noted, however, that De Jonge offers his interpretation within the context of a strictly verifiable development of *ideas* and *perceptions* of people. He hardly considers the possibility of new experiences or expressions that might create new perceptions. His point of departure is the continuity of perceptions and

---

11. James W. Thompson, *Preaching like Paul: Homiletical Wisdom for Today* (Louisville: Westminster John Knox Press, 2001), p. 15.

12. Richard Lischer, *The End of Words: The Language of Reconciliation in a Culture of Violence* (Grand Rapids: Wm. B. Eerdmans, 2005), p. 96.

The Mystery of Christ

ideas. His starting point is that the idea of the resurrection resulted from an interpretation of the disciples immediately after Jesus' death, and he argues that this thought fits with the idea of a martyr who is rehabilitated by God. Jesus' death was not a fiasco; De Jonge asserts that the disciples were convinced that "God had rehabilitated Him as a righteous man and vindicated Him as a martyr, and raised Him from death into heaven." By confessing Jesus' resurrection so soon after his death, the disciples emphasized how Jesus had received his role as the inaugurator of God's rule from no one else but God himself. The resurrection was God's vindication, and thereby his authorization, not just of Jesus as a righteous man and a martyr, but, in particular, of Jesus as the one who had inaugurated the eschatological reign of God.[13]

In itself, this interest in the historical development of perceptions and ideas is important for our understanding of the New Testament. This also applies to faith in the resurrection of Christ. The analogy and the parallels with other perceptions and time aspects may contribute to a better understanding. But De Jonge places such a strong emphasis on historical comparability and verifiability that he will not consider the *unicity* of the event and the possibility of a *transcendental* experience. Because of his point of departure, he reduces faith in Christ to a human phenomenon and a human perception.

Riemer Roukema points out that New Testament scholars do not always define "historical" in exactly the same way. The role of the "historical" Jesus is, in itself, already a complex matter. Furthermore, he believes that it is rather difficult to separate the "real" Jesus from the theological interpretation of the early church. As he explains, "There appears to be an overlap between the concepts 'historical' and 'theological' as well. First of all there is the appearance of the 'historical' Jesus. Secondly, accounts have been made of this that bear witness to the theological convictions of the authors."[14]

We already noted how Bultmann created an enormous issue by saying that many of Jesus' statements are, in fact, the product of the early church. Roukema suggests that current opinion tends to be different. Even though, historically speaking, we cannot go back to the person of Jesus himself, scholars (as, for instance, James Dunn) are now more optimistic about the credibility of the tradition of Jesus. Marinus de Jonge has also pointed out that current New Testament scholarship pays more attention to the connec-

---

13. H. J. de Jonge, "Ontstaan en ontwikkeling van het geloof in Jezus' opstanding," in *Waarlijk opgestaan!*, ed. Van Gennep and Zuurmond, p. 46.
14. Riemer Roukema, *Jesus, Gnosis, and Dogma* (London: T&T Clark, 2010), p. 4.

tion between the "historical Jesus" and the "risen Christ." The post-Easter conviction that God's rehabilitation of Jesus inaugurated a new era became as prominent as it did because already prior to Easter the dynamic presence of the kingdom had been recognized in the life of Jesus, and had already led to the expectation that a complete fulfillment was imminent.[15]

Therefore, we cannot separate the historical Jesus from the risen Christ. The convictions regarding the risen Lord cannot be separated from those regarding Jesus' suffering and death. And these latter convictions about the historical Jesus are based on concrete experiences with Jesus. It is true that these beliefs, in turn, have been colored and shaped by faith in the resurrection — hence the impossibility of separating the "true" Jesus from the events in the early church. But it is going too far to state that this is where these beliefs originated. If we want to understand the Gospels correctly, we must not forget that the risen Lord is identical with the "historical" Jesus. It is precisely because the disciples saw and experienced the uniqueness of Jesus in their contact with the earthly, historical Jesus that they could believe in the risen Lord. They recognized him as one and the same. After the resurrection their understanding became more profound, as is clear from the appearances of Jesus. At the same time, what they saw and experienced with the earthly Jesus (his trust in God, his obedience in his suffering, the signs of the reign of God that he performed) made faith in the resurrection of their Lord more plausible.

We must avoid getting caught up in a play on words or ending up in confusion. Therefore, we must not just look at things from a literary and a textual angle; we should also consider how the *descriptions* relate to *experiences* and *events*. These are not always on the same plane. Naturally, literary-historical approaches are limited to literary categories and to the way in which things are perceived. But that is not the end of the story. Our use of language also has social and referential dimensions. Paul Ricoeur rightly remarks that the words that we use point to the speaker as well as to the world: "This correlation is not fortuitous, since it is ultimately the speaker who refers to the world in speaking. Discourse in action and in use refers backwards and forwards, to a speaker and a world."[16] In this way Ricoeur does justice to the subjective dimension of language. At the

---

15. Marinus de Jonge, *Jesus, the Servant-Messiah* (New Haven: Yale University Press, 1991), p. 96.

16. Paul Ricoeur, *Interpretation Theory: Discourse and the Surplus of Meaning* (Fort Worth: Texas Christian University Press, 1976), p. 22.

same time, this permits him to attach value to human experience and its reference to reality. I realize that this observation is based on a distinction between oral discourse and written text. That, however, is not relevant to my argument. What is relevant is the distinction between human intentionality (and subjectivity) and our reference to the world. A story cannot exist without an author, without his experiences and observations. These are the minimal *ontological* conditions for putting things into language. In dealing with the statements concerning the resurrection of Christ, we will have to ask ourselves about the relationship between verbal statements, convictions, experiences, and events. These are not all on the same level and do not all share in the same ontological status. It is quite possible that people with a certain perception of the resurrection may have used a particular literary format.[17] But that does not exclude the possibility that the first witnesses of the resurrection may have developed a particular perception of it as a result of the *experiences* they had. The question, however, remains: Should these experiences be explained as purely mental or psychological processes, or might we also consider them as experiences of *events*? And what was the nature of these events? It seems as if most exegetes limit themselves to what has been written down, without asking these questions. This is quite strange, since these written statements also express the nature of these experiences and events. It is quite plausible that the experiences of the disciples with Jesus during his earthly life, the signs they saw of the kingdom of God, and their familiarity with the perceptions and the formulations which were current at the time — that all these factors, in turn, also contributed to the manner in which they observed and defined his appearances. Seen against this background, it is not at all strange that the risen Christ appeared to those who were with him during his life on earth. During his life the disciples time and again saw the signs of the eschatological salvation. While they sojourned with him, they experienced how the kingdom had come near in his very person. The Risen One was the same person as the Jesus with whom they had associated. And, therefore, it is not so strange that the words Jesus spoke and the acts that he did during his life offered the framework for understanding his post-resurrection appearances. Although the testimony of the resurrection and of the appearances throws a new light on the historical Jesus, this is no reason to attribute the "mythical-ontological" dimension mainly to the faith of the early church.

---

17. M. de Jonge, "De hoofdzaken," in *Waarlijk opgestaan!*, ed. Van Gennep and Zuurmond, p. 79.

The Ontological Character of the Resurrection

The Realness of the Resurrection

In his study on Paul, J. Christiaan Beker has pointed out that the resurrection has an ontological-cosmological dimension. He bases this on the idea that the future apocalyptic resurrection of the dead undeniably has a physical component. Beker believes that the personalistic-existentialistic interpretation of Bultmann is seriously inadequate. Bultmann reduces the resurrection to a mere mental or existential phenomenon, which is limited to the world of human decisions. Thus the ontological-cosmological dimension completely disappears.[18] Beker sees the resurrection event as a "historical-ontological category, manifesting in this world the dawning of the new age of transformation."[19] Beker places the resurrection event within the framework of the apocalyptic and remarks that Paul does not refer to the apocalyptic as an accidental historical phenomenon to shed some light on the resurrection of Christ. On the contrary. The apocalyptic aspect expresses a crucial thought: "Although the death of Christ is a 'once and for all event,' the resurrection of Christ is not 'completed' in its full meaning and consequence until the future resurrection of the dead. Therefore, the resurrection of Christ cannot be asserted apart from the future apocalyptic resurrection, because it derives its meaning from its future referent."[20] Beker explains that the resurrection has two foci: the resurrection of Christ and the ultimate apocalyptic resurrection of the dead. This future resurrection has a material, corporeal component. The *being-in-Christ* can therefore not be spiritualized into an existential attitude of faith. It points in a real way to the *parousia* as a future event. For Paul, the resurrection unquestionably has a historical-ontological character: it is confirmed by eyewitnesses (1 Cor. 15:6) and is not merely a kerygmatic event. In opposition to Bultmann (who sees the mythological apocalyptic as a husk of first-century language that we should demythologize in order to arrive at the core of the gospel, the *kerygma*), Beker argues that the apocalyptic framework is essential for Paul's understanding of the resurrection. He regards it as typical that the word "eschatology" has pushed the word "apocalypticism" aside.[21] Paul does

---

18. J. Christiaan Beker, *Paul the Apostle: The Triumph of God in Life and Thought* (Minneapolis: Fortress Press, 1980), p. 154.
19. Beker, *Paul the Apostle*, p. 153.
20. Beker, *Paul the Apostle*, p. 167.
21. Beker, *Paul the Apostle*, p. 18.

The Mystery of Christ

not treat the apocalyptic resurrection as something that we can do without, but as the inalienable core of the gospel.

Modern Protestantism is inclined to approach the reality of religion (the ontological questions) from an anthropological perspective. This fits with the Protestant emphasis on the role of faith. Thus the sacred is approached from the point where we may *access* the sacred, or from the *impact* of the sacred on the human spirit, or from its being a *construct* in the development of human culture. As a result, the more ontological and metaphysical aspects of faith are primarily approached through anthropology. And, thereby, the divine reality, the reality of the Holy Spirit, is directly related to the traces of God's presence in our spiritual life. There is something to be said for this approach. For it concerns the communion of faith, the bond between God and humankind. Or, to put it in Christian language, it concerns our relationship with Christ, the risen Lord. Paul even speaks of "Christ among us" and "Christ in us." But we cannot evade certain questions. Does Christ merely exist in the human mind? Or in the story? Does he exist in the ideas and theories that are current within a particular culture? What kind of "existence" might this be? In the final analysis, is the risen Christ a creation of the human mind, or is the perception in the human mind rather a result of Christ's resurrection, a human way of understanding the resurrection event? Modern Protestantism is inclined not to attribute to Christ (or God) any ontological or metaphysical dimension that is independent of us as human beings.[22] Bultmann is a good example of this type of thinking. He spiritualizes the resurrection. And Beker justifiably criticizes him with regard to the ontological character of Paul's apocalypticism. In this connection I want to refer to Edward Schillebeeckx, who states that some Protestant theologians (Bultmann among them) are inclined to interpret Jesus' resurrection as the renewal of life. But Schillebeeckx firmly believes that we cannot separate Jesus' resurrection from the apostolic faith that Christ was risen. It is clear, he says, that "no Easter experience of renewed life was possible without the personal resurrection of Jesus — in the sense that Jesus' personal-cum-bodily resurrection (in keeping with a logical and ontological priority) . . . 'precedes' any faith-motivated experience."[23]

F. O. van Gennep differentiates between the *ethical* and the *mystical*

---

22. See my book titled *Faith: A Practical Theological Reflection* (Grand Rapids: Wm. B. Eerdmans, 2005), chap. 12.

23. Edward Schillebeeckx, *Jesus: An Experiment in Christology* (New York: Crossroad, 1985), p. 645.

significance of the resurrection. The ethical aspect, he believes, has to do with the way in which a Christian lives his life, based on his faith in the resurrection. As Van Gennep says, "For me the meaning of the resurrection experience is that there is justice, that death does not have the final word, nor the extorters, the murderers. That I may believe this has gripped me with inexpressible joy. To this I have committed my life: there is a future. I believe in this justice. If I could no longer do this, my life would be without meaning and significance."[24] Even though Van Gennep states that he does not believe in a bodily resurrection, or in miracles, he considers the resurrection of Christ to be the core of Christian faith.[25] In line with modern Protestantism, he refers to the resurrection experience and its relevance for our present life. But that is not all. Van Gennep also speaks of the *mystical* dimension of the *resurrection event*:

> For one can also see the experience of the resurrection, as reported in the gospels, as a totally new and surprising experience that completely changed the life of the disciples and the friends of Jesus. The term "mystical" may not be fully adequate, because it may point too exclusively to an inner experience. I believe it is possible for us to read the gospels in such a way that we see a description of a "sublime experience" that radically changed the life of the early Christians.[26]

Remarkably enough, Van Gennep refers to this mystical dimension in the context of, on the one hand, "experience" and, on the other hand, a "resurrection event." This implies that he does not reduce the resurrection to a mental experience or a human idea. In line with the (older) Pauline studies of Gustav Deissmann, he refers to a "Gemeinschaftsmystik." He wants to stress that it concerns a mystical element, "a human reaction to a divine initiative." Thus Paul's encounter with Christ becomes "a response to the speaking of the living Lord."[27]

Much has been written about the mystical element in Pauline thought.[28] My present concern is to underscore how this mysticism points to a realistic

---

24. F. O. van Gennep, *Naam geven wat ik zoek, preken* (Baarn: Ten Have, 1991), p. 69.
25. F. O. van Gennep, "Het is beslist," in *Waarlijk opgestaan!*, ed. Van Gennep and Zuurmond, p. 16.
26. Van Gennep, "Het is beslist," pp. 17-18.
27. Van Gennep, "Het is beslist," p. 18.
28. See, for example, Albert Schweitzer, *Die Mystik des Apostels Paulus* (Tübingen: Mohr Siebeck, 1930).

dimension in our communion with Christ. Dying and rising with Christ not only brings a new mode of existence (a new manner of life), but also presupposes a genuine (and not just a symbolic) union with Christ. Paul does not spiritualize the resurrection to the extent that it becomes solely an ethical category. This mystical interpretation concerns an event with a "naturhafte" dimension. Albert Schweitzer refers to an "objektive *Mystik der Tatsachen*" (the objective mysticism of facts) and says that being-in-Christ is not just an inner and spiritual state.[29]

The New Testament scholar N. T. Wright has concluded that faith in the resurrection must ultimately be grounded in the resurrection event itself, and cannot be explained from the development of the church's theology.[30] He believes that the empty tomb and the appearances of Jesus are sufficient conditions for the early Christian faith in the resurrection. "Early Christian belief in the resurrection is clearly not something derived from any form of paganism," he says; "it is a mutation from within Judaism, or rather six mutations." His point is that the idea of a bodily resurrection was a tremendous shift from contemporary thinking in Judaism and in the Hellenistic culture. How could this shift happen? According to Wright, the early Christians would say that it was possible because of the bodily resurrection of Jesus from death.[31]

The Pneumatic-Anthropological Impact of the Resurrection

Christian faith is intrinsically related to the salvific events in Christ, and to the ensuing transformation of life.[32] This implies that the cross and the resurrection find their echo in the life of the believer. This connection is already apparent in the expression "salvific event." The life and death of Jesus comprise an event that brings salvation — both for humanity and for creation. The Reformation recognizes a close connection between the cross and the resurrection of Christ, on the one hand, and the renewal of life on

---

29. Schweitzer, *Die Mystik des Apostels Paulus*, pp. 100, 127.
30. N. T. Wright, *The Resurrection of the Son of God* (Minneapolis: Fortress Press, 2003).
31. *The Resurrection of Jesus: John Dominic Crossan and N. T. Wright in Dialogue*, ed. Robert B. Stewart (Minneapolis: Fortress Press, 2006), p. 18.
32. Charles Taylor, *A Secular Age* (Cambridge: Belknap Press, 2007). Taylor argues that Christian faith presents a dual aspect: "the belief in transcendent reality, on the one hand, and the connected aspiration to a transformation which goes beyond ordinary human flourishing, on the other" (p. 510).

the other. The true effectiveness of Christ is not primarily understood in terms of a sacramental mechanism, but is linked to an act of faith. For this close linkage between resurrection and the newness of life, we may appeal to biblical texts such as these:

> We were buried therefore with him by baptism into death, so that as Christ was raised from the dead by the glory of the Father, we too might walk in newness of life. (Rom. 6:4)

> But if we have died with Christ, we believe that we shall also live with him. (Rom. 6:8)

> Blessed be the God and Father of our Lord Jesus Christ! By his great mercy we have been born anew to a living hope through the resurrection of Jesus Christ from the dead. (1 Pet. 1:3)

What Romans refers to as "living in Christ" is described in the letter by Peter with the term "born anew." Paul lays great stress on the assimilation with Christ: becoming one and being simultaneous with Christ. We are one with him in his death, and thus we may also share in his resurrection. Through his baptism and through faith, believers participate in the Christ event. On that basis Paul can state with force, "So you also must consider yourselves dead to sin and alive to God in Christ Jesus" (Rom. 6:11). This is not the place to discuss whether we should see this assimilation with Christ mainly as a forensic-eschatological, a mystical, or a sacramental union. The point is that the appeal that issues from the cross and the resurrection brings a change in the life of human beings. Our "old man" is crucified with Christ. This creates a totally new dynamic in the lives of human beings. It causes a struggle between old and new that Paul captures in Romans: "But if Christ is in you, although your bodies are dead because of sin, your spirits are alive because of righteousness" (Rom. 8:10). In other words: Paul suggests that the possibility of a connection between God and humans lies in the domain of the spirit *(pneuma)*:

> If the Spirit of him who raised Jesus from the dead dwells in you, he who raised Christ Jesus from the dead will give life to your mortal bodies also through his Spirit which dwells in you. (Rom. 8:11)

So, God does something with us. But how can we describe what he does? George van Kooten points out that Paul's anthropology seems to suggest that the human spirit will begin to communicate with the Spirit of God, or of Christ, as soon as it starts functioning correctly.[33] When a spiritual person considers the things of the Spirit, he will begin to combat sin and the desires of the flesh. This produces an inner struggle, for the Spirit of God is the Spirit of life (Rom. 8:20) and fights the desires of the flesh. "For those who live according to the flesh set their minds on the things of the flesh, but those who live according to the Spirit set their minds on the things of the Spirit. To set the mind on the flesh is death, but to set the mind on the Spirit is life and peace" (Rom. 8:5-6).

Van Kooten distinguishes three dimensions in Paul's view of man: body, psyche, and spirit. We find this tripartition, for instance, in 1 Thessalonians 5:23, where Paul writes, "May the God of peace himself sanctify you wholly; and may your spirit [*pneuma*] and soul [*psyche*] and body [*soma*] be kept sound and blameless at the coming of our Lord Jesus Christ." These three facets characterize man. Paul differentiates between the *spiritual* man (the *pneumaticus*) and the unspiritual, *psychic* person (the *psychicus*): "The unspiritual man does not receive the gifts of the Spirit of God, for they are folly to him, and he is not able to understand them because they are spiritually discerned" (1 Cor. 2:14). The unspiritual are those who live according to their psyche, who, in fact, live in accordance with the *flesh* (1 Cor. 3:1) and miss a guiding principle. The *pneumatici* are those who are able to think of spiritual things, and who live in accordance with God's *pneuma*, and in accordance with the Spirit of Christ. Apparently, the *pneumatici* recognize the value of being crucified with Christ and of having risen with him, and this determines the reality of their life. Van Kooten says that the terms *pneuma* and *nous* are used to refer both to the divine and to the human spirit.[34] There is in the human spirit a place of contact between God and us. When the Spirit of Christ enters that place, we regain control over our lives, because the Spirit enables us to become spiritual persons. By sharing in the death and resurrection of Christ, we walk according to the way of the Spirit *(pneuma)*. Through communion with Christ, the right direction and the correct judgment are restored.

It becomes clear that the death and resurrection of Christ have an impact on the believer. The ethical dimension (involving the exhortation towards renewal and sanctification) is not detached from what the *human*

---

33. George H. van Kooten, *Paul's Anthropology in Context* (Tübingen: Mohr Siebeck, 2008), p. 378.
34. Van Kooten, *Paul's Anthropology in Context*, p. 307.

self can do. Paul refers to the *human self* not only as "spirit," "soul," and "body," but also as "heart." The term "heart" has connotations of passions, intentions, affections, and desires, while another word that Paul also uses, *nous* (spirit), refers primarily to the capacity of thought. We are addressed as thinking creatures who are responsible, intentional, and capable of making judgments. We note, however, how all these anthropological terms point to real human existence — and in such a way that human decay and sin can also enter the picture. We can get ourselves mixed up in sin, can act from a wrong disposition, can surrender ourselves to passions and desires, and can live in opposition to God.

Paul also distinguishes between our inner and outer nature: "Though our outer nature is wasting away, our inner nature is being renewed every day" (2 Cor. 4:16). This points to the struggle that we as believers are engaged in: "We know that the law is spiritual [*pneumatikos*]; but I am carnal [*sarkinos*], sold under sin" (Rom. 7:14). We must be freed from the sinful disorder of life so that we may once again possess that inner nature with which we may serve God. In communion with Christ, life is so enriched that we no longer lose ourselves in the affectations of our bodies and our psyches. The Spirit guides us towards a renewal of his thought *(nous)*, ". . . that [we] may prove what is the will of God, what is good and acceptable and perfect" (Rom. 12:2). Believers, Paul says, must allow themselves to be guided by the Spirit of Christ, and no longer by the affectations of the body and the psyche. "For you did not receive the spirit of slavery to fall back into fear, but you have received the spirit of sonship" (Rom. 8:15).

Paul Althaus maintains that the central concepts in Paul's theology demonstrate a kinship with the Old Testament as well as with the Hellenistic mystery religions. But this does not mean that Paul derives his thinking from those mystery religions. The origin of Paul's theology is "the insight of how Christ stands in contrast with man and how He has a renewing significance for man."[35] The Spirit penetrates our feelings, our thinking, and our will, but, at the same time, stands, as the Spirit of God, in contrast with us as human beings. Clearly, renewal and conversion find their basis and source in our assimilation with the death and resurrection of Christ. In Pauline theology and anthropology we see clearly how the cross and the resurrection of Christ take hold of our life. In this process, the human self experiences the attraction of the Spirit of Christ. As a result, there is a movement of Christ

---

35. Paul Althaus, *Der Brief an die Römer,* NTD (Göttingen: Vandenhoeck & Ruprecht, 1949), p. 75.

— through the message of the gospel, the sacrament of baptism, and the impact of God's Spirit — towards us in the here and now. The resurrection is not an extrapolation of true believers hoping for the possibility of renewed life; rather, the message of Christ as the risen Lord brings conversion and renewal. This involvement with Christ as a reality that precedes faith and renewal is crucial in the Christian praxis of faith and in the worldview of the believer. Here, central concepts like grace, freedom, and faith find their origin. "But God shows his love for us in that while we were yet sinners Christ died for us" (Rom. 5:8). It is precisely this divine reality that enters the reality of us and of our human culture, and there creates a new dynamism. "For freedom Christ has set us free; stand fast, therefore, and do not submit again to a yoke of slavery" (Gal. 5:1).

A Liminal Event and an Independent Person

The cross and the resurrection are the heart of the worship service and of the Christian Year. But the mystery remains. Without imagination and spiritual insight, without some mastery of religious language and an openness to the transcendent, it remains something strange. No wonder that the discussion about this mystery of faith continues. When, on the Areopagus, Paul began to talk about the resurrection, some said, "We will hear you again about this" (Acts 17:32), while others ridiculed him. Nonetheless, Dionysius the Areopagite joined the apostle.

"That is why our faith halts when Easter comes in view," O. Noordmans says. "Until we come to the cross, everything seems fine. But then the gospels bring us to that critical chapter. At that point the same reluctance and fear come over us, as happened to the women, and, a little later, to Peter and John, and we experience the same confusion as the men on the road to Emmaus (Luke 24:22), and even the same disbelief that we find with Thomas" (John 20:24-31).[36] We cannot fit the Easter event into a closed, naturalistic or idealistic worldview. Without the imagination of the eschatological and transcendental dimension, we get stuck in the realism of the laws of nature. Or we succumb to the temptation to let the resurrection be absorbed into the "myth" or the "story" of the deepest desires and human ideals. But this no longer has the power of an actual event that breaks through and renews. Paul says that Jesus Christ is revealed in him

---

36. O. Noordmans, *Verzamelde Werken*, vol. 8 (Kampen: Kok, 1980), p. 310.

(Gal. 1:12) — that is to say, in Christ he is confronted with a new reality. The resurrection is the opening act in a new drama: our own redemption and the redemption of the world. This redemption not only has an ontological-eschatological dimension, but also an ethical-religious one. In the Christian faith, Christ is the pivot of everything. He is the firstborn from the dead (Col. 1:18). He is God's mystery, "in whom are hid all the treasures of wisdom and knowledge" (Col. 2:3).

If we acknowledge that, indeed, Christ is the living Lord, does it no longer matter *how* we conceptualize this? Does it not suffice that we imagine an event that is at the boundaries of our world, a mystery that breaks through the limits of time and space, a mystical awareness of, and participation in, the Christ event? As long as there is, on the one hand, this imagination of this mysterious event, and there is, on the other hand, its renewing power and inspiration — as long as both dimensions are present, does this guarantee the fundamental pillars of the Christian faith?

Here I want to make two remarks. First, we should bear in mind that human faith does not generate the "idea" or the "imagination" of the resurrection; on the contrary, the event of the cross and the resurrection results in the Christian faith. The initial state of mind of the disciples was not exactly one of faith. The theory that their faith resulted from visions — a view that was popular in the nineteenth century — is not very convincing and reduces faith in the resurrection to a matter of psychology. The resurrection of Christ is the pillar and the guarantee of our salvation and of the redemption of the concrete life of humankind and creation. Second, regardless of the degree to which the appearances of Christ are presented as liminal events between two worlds, it is nonetheless clear that Christ is *one and the same* person as the historical Jesus. Therefore, the resurrection of Christ is not the mere personalization of an idea or ideal, but the return to life of an independent person, of Jesus of Nazareth as the Messiah. After the women heard the news from the angels that he had risen, Jesus meets them, and they grip his feet (Matt. 28:9). The words of Christ in the Gospel of Luke are abundantly clear: "See my hands and my feet, that it is I myself; handle me, and see; for a spirit has not flesh and bones as you see that I have" (Luke 24:39). When Christ appears, the mystery is revealed. He proceeds to a new mode of existence: "Do not hold me, for I have not yet ascended to the Father," he tells Mary (John 20:17). He comes and goes in a mysterious manner (Luke 24:36). He appears in another form (Mark 16:12). For that reason Paul speaks of a "spiritual body." In short, it is the dialectic of the glorified Lord on the one hand being identical with Jesus on earth and on the other hand as having moved into another mode of being.[37]

Confessing Christ as the risen Lord is fundamental for the praxis of faith and the worship service. He is the Christ of faith who is *present*. When Paul says that "it is no longer I who live, but Christ who lives in me" (Gal. 2:20), he points to a personal submission to, and connection with, the risen Christ. We cannot reduce this to a remembering of the historical Jesus. For it is more: there is a personal tie, a communal life — in such a way that we experience Christ as One who may be encountered in a personal manner. Our faith has to do with a personal relationship with the living Christ. These dimensions are also implied in the *remembrance of Christ* in the celebration of the Lord's Supper. The constant background of the sacrament is that God himself is personal and that God himself is spirit — that is to say, a subject. God is a person, a self, with a spiritual character who enters into a covenantal relationship. Humans are made in the image of God and commune with God, and in the same manner, believers commune with the risen Christ. Richard Niebuhr says, "When we reflect on the life of faith in and with Jesus Christ as the companion of the trusting and would-be loyal self, we find that what is present is not a Jesus of history but the Christ of faith, not Jesus incarnate, but the risen Lord. . . . The Jesus Christ we acknowledge in personal trust and loyalty . . . is Jesus Christ risen from the dead, Jesus Christ among us. . . . In other words: We remember Jesus Christ *in our very co-existence with him*."[38]

At this crucial point we must note that we should not play the psychological dimension and the objective dimension of faith off against each other, but should keep them together. For faith in the risen Christ implies a mental, psychological habit on the part of believers. Religious faith is part of our mental and psychological infrastructure. Here we find the connections and intersections with other convictions, insights, and motivations. At the same time, believers have certain ideas about *who* God is. There is also an objective dimension: we have convictions about God, Jesus Christ, and the Holy Spirit. We cannot reduce this dimension to psychological processes. If we want to have a good understanding, we must distinguish three aspects. First, we must distinguish the level of the mental and psychological processes (the psychosocial dimension); second, the noetic content (the confessional dimension);

---

37. Hendrikus Berkhof, *Christian Faith*, rev. ed. (Grand Rapids: Wm. B. Eerdmans, 1986), pp. 315, 316.

38. H. Richard Niebuhr, *Faith on Earth* (New Haven: Yale University Press, 1989), pp. 87, 89.

and third, the reference to God himself (the referential dimension).[39] This third dimension is of crucial importance not only for faith in God, but also for faith in Christ, the risen Lord. We encounter Christ in a personal way. According to the New Testament witness, Jesus Christ presents himself as the risen Lord. Just as God takes the initiative in the encounter with us; Christ proceeds to meet his disciples and his church. Religious life is characterized by the fact that the believer is touched by the Other. That is where we find the redemptive mystery and the receptivity that is so important in religion. The anchor of faith is the reality of God, of Christ, and of the Holy Spirit as the *referential* other. The noetic content (confession) and the psychological dimension (spirituality) are in a dependent relationship with regard to the divine subject. Without this ontological order, faith ceases to exist.

Holy Presence

When the church assembles on the day of the resurrection, *the people are touched by the sacred*. In and through the actions of the church, faith is activated. The sacred "happens" in a concrete interaction between the human self and the Spirit of Christ. The communion with Christ becomes a living reality. Christ as the risen Lord interacts with the human selves of the participants. The world of the cross and the resurrection comes alive. The human self is activated — not just his rational aspect, but also his emotions and his will. The entire human self — with all the functions of the human spirit — is involved. The relationship with Christ is an activity of the human self, *an act of faith*.

The liturgical agenda and the Christian Year provide the framework within which the sacred may touch us. The liturgy projects a picture of the reality that enables worshippers to exercise their faith. This setting brings the worshippers to "enlightenment" and offers moments of "revelation" — revelation in the sense that the setting sheds light on the path they travel, on their spiritual considerations, on the praxis of their daily life, and on the events in the world at large. It is a revelation in the sense that they understand anew *who* God is and *what* salvation is all about. This occurs in the

39. See F. Gerrit Immink, "Homiletics: The Current Debate," *International Journal of Practical Theology* 8, no. 1 (2004): 120; and F. Gerrit Immink, *Faith: A Practical Theological Reconstruction* (Grand Rapids: Wm. B. Eerdmans, 2005), pp. 26-42, 238-66. See also Robert Audi, "Belief, Faith, and Acceptance," *International Journal of Philosophy of Religion* 63 (2008): 90. Theologians often refer to the attitude of faith as *fides qua*, or as "intentional faith."

hymns and the prayers, in the preaching of the Word, and in the sacrament. Thus the worship service has moments of *disclosure.* But there may also be moments of estrangement, of want, of being abandoned by God, of personal insufficiency and disbelief. The service always concerns an existential level of relationships. There are moments of awareness, of insight, of joy, of remorse, of humility, of hope and desire, of conviction, of inspiration. We may experience a direct sense of God's goodness and redeeming power, or we may find ourselves in a more contemplative situation in which we focus on our own state of mind or think about, and weigh, an insight of faith. This gaining of awareness, or becoming conscious of something important, is an activity of the human self, but it is set in motion through the *performance* of the worship service. This *performance* is about something: it is about the world of faith, about salvation in Christ, about Christ, about everyday life, about disappointment and grief, about sin and forgiveness, about life and death. In the *performance* (of word and act), "worlds" and "realities" come into the spotlight — that is to say, there is a certain "aboutness," there is (propositional) *content, there are realities* with which the human self becomes involved.[40]

The worship service as *performance* has an activating and actualizing function. This also includes the *becoming-present* of Christ. In and through the speaking and acting of the church, the Spirit of God activates the human self. He does this in such a way that he not only brings about human receptivity but also presents a gift. Christ and his salvation are actually *given.* There is a genuine *presentation* on the part of God. With regard to the participants, this means *experience and ownership* as well as receptivity. In the *performance,* faith is not a matter of accepting particular opinions as true; it is a struggle for truth and evidence. The truth is discovered, praised, and believed. Or the evidence does not convince, doubt strikes, and the chasm increases.

The story of the two men on the road to Emmaus (Luke 24) shows something of the relationship between *performance* and becoming-present. Two disciples who are on their way home discuss what has happened. While they are talking, Jesus joins them. As they talk, the disciples' sight remains unclear, and they fail to recognize him. They are confused because of the message of the women, who say that Jesus lives. They have received a message from heaven, from an angel of God; still, it does not register in the minds of these disciples. It is only after the Scriptures have been opened,

---

40. Niebuhr, *Faith on Earth,* pp. 23-30.

and after it has been explained what Moses and the prophets said about the Messiah, and as the bread is being broken — it is only then that the disciples discover that Jesus himself is present. Here a situation is presented that may be compared to a worship service. People come together, and there is a discourse. And the Risen One joins the discourse; he takes part in it. It is significant to note the role of language in the disciples' experience. This discourse, however, does not suffice to discover the living Lord. When the Scriptures are opened, they shed light on the recent events. And the eyes of the disciples are opened as the bread is broken and the Scriptures are explained. "Did not our hearts burn within us while he talked to us on the road, while he opened to us the scriptures?" (v. 32). The becoming-present is linked to the words of Scripture and to the holy act of the breaking of the bread. This is how the recognition takes place. The eyes of the disciples are opened, and they recognize him.

A Multi-layered Existence: Creation and Redemption

On the first day of the week, the church meets to joyfully bring thanks to God the Father for the fact that he has become involved, in a decisive way, with this world in his Son. The church lives in the expectation that, from this decisive event onwards, God's Spirit will remain involved with the world. The church that has gathered together does not look upon the world as a lawless mess. The world is a work of creation, and the church lives in the expectation that God will finish his creation. God is confessed and served as a trustworthy Source of love. That is why the church in its earthly existence prays to God. The prayer is not an empty cry that emerges from human impotence, but something that emerges because of the mystery of a living God who in his love remains connected with his creation. It stems from the joy that God has not forsaken the world and human life. In the worship service, the church does not succumb to the idea of the world as a cold and blind order; instead, it counts on the creative and renewing power of the living God.

We already noted that the worship service follows a Trinitarian model. This is expressed in the praises and prayers of the church. Worshippers praise God for the redemption in Christ: "Blessed be the God and Father of our Lord Jesus Christ, the Father of mercies and God of all comfort . . ." (2 Cor. 1:3). In the celebration of the Lord's Supper, this praise to God as the Creator is directly connected to gratitude for the redemption in Jesus Christ:

The Mystery of Christ

> We thank You,
> Lord our God,
> everywhere and always,
> through Jesus, our Lord,
> for You have created us. . . .

In the liturgy the communion with God is enacted from a number of different perspectives. God is confessed as the Creator, and worshippers are invited to understand themselves as made in the image of God. At the same time, the awareness is evoked that human life is a life where evil dwells, and where a rebellion against God has broken out. This is expressed, for instance, in the prayers of confession and in the Kyrie. As human beings, we lead a life that is in disarray; the world in which we live is no paradise. We see destruction, tyranny, guilt, and tragedy. Paul's letter to the Romans underscores this truth: "For the creation was subjected to futility . . ." (Rom. 8:20); "We know that the whole creation has been groaning in travail together until now" (Rom. 8:22). But the very expression "groaning in travail" implies that the creation will be finished. We long with great desire for the glory. And thus, in the proclamation of God's grace and in the hymns of glory, the redemption in Christ is expressed in words.

Faith in the resurrection thus opens a new perspective on daily life. Because of the resurrection of Christ, the church has a firm reason to expect a real transformation of this world. This means that in the midst of the ambivalence of our present world, the church knows that the evil powers will not continue to keep us in their grip.

Therefore, hope is a fundamental part of Christian life. This hope is directed towards the re-creation, the glory that will come to us. The *hoped-for reality*, J. Christiaan Beker says, is the renewal of all that exists in apocalyptic time.[41] Precisely because Christ has conquered death, the church is able to look and live in a new manner. Paul says that the Spirit lives in believers: "If the Spirit of him who raised Jesus from the dead dwells in you, he who raised Christ Jesus from the dead will give life to your mortal bodies also through his Spirit which dwells in you" (Rom. 8:11). This indwelling Spirit groans within us and sets this expectation ablaze: the redemption of our body. The Spirit has been given to us in our hearts as a security, a guarantee (2 Cor. 1:22). Therefore, the believer is not just convinced that the full salvation in Christ is realized (and is given as security), but he looks ardently for the completion of that salvation. It makes his joy and praise complete.

---

41. Beker, *Paul the Apostle*, p. 152.

The meaning of all of this in people's lives is the constant concern of the worship service. Both the minister and the worshippers are focused on this. Empirical research by Theo Pleizier has shown that participants in worship do not consider the eschatological dimension as an escape from the misery of daily life. On the contrary, they see it as something that gives depth to life. Through this hope they have access to a deeper level of their existence.[42] As they begin to discover such notions as atonement and redemption, hope and forgiveness, worshippers learn to deal in a new way with the brokenness of life.

---

42. Theo Pleizier, *Religious Involvement in Hearing Sermons: A Grounded Theory Study in Empirical Theology and Homiletics* (Delft: Eburon, 2010), pp. 261-64.

CHAPTER 4

Backgrounds and Dilemmas

In the previous chapters we saw how the gathering of the church on Sunday morning is connected with the redemptive events in Jesus Christ. The Christian church meets in the name of the Father, the Son, and the Holy Spirit. Worshippers expect that the Triune God will be actively present in their midst. In the second part of this book, I will elaborate on the praxis of the worship service. We will look at the prayers and the hymns, the sermon, and the Lord's Supper. But before we do so, we must be aware of the backgrounds and dilemmas that play a role in the structure of the worship service. *Word* and *sacrament* are essential elements in the tradition of the Christian church. We already studied the central role of the *epiclesis* (the prayer for the presence of the Holy Spirit) in the Protestant worship service. The risen Christ works through the power of the Holy Spirit. This applies to the effect of the Word as well as of the sacrament. We have noted that there are some differences between Rome and the Reformation with regard to *epiclesis* and consecration. But there are other differences as well. One can hardly think of a Roman Catholic worship service without the Eucharist, while a Protestant service without the proclamation of the Word is similarly unlikely. What is the background, and what are the differences? Does Rome have reason to blame the Reformation for having broken the unity between Word and sacrament? Does this unity between Word and sacrament presuppose that the Lord's Supper should be celebrated every Sunday? The first part of this chapter will deal with this question. Then I will study the role of the Scriptures and of the sermon in the worship service. The Reformation gave the Bible a central role in the worship service by giving a substantial place to the proclamation of the Word and to the reading of the Scriptures. But some questions may be raised. First, do the Scriptures exercise some real authority over the sermon? What has happened through the centuries (in particular as a result of the Enlightenment) regarding the authority of the Bible? Second, we must realize that the sermon is a free discourse in which eloquence plays an important role. A sermon must be pleasant to listen to and must be able to retain the attention of the audience. How does this happen? How risky is it to connect the *presentia Christi* with human discourse? The second part of this chapter will deal with these kinds of questions and backgrounds. Finally, we will discuss baptism. The Reformers advanced their own arguments with regard to baptism, but stayed within the tradition of the church. The Anabaptists reintroduced adult baptism and rejected the baptism of infants. The growth of the Pentecostal churches and the influence of the evangelical movement have resulted in the rekindling of this discussion in the Protestant churches. Is infant baptism legitimate? How do we respond to people who want to renew their baptism?

The Lord's Supper: A Departure from Tradition?

A weekly communion service on Sunday is not part of the Protestant tradition. In some congregations the Lord's Supper is celebrated about once every six weeks, and in others, once a month. Churches with a weekly celebration are quite rare. But Christ said emphatically, "Do this in remembrance of me" (Luke 22:19). Would that not be reason enough to celebrate the Lord's Supper every Sunday? Is, in fact, every "ordinary" Sunday-morning worship not an "incomplete" service? Movements for liturgical renewal have emphasized the unity of Word and Table. In the Netherlands, for example, the new liturgical handbook (*Dienstboek*, 1998) takes the unity of Word and Table as its basis. For M. A. Vrijlandt, things are quite clear:

> There is enough evidence from the New Testament (Acts 20:7) and from the tradition of the early church (Justin Martyr, *Apology*), to conclude that the sacred meal was celebrated every Sunday. In the Middle Ages we discover the schizophrenic situation that the priests are obliged to celebrate the Eucharist every day, while the laity is required to do so once a year (at Easter). However, the preference is that they do so four times a year at the time of the principal feasts: Christmas, Easter, Pentecost, and once in September. The people would also confess their sins four times a year. After having done penance, they could partake from the meal.

How strangely things can turn out, says Vrijlandt. The Reformation wanted to go back to the New Testament, but remained stuck in a medieval aberration. He argues that Calvin (and even Zwingli) had wanted a different course, but were unable to convince the city government, which was afraid of a weekly, large-scale participation of all believers.[1]

In most parts of the Protestant Church, the communion service follows the Protestant ecumenical pattern. This means that the main prayer of thanksgiving is spoken at the table. This does away with the radical change in the order of the liturgy that dates from Reformation times. The Reformers removed the *Canon Missae* because of the dominant presence of the idea of sacrifice. By removing the *Canon,* they dismantled the prayer of consecration. This led to the practice of beginning the celebration with a quotation from 1 Corinthians 11: "Beloved in the Lord Jesus Christ, listen to the words that Christ spoke when He instituted the sacred Supper, as recorded for us by the holy apostle Paul. . . ." The phrase "Words of Institution" is spoken before the Scripture reading, which is followed by instructions for the actual celebration. The underlying thought is that the word of Christ, "Do this in remembrance of me," is directed to the church. Calvin therefore thought that these words should not occur in a prayer to God.[2]

As a consequence, different traditions for the Lord's Supper continued to co-exist. The Dutch *Dienstboek* of 1998 gives both the Protestant ecumenical order and the old Reformed order. We may note that in the American *Book of Common Worship* (1993 edition), the option is given not to include the institutional words of the "great thanksgiving" prayer. And this is not just theory, for there are many churches in which the main prayer of thanksgiving is clearly separated from the Words of Institution. Following the prayer, the minister repeats the words whereby Christ instituted the Supper, while breaking the bread and pouring the wine. Then the communion takes place.

The re-introduction of the Table Prayer signals a return to pre-Reformation tradition. What was this tradition like? H. A. J. Wegman points out that the Table Prayer originally consisted of three parts:

1. Praise is sung to the glorious name of the Lord.
2. We are called to remember the life, death, and resurrection of Christ.
3. A plea is uttered for the presence of the Holy Spirit.[3]

---

1. M. A. Vrijlandt, *Liturgiek* (The Hague: Commissie voor de kerkmuziek, 1987), p. 225.

2. Ronald P. Byars, *Lift Your Hearts on High: Eucharistic Prayer in the Reformed Tradition* (Louisville: Westminster John Knox Press, 2005), p. 79.

3. H. A. J. Wegman, *Riten en mythen. Liturgie in de geschiedenis van het christendom* (Kampen: Kok, 1991), pp. 87, 88.

The three parts of the prayer suggest that it has a Trinitarian structure. It focuses on giving thanks to the Father, remembering Jesus Christ, and making a plea for the presence of the Holy Spirit. After Vatican II, this plea visibly returned in the Roman Catholic liturgy. In the *Missale Romanum* of 1570 (the result of the Council of Trent), the *epiclesis* was hardly present.

The Reformers thus caused a significant departure from the liturgical traditions of the past. The "Swiss Reformation," in particular, had a crucial role in this process. Zwingli went even further than the other Reformers in dismantling the traditional celebration of the mass. He developed a Sunday worship service that followed the pattern of the *Pronaus* service: a practice in southern Germany and Switzerland that focused on the Word, without a celebration of the Eucharist. It is often said that Calvin was keen to reform the classical celebration of the mass (as his work in Strasbourg may lead us to think), but that he failed because of the attitude of the city government of Geneva.

The reason for the radical change was the sacrifice of the mass. The Roman Catholic Church regarded the mass as a sacrifice — "not a sacrifice that Christ brings, but a sacrifice that we may bring together with him *(offerimus)*."[4] Luther rejected this idea of a sacrifice in the strongest possible language: he spoke of a foolish abomination that was composed of many different elements. He wanted to see the mass as a "Segnung" (blessing), as "the table of God, or the supper of the Lord, or a remembrance of the Lord."[5] Zwingli also wanted to discontinue the *Canon Missae*. Instead, he suggested four new prayers, with the Lord's Prayer at the end.

The Swiss Reformation (Zwingli in particular) is often heavily criticized in discussions about liturgical renewal.[6] It was thought that the Swiss broke the unity between Word and Table by developing a worship service that was patterned after the *Pronaus* model. Movements for liturgical renewal usually plead for the restoration of the liturgy as a cultic event, and for the inclusion of the age-old traditions and rites. The Swiss Reformation (and Zwingli in

---

4. Josef Andreas Jungmann, *De eredienst van de Katholieke Kerk* (Roermond: Romen, 1959), p. 153.

5. *Evangelischer Gottesdienst. Quellen zu seiner Geschichte*, ed. Wolfgang Herbst (Göttingen: Vandenhoeck & Ruprecht, 1992), p. 21.

6. Theophil Müller, *Evangelischer Gottesdienst. Liturgische Vielfalt im Religiösen und Gesellschaftlichen Umfeld* (Stuttgart: Kohlhammer, 1993), pp. 19, 20. Christoph Albrecht comes to this conclusion with regard to the Lutheran tradition in the Enlightenment era: "During the first three centuries of its history, the history of evangelical worship is one of liturgical deterioration." See his *Einführung in die Liturgik* (Göttingen: Vandenhoeck & Ruprecht, 1989), p. 31.

particular) and the ongoing Enlightenment in the eighteenth and nineteenth centuries are blamed for the destruction of the liturgical structure (especially the unity between Word and sacrament). Rudolf Stählin makes a very bold statement in this regard: ". . . the Protestant 'Aufklärung' (Enlightenment) resulted in a total destruction of the liturgy of the church. . . . The only aspect that continues to be considered as meaningful for a worship service is related to admonishment and moral improvement. Everything else has become meaningless and has been destroyed — very thoroughly!"[7]

Preaching and the Lord's Supper

Nonetheless, the Protestant worship service is not to be viewed in all respects as a total break with ecclesial tradition. There has been preaching as long as the Christian church has existed, and the sermon was always preached in the vernacular. The ministry of the Word played an important role in the medieval worship service, even though at times this aspect was largely ignored. Repeatedly Charlemagne urged the synods to ensure regular preaching.[8] The sermon was intended to educate the people with regard to the basics of the Christian faith. Often the Apostles' Creed and the Lord's Prayer served as topics for the sermon. W. F. Dankbaar argues that since the ninth century a number of well-established liturgical elements in the vernacular were in common use, and were linked to the sermon. These were never authorized by any papal decree, and yet they were widespread in the Late Middle Ages — in Germany, in France, and even in England. Together with the sermon they formed a liturgical unit, between the mass for the catechumens and the mass of the faithful.[9] Among these liturgical elements, Dankbaar states, were the Apostolicum, the Lord's Prayer, the general prayer for all needs in Christendom, and the public confession of sin *(Offene Schuld)*. Precisely these liturgical rubrics played an important role in the shaping of the Reformed liturgy in Switzerland. Therefore, the sermon as popular catechesis, surrounded by the classical liturgical rubrics, was a well-known phenomenon, in particular in the cities of southern Germany. In this context it is important to mention the popular *Manuale Curatorum* of Johann Ulrich

---

7. Rudolf Stählin, "Die Geschichte des Christlichen Gottesdienstes," in *Leiturgia*, vol. 1 (Kassel: Stauda Verlag, 1954), p. 72.

8. W. F. Dankbaar, *Hervormers en Humanisten* (Amsterdam: T. Bolland, 1978), pp. 221-36.

9. Dankbaar, *Hervormers en Humanisten*, p. 228.

Surgant that was published in Basel in 1503. Surgant was a priest and a professor at the University of Basel. The book, which was reprinted many times, was intended as a guide for preaching and liturgy, especially for young clergy. The book showed how several liturgical elements surrounded the sermon: the reading of the text on which the sermon was based, the general prayer to which the church would respond with the Lord's Prayer and the Ave Maria, announcements, the Apostolicum, the Ten Commandments, and the *Offene Schuld*. The liturgical sections were not always cited verbatim; they might be paraphrased.

According to J. Schweitzer, the Swiss Reformation based its reformation of the worship service primarily on the liturgical elements that surrounded the sermon. He believes that the Reformed churches in the German-speaking part of Switzerland did not develop a completely new liturgy, but adapted existing traditions.[10] He points to the fact that the *Pronaus*, in contrast to the liturgy of the mass, does not contain any responsive formulas, and therefore we find no responsive formulas in early Reformed liturgies. Every reminder of the dramatic re-enactment of the Christ event is left out. Schweitzer thinks that the lack of an organic link between the celebration of communion and the weekly worship service in the Swiss tradition resulted from the dislike for the sacrifice of the mass and the emphasis on the proclamation of the Word. "Without any objection," he says, "an order of service was borrowed which attributed a rightful place to the proclamation of the Word, but failed to provide reasonable arguments for the administering of the sacraments in the Sunday service."[11] This caused a separation between the preaching of the Word and the celebration of the Lord's Supper, which henceforth characterized the further development of the Reformed tradition.

In the fifteenth century we find not only churches where the priests celebrated the mass on a daily basis, but also services with a proclamation of the Word without the Eucharist — services that were primarily focused on catechetical instruction and the practical aspects of daily life. And when the Reformation gained a stronger foothold, it was to be expected that the pattern of *Pronaus* worship would become the leading principle for the Reformed tradition — all the more so because the urban populations manifested an increasing openness towards new developments, and turned more

---

10. J. Schweitzer, *Zur Ordnung des Gottesdienstes in den nach Gottes Wort Reformierten Gemeinden der Deutschsprachigen Schweitz* (Zurich: Zwingli Verlag, 1944), p. 8.

11. Schweitzer, *Zur Ordnung des Gottesdienstes in den nach Gottes Wort Reformierten Gemeinden der Deutschsprachigen Schweitz*, p. 12.

and more against the ecclesial hierarchy. Schweitzer argues that the Reformers were aiming not at a reformation of the mass, but at the creation of a new pattern for the worship service that would closely follow the tradition of the *Pronaus*. The celebration of communion was an *addition*. Following the proclamation of the Word, the Words of Institution, together with a short instruction, were read, and then communion was celebrated. Calvin preferred a weekly communion service because of the importance that he attached to the Lord's Supper — not because he wanted to maintain the unity of the liturgy.[12] However, Calvin accepted the practice of German-speaking Switzerland, where the Lord's Supper was celebrated quarterly.

Those who want to see a liturgical renewal and a restoration of the early Christian form of the Table Prayer have often suggested that Calvin saw the liturgy of Strasbourg as the ideal: it restored the role of the sermon in the worship service, and it purified the mass and transformed it into the Lord's Supper.[13] Hence the unity of Word and sacrament. However, Calvin remained unsuccessful in his efforts because the views of the early Swiss Reformers (e.g., Zwingli) had already resulted in an established practice. Howard Hageman comments, "Whether or not you want to believe it, in actual practice Zwingli became the liturgical teacher for the Reformed. . . . Many Calvinist churches are Reformed in their theology, but Zwinglian in their liturgy and their view of the sacraments."[14]

A Swiss Accent

The first proposal for new communion liturgies in Reformation times showed a shift from consecration to communion. This development took place in a relatively short period, between 1523 and 1526. In these years both Luther and Zwingli gave a new format to the celebration of the Lord's Supper.[15] Both men emphasized the unrepeatability of Christ's sacrifice on the cross. Zwingli, however, differed from Luther in his emphasis on the Lord's Supper as an act of the congregation — an emphasis characteristic of the Swiss Reformation. We notice this, for example, in the title of a publication in

---

12. Schweitzer, *Zur Ordnung des Gottesdienstes in den nach Gottes Wort Reformierten Gemeinden der Deutschsprachigen Schweitz*, p. 20.

13. Vrijlandt, *Liturgiek*, pp. 86, 87.

14. Howard G. Hageman, *Pulpit and Table* (Richmond, Va.: Wipf & Stock, 1962), p. 34.

15. J. Schweitzer, *Reformierte Abendmahlsgestaltung in der Schau Zwinglis* (Basel: Reinhardt, 1954), pp. 69-89.

which Zwingli introduced the new manner of celebrating the Lord's Supper on Easter Sunday 1525: *Aktion oder Bruch des Nachtmals* (Act or Custom of the Evening Meal).

What did the actual celebration look like? The altar was removed from the choir, and a table was placed in the aisle of the church. The glory and glitter was gone: away with the silver cups, the magnificent garments, the communion on a podium in the choir of the church. The church now assembled in the aisle of the church around the table, on which wooden vessels were placed. From now on, the celebration of communion was visible to all, and worshippers could participate. The minister was a *servant* of the church. In this act, in which both the church and the servant were the performers, the command of Jesus — "Do this in remembrance of me" — was implemented. Zwingli incorporated the Lord's Supper in the preaching service by removing communion from the choir and placing the table in the part of the church where the people were. Thus communion "is not an act *on behalf of* the congregation, but an act *of* the congregation, that is, of the congregation that is brought together under the Word."[16] Zwingli quite clearly used the Pauline quotation as the formula that instituted the Lord's Supper, but not in the sense of a consecration. The *Aktion* is an act of the congregation, a response to the act of Christ — an act in which Christ himself is active.

If we want to arrive at a good understanding of the Reformed communion praxis, we must remember that Calvin as a Reformer appeared somewhat late on the ecclesial scene. When he began his work, a certain tradition with regard to the format of the worship service had already been established in the southern German and Swiss cities. At first, attempts were made (in particular in Strasbourg) to eliminate all sacrificial elements of the *Canon* prayer from the mass (something even Zwingli wanted as late as 1523), but rather soon the entire *Canon* prayer was removed, and the words that instituted the Lord's Supper came to function as the Scripture reading. In the actual order of the liturgy, a short instruction and admonition followed or preceded these Words of Institution, but almost immediately these were followed by the communion of bread and wine. In any case, the Words of Institution and the communion were close together.

Here, however, Calvin embarked on a new path. In Geneva in 1542, he placed the excommunication of the unrepentant directly after the Words of Institution. Only then came the exhortation to examine oneself, and the

---

16. Markus Jenny, *Die Einheit des Abendmahlsgottesdienstes bei den Elsässischen und Schweitzerischen Reformatoren* (Zurich: Zwingli Verlag, 1968), p. 50.

invitation to participate in the Lord's Supper. Perhaps this proved somewhat severe for the Dutch churches, for in the classical text for communion in the Dutch Reformed Church, the self-examination is brought forward, but the excommunication is toned down. The intention, however, is the same: the exhortation for self-examination has a more or less instructional form. Over time, this Calvinist liturgy has received much criticism. J. A. M. Mensinga (nineteenth century) saw it as a remnant of the medieval doctrine of sin. He claimed that "this self-examination is nothing but an ecclesial tradition which has its basis in the auricular confession of the Roman Church."[17] In the explanatory notes of the *Oecumenisch Ordinarium* (1968), Calvin's didactic structure is disdainfully disregarded: "The entire idea is reminding the participants at the table of things they apparently did not yet fully learn during their catechetical instruction."[18]

The Unio Mystica

This criticism — though in itself understandable — was, however, also influenced by its context. The dominant theology of the nineteenth century did not favor the classical theology of atonement, and the liturgical movement of the twentieth century objected to the didactic element in the Reformed liturgy. The question may well be asked, however, whether this criticism does justice to the unique character of the communion with Christ that is expressed in the Reformed celebration of communion. The basic thought is that the communion with Christ is an actual reality, and not a matter of the *presentia realis* in the elements. With his emphasis on self-examination, Calvin places the communicant in the center. The self-examination promotes the awareness of the participant in communion. The instruction is intended to strengthen the process of spiritual union with Christ. Something real happens when the Lord's Supper is celebrated, but this does not occur without the involvement of the believer. It is a *unio mystica* of the believer with Christ rather than a *presentia realis* in the elements. The prayers and the wording of the *Sursum Corda* underscore how the celebration is an exercise of faith. In a prayer in preparation for the celebration, Calvin says,

---

17. J. A. M. Mensinga, *Verhandeling over de liturgische schriften der Nederlandse Hervormde Kerk* (The Hague: Thierry en Mensing, 1851), p. 247.

18. *Proeve van een oecumenisch ordinarium. Toelichting en verantwoording* (Amsterdam: Prof. Dr. G. van der Leeuw Stichting, 1968), p. 36.

> Help us, O God, through Your mercy, that we may truly enjoy, through the certainty of faith, His body and blood, yes, Him, our very Savior, truly God and truly man, the only true heavenly bread; . . . that He may live in us and effectuate a holy, blessed, and eternal life in us. . . .[19]

In the celebration of the Lord's Supper, something real takes place. The Spirit ensures that we may have Christ in us and that he will remain with us. In the communion praxis of Reformed Protestantism in the Netherlands — particularly in the more Pietistic traditions — the "pious communicant" occupies a central place.[20] The self-examination of the communicant with regard to his own moral and spiritual situation becomes a central part of the celebration of the Lord's Supper.[21] Wilhelmus à Brakel defines the relationship between the *sign* and the *signified* as follows:

> So that it will not be a union that results from human imagination, but a true unity — not a local or physical union, but a spiritual one that finds its ground and truth in what Christ instituted. That the union is therefore not in the substance of bread and wine, in themselves, or in the plate and the cup, and other things that may be used, but a union that results from the active faith of the communicant, as Christ instituted it, considering the relationship between the sign and what it signifies — as a stone that is taken out of a heap of stones, and is used as a boundary marker for a piece of land, will not be changed as far as its nature is concerned, but in how it is viewed.[22]

This quotation appears to point in the direction of trans-signification rather than transubstantiation. In the celebration of communion, an existential relationship between Christ and the believer is brought about.

This is not just an accidental Dutch variant of the Reformed tradition. The *Westminster Directory* of 1644 asks in the communion prayer "for God's gracious presence and [the] effective presence of his Spirit in us . . . , so that Christ may be one with us, and we with Him; and that He may live in us, and we in Him, who loved us and gave Himself for us." It is precisely in the Reformed tradition and in groups (e.g., the Puritans) with Reformed roots

---

19. Calvin, in Mensinga, *Verhandeling over de liturgische schriften der Nederlandse Hervormde Kerk*, p. 219.

20. Petrus Immens, *De godvruchtige avondmaalsganger* (Nijkerk: I. J. Malga, 1874).

21. A. A. van Ruler, *Reformatorische opmerkingen in de ontmoeting met Rome* (Hilversum: Paul Brand, 1965), p. 211.

22. Wilhelmus à Brakel, *Redelijke Godsdienst*, vol. 1 (Nijkerk: n.p., 1870), pp. 989, 990.

Backgrounds and Dilemmas

that the idea of the effective impact of the communal aspect of the Lord's Supper is alive and is not detached from the subjective faith experience of the communicant.

Appealing to the Traditions of the Bible

The classical Reformed communion liturgy originated in the Reformation struggles and breathes a Pauline concept of atonement.[23] Alternatively, the communion liturgy in the Protestant ecumenical tradition has a tone of celebration and breathes the spirit of the Easter mystery. Joop Boendermaker states that the meal of the Lord symbolizes "the great mystery of the removal of life's restrictions through Christ, who went through the utmost depth and prepared our way."[24] The Lord's Supper points to the secret of his new presence. The story of the men on their way to Emmaus functions as the key text: they recognize the Lord as he breaks the bread. And there is an additional emphasis: attention to the Jewish roots of Christian worship.[25] The celebration of the Lord's Supper cannot be detached from "the source where it originated: the celebration of the Jewish Pascha. In our Communion celebration the miracle of the Messianic passage across the border of the possible lives on."[26]

However, it is not so simple to justify the current communion tradition and practice through an appeal to the Bible. Over time, various theories have been proposed regarding the way that communion was practiced in the New Testament. But the texts do not give a uniform picture. Moreover, it is not difficult to discover in these different hypotheses clear traces of the theological interests of the scholars. In a thorough study that is still worth reading, Hans Lietzmann (in 1926) suggested that the New Testament knew of two kinds of communion celebrations: the Jerusalem type and the Pauline type. We find the first type in the Acts of the Apostles. We read in Acts 2 about the early disciples: "And they devoted themselves to the apostles' teaching and

---

23. See F. Gerrit Immink, "Heilig avondmaal: klassiek-gereformeerd," in *De weg van de liturgie. Traditiies, achtergronden, praktijk*, ed. M. Barnard and F. G. Immink (Zoetermeer: Meinema, 2008), pp. 245-56.

24. Joop Boendermaker, "Maaltijd van de Heer; Oecumenisch Protestant," in *De weg van de liturgie*, ed. Barnard and Immink, p. 226.

25. R. Boon, *De joodse wortels van de christelijke eredienst* (Amsterdam: Prof. G. van der Leeuw Stichting, 1973), p. 2.

26. Boendermaker, "Maaltijd van de Heer; Oecumenisch Protestant," p. 227.

fellowship, to the breaking of bread and the prayers" (2:42). The breaking of the bread is explicitly mentioned. We notice the same in other texts. However, only the breaking of the bread is mentioned, and not the drinking of the wine, as we also see in the story about the men from Emmaus. We find the same manner of celebrating communion in the early Christian document *Didache*. Lietzmann considers this to be the most original form of the Lord's Supper. He describes it (quite idealistically) as follows: "The Jerusalem church forms itself into a union after it has experienced that the Lord is truly alive and has not remained dead. And what happened in the sunny times of his journeys through Galilee is now experienced in a new way.... The 'fellowship at the table' that began with the 'historical' Jesus is now continued with the risen Lord."[27] How is this done? Someone pronounces the blessing, breaks the bread, and shares it with the others. Thus the meal is begun. There is no cup and no prayer of thanksgiving. The meal has strong eschatological connotations. It is a joyful meal in the expectation of the return of the Son of Man. This is where the "Maranatha" finds its place. We note the jubilation, which we read about in Acts 2:46: "... they partook of food with glad and generous hearts."

The Pauline type of communion is thought to have originated with Paul (and Mark), and was supposedly linked to the Last Supper (the communion) that Jesus had with his disciples. In this tradition the meal is primarily a commemoration of Christ's death. Moreover, we read of bread and wine. The wine is a sign of the blood that was shed and of the sacrificial animal that died, and this seals the new covenant. In taking part in this meal, the church commemorates and thus proclaims the death of the Lord. According to Lietzmann, the order of communion in 1 Corinthians 11 is as follows: An *agape* meal is held. All members bring food and wine as they are able. The acts of communion are tied to this meal: the meeting is opened with the blessing and the breaking of the bread — and concluded with the blessing and the drinking of the cup. Lietzmann describes it thus: "The blessing of the bread at the beginning, the blessing of the wine at the end, and in between the actual meal." Lietzmann says that this type of celebration also undergoes a further development that makes it somewhat similar to Hellenistic commemorative meals. The table fellowship gradually becomes a mystical *koinonia*. The believers joyfully partake of the body of Christ, and thus form one body with him. Lietzmann believes that this Pauline type of communion

---

27. Hans Lietzmann, *Mass and the Lord's Supper: A Study in the History of the Liturgy* (Leiden: Brill, 1979), pp. 187, 204.

eventually pushed the Jerusalem type aside and thus developed into the celebration of the Eucharist of the early church.[28]

Lietzmann's proposal shows the existence of a tension between, on the one hand, an original (and therefore early) meal that was related to the historical Jesus, and, on the other hand, a meal of commemoration, as it was known in the Hellenistic world. It should be noted that the Pauline type is also of an early date. These differences indicate that the earliest praxis of communion was not unambiguous. The Dutch liturgical movement strongly emphasized the eschatological dimension (communion as a joyful meal) and its link with the Jewish Passover. This seems quite obvious when we connect communion with the story of its institution. Yet, some recent research points — in line with Lietzmann — to a Hellenistic setting of the New Testament communion praxis.

The hypothesis of H. J. de Jonge presents a good example of this line of reasoning. He argues that the early Christian weekly gathering is a continuation of the Hellenistic communal meal with its two aspects. De Jonge does not believe that the Lord's Supper should be linked to the tradition of the synagogue: "If you want to have a general idea of the Christians of the two first centuries, you would not be widely off the mark if you would picture them first of all as 'dining-clubs': communities that would meet regularly in the home of one of its members, where they would meet in the dining room to enjoy together the main meal of the day, the *deipnon* or supper, followed by a conversation in an after-meeting with wine, the *symposion*."[29]

De Jonge believes that the formula of interpretation ("This *is* . . .") and the formula of institution ("*Do* this in remembrance of me") did not occur. The early Christian document *Didache* does not include the words of interpretation and does not regard the meal as a form of becoming one with Christ. But it does interpret the eating and drinking as an anticipatory participation in the coming kingdom of God. According to De Jonge, even in the third and fourth centuries, celebrations occurred without the Words of Institution. He maintains that with Paul new interpretations emerge, which we notice in (what he refers to as) the explanatory notes in 1 Corinthians 11. Paul still seems to have known a practice without words of interpretation and of institution (1 Cor. 10), but he connected this praxis with the story of the Last Supper, with the result that the words of interpretation and the Words of Institution became

---

28. Lietzmann, *Mass and the Lord's Supper*, p. 185.

29. H. J. de Jonge, *Avondmaal en Symposium. Oorsprong en eerste ontwikkeling van de vroeg-christelijke samenkomst* (Leiden: Universiteit Leiden, 2007), p. 4.

part of the celebration. De Jonge says, "This is what we call an etiology of the ecclesial Communion; it originated as an etiology, somewhere in the third or fourth decade of the first century, possibly in Jerusalem."[30] Whatever the case may be, Paul stresses the corporative union with Christ. Partaking of the bread and wine is regarded as communion with the body and blood of Christ. This Pauline approach is clearly present in the Reformed communion liturgy.

The Word of God and the Sermon

In the worship service the Bible has the status of *canonical text*. The church thereby confesses that God speaks in and through this book to us. For this reason, the Bible is referred to as the Holy Scriptures or the *Word of God*. The authority of the Scriptures as God's Word may be expressed in the liturgy in different ways. In the Protestant worship service, the open Bible is usually placed on the pulpit. The church assembles around the open Word. In the Roman Catholic worship service, the congregation stands when the gospel is read, and this reading is done by an ordained priest.[31] As a result, this reading of the gospel acquires a sacramental connotation, and it suggests that the risen Lord himself is speaking. When he finishes his reading, the priest lifts up the Holy Scriptures and says, "The Word of God." In Protestant circles, the Scripture readings may be concluded in various ways:

>
> Minister: Thus speaks the Lord.
> Congregation: We thank God.
>
> Minister: Blessed are those who hear the Word of God and keep it.
> Congregation: Thine be the honor, the praise, and all the glory, Father, Son, and Holy Spirit in all ages of ages.

These words show that the Bible is an authoritative book in the worship service, and this is underscored by the term "Word of God." Moreover, in the Protestant worship service the sermon is often referred to as the administering or service of the *Word of God*.

---

30. De Jonge, *Avondmaal en Symposium*, p. 10.
31. Vrijlandt, *Liturgiek*, pp. 194, 195.

Backgrounds and Dilemmas

In the Bible we meet a God who speaks to human beings when he approaches them. The calling of Abraham is a significant example: "Now the LORD said to Abram, 'Go from your country and your kindred and your father's house to the land that I will show you. And I will make of you a great nation, and I will bless you, and make your name great, so that you will be a blessing'" (Gen. 12:1-2). God calls Abraham and promises his blessing. The God-human relationship is, on the one hand, characterized by the concepts of calling and promise, and is, on the other hand, characterized by a response of faith and trust. The motif of a speaking God and a human being who responds in faith and trust is an important theme in the Protestant praxis of faith. Martin Luther once said that God "never has dealt, or does deal, with men in any other way than by the word of promise. Again, we can never deal with God in any other way than by faith in the word of His promise."[32] We find similar statements by Calvin: "We make the freely given promise of God the foundation of faith because upon it faith properly rests." Calvin does not say that the Word encompasses nothing more than the promise, but "... we do point to the promise of mercy as a specific element for our faith."[33] Even though this focus on the promise betrays an Old Testament background, the theology of Paul plays a decisive role in the development of this theological structure. For Paul specifically emphasizes that in Jesus Christ all promises have been fulfilled (2 Cor. 1:20). In his explanation of the breadth of the redemption in Christ, Paul refers back to the calling of Abraham, and specifically to the thought that Abraham trusted God and that God "reckoned it to him as righteousness" (Gen. 15:6). This is the basis of the Word-response concept in the worship service. The communion between God and humankind is the core, and this is expressed in the dynamic of Word and faith.

This approach has received broad support from within the Protestant tradition. However, in this paragraph I hope to clarify that different aspects may be distinguished in this mutuality of Word and faith. On one end of the spectrum, the emphasis is on the faith experience and the inner enlightenment through the Spirit. At the same time, there may be a significant fear regarding an external authority of the Word as the formal authority of the Scriptures. On the other end of the spectrum, there is a strong emphasis on the revelatory aspect of God's promise — on the "oth-

---

32. Martin Luther, *The Ninety-five Theses and Three Primary Works by Dr. Martin Luther* (Grand Rapids: Christian Classics Ethereal Library, 1885), p. 192.

33. Calvin, *Institutes of the Christian Religion*, Book III.2.29, p. 575.

erness" of the Word as the Word *of God*, and the proclamation of Christ as a *gift of salvation*. However, though the emphases may differ, because the promise is characterized by grace, the Reformation takes God as its point of departure. G. J. Heering points to the fact that the Reformation regarded God's grace as "the one and all, and certainly the beginning of everything.... This view of grace and of the Holy Spirit determined the understanding of the Reformers of the origin and nature of faith. The origin of faith is in all respects the result of divine intervention, the work of His Spirit, and likewise its nature is not an attribute of man, . . . but only the fruit of God's grace, the work of His Holy Spirit inside man."[34] What happens in the inner person, Heering says, may be the most important aspect, but it is nonetheless dependent upon the priority of God's Spirit inside man. If not, then faith would cease to be faith.

The Effect of the Word

To arrive at a clear understanding of the term "word" as a theological concept, I want to make a few remarks about the biblical view. In the Old Testament, the word-event is an important revelatory form. God acts in history, his glory appears, and we encounter events with the character of a theophany. Yet, generally speaking, the word has a primary role in the relationship between God and us. When God appears, he usually appears as the One who speaks: "Thus says the Lord . . ."; "The Lord said. . . ."

Th. C. Vriezen considers the word as a revelatory form: It is "proof for, on the one hand, an immediate personal relationship between God and man, and, on the other hand, for the spiritual character of that relationship."[35] In the Old Testament the divine word has a force that brings things about: "The divine revelatory word does not only proclaim salvation, but it also brings it near and actualizes it."[36]

Likewise, in the New Testament, God is represented as a speaking God. "In many and various ways God spoke of old to our fathers by the prophets; but in these last days he has spoken to us by a Son" (Heb. 1:1-2).

---

34. G. J. Heering, *Geloof en openbaring*, vol. 2 (Arnhem: Van Loghum Slaterus, 1935-1937), p. 257; see also F. Gerrit Immink, *Faith: A Practical Theological Reflection* (Grand Rapids: Wm. B. Eerdmans, 2005), pp. 167, 168.

35. Th. C. Vriezen, *Hoofdlijnen der Theologie van het Oude Testament* (Wageningen: H. Veenman, 1966), p. 241.

36. Vriezen, *Hoofdlijnen der Theologie van het Oude Testament*, p. 238.

The Christ event *is God speaking to us*.[37] In the past there may have been different channels of information, but now all converge in the Son. But, once again, it is God who is *speaking*; it is a word that *he wants to be heard*. Look at the remarkable statement in Hebrews 4:2: ". . . but the message which they heard did not benefit them, because it did not meet with faith in the hearers."

In Romans 10:8, Paul links "the word of faith which we preach" explicitly with Jesus Christ. Through the apostles, the Christ event comes to the people as the proclamation of salvation. Thus proclamation and faith are closely intertwined. It is clear that the Christ event constitutes the content of the proclamation: ". . . if you confess with your lips that Jesus is Lord and believe in your heart that God raised him from the dead, you will be saved" (Rom. 10:9). Just as Moses, at the end of the book of Deuteronomy, points the people of Israel to the commandment, so the apostle now focuses on the proclamation of the *word of faith*.

The sermon acquired its central role (as a ministry of the Word of God) in Protestant worship because of its relationship to the fact that the speaking God revealed himself in Christ. The Christ event is the good news, and this good news is spread around the world as the Word of God. Paul writes that the gospel is proclaimed everywhere: "For I delivered to you as of first importance what I also received, that Christ died for our sins in accordance with the scriptures" (1 Cor. 15:3). He brings the gospel of God; he hands it down. This handing down, announcing, instructing — or whatever terms we may use — is far more than a sharing of information about a past event. This sharing of the gospel as such is a power of God: "For I am not ashamed of the gospel: it is the power of God for salvation to everyone who has faith . . ." (Rom. 1:16). The Word possesses a renewing power; hence the appeal and the admonition: "We beseech you on behalf of Christ, be reconciled to God" (2 Cor. 5:20).

The proclamation may be a human activity, but in the meantime something happens in which God has a part. Paul writes to the church in Thessalonica, "When you received the word of God which you heard from us, you accepted it not as the word of men but as what it really is, *the word of God*, which is *at work in you believers*" (1 Thess. 2:13; italics mine). We notice that the oral proclamation of the gospel is referred to as the word of God, and this oral transmission instills faith. Romans 10:17 also points to

---

37. Otto Michel, *Der Brief an die Hebräer* (Göttingen: Vandenhoeck & Ruprecht, 1966), p. 95.

the connection between oral proclamation and faith: "So faith comes from what is heard, and what is heard comes by the preaching of Christ." In the First Letter of Peter we find the same thought (1:25): ". . . but the word of the Lord abides for ever." That word is "the good news which was preached to you." The expression "word of God" does not just cover the moment when the word is delivered. As James Thompson explains, "Preaching contains the summons to the hearers to receive it, believe, repent, and be incorporated into the people of God."[38] It would therefore be a one-sided approach to fully identify the preaching with the *kerygma* concept. For the idea of *paraclesis,* the notion of an appeal, is also typical for how we understand the word of God. The proclamation of Jesus Christ is both the announcement of salvation in his name and the appeal to live in accordance with it. Paul did all he could to instruct and equip the new communities of believers through his preaching and teaching.

The congregation hears the reading of the Holy Scriptures during a worship service as the Word of God, and it trusts that the sermon — to the extent that it "serves" the Word — will also become operative as a word from God. The *epiclesis* prior to the Scripture reading nurtures this confidence that the entire word-event will awaken and strengthen our faith. And so, Calvin was convinced that God himself speaks to the church through the preaching:

> For God nothing is higher than the preaching of the gospel. For this is His reign by which He wants to rule in this world. The preaching is the instrument that leads the people to salvation. . . . For the only means through which people can come to salvation is by being instructed in the teaching of the gospel.[39]

Heinrich Bullinger phrased this close link between Word and sermon very aptly in the *Confessio Helvetica posterior* (1566): "Predicatio verbi Dei est verbum Dei." The preaching of the Word of God itself becomes a word of God. In this confession we read about the effect of the Word: "When today this Word is preached to the congregation by God's lawfully ordained servants, we believe that it is God's Word that is being proclaimed and is being received by the believers." Calvin was of the same opinion. The preaching

---

38. James W. Thompson, *Preaching like Paul: Homiletical Wisdom for Today* (Louisville: Westminster John Knox Press, 2001), p. 52.

39. This is a statement from one of Calvin's sermons. See W. H. Th. Moehn, *God roept ons tot zijn dienst* (Kampen: Kok, 1996), p. 256.

Backgrounds and Dilemmas

in the worship service is God's word, in the sense that it has the same powerful effect as the initial speaking of God. The repetition (in the sermon) does not weaken it and does not lessen it as the Word of God.[40] Luther also made similar statements, such as this one: "The voice of the preacher that I heard was not his, but it was the word and the preaching of the Holy Spirit, who, through this external instrument, awakens the faith in us and thus sanctifies us."[41] The central role of the preaching in the worship service is supported by the conviction that God not only spoke in Jesus Christ and in the Scriptures, but that he also speaks here and now through the preaching of his Word.[42]

The Power of the Word and the Vulnerable Authority of the Scriptures

The Reformers were convinced of the authority of the Scriptures. They had discovered this authority as they read and studied the Scriptures. For them this was not a formal, external authority, but an insight of faith.[43] For that reason, the church cannot enforce the authority of the Scriptures in any formal way. But their truth is evident to whoever wants to discover it. And if we might ask how we are convinced that the Scriptures originate with God? That would be the same, Calvin claims, as asking how we would distinguish light from darkness, white from black, and sweet from bitter: "Indeed, Scripture exhibits fully as clear evidence of its own truth as white and black things do of their color, or sweet and bitter things do of their taste."[44] We receive this sense of self-authentication through the Holy Spirit as our internal teacher:

> Let this point therefore stand: that those whom the Holy Spirit has inwardly taught truly rest upon Scripture, and that Scripture indeed is self-authenticated; hence, it is not right to subject it to proof and reasoning. And the certainty it deserves with us, it attains by the testimony of the Spirit. . . . Therefore, illumined by His power, we believe neither by our

---

40. T. H. L. Parker, *Calvin's Preaching* (Louisville: Westminster John Knox Press, 1992), p. 24.

41. Martin Luther, Weimarer Ausgabe (W.A.), 45, 616, p. 32.

42. A. Niebergall, "Die Geschichte der Christlichen Predigt," in *Leiturgia*, vol. 2, ed. Walter Blankenburg and Karl Ferdinand Müller (Kassel: Stauda, 1954), p. 257.

43. Parker, *Calvin's Preaching*, p. 2.

44. Calvin, *Institutes of the Christian Religion*, Book I.7.2, p. 76.

own nor by anyone else's judgment that Scripture is from God; but above human judgment we affirm with utter certainty (just as if we were gazing upon the majesty of God Himself) that it has flowed to us from the very mouth of God by the ministry of men.[45]

The Scriptures give human beings insight. They produce the immediate realization that the promises concern us and impact our concrete daily life. But in recent history we have seen how vulnerable Protestantism tends to be on this point. As modern scholarship developed (in particular through the historical-critical approach), a debate has arisen regarding the authority of Scripture. Nonetheless, the Bible has continued to function as the source of preaching. Protestant worship has remained Word-oriented. This is, however, not so strange, for the Word of God (as an active force) was never identified with the Scriptures as a book.

Even though the authority of the Scriptures has been strongly debated, the Bible has retained its special status in the worship service. However, different arguments have been advanced for the belief that the Bible is the *Word of God*. For some, the authority of the Bible is connected with inspiration; for others, its authority comes from divine authorship; while for others still the authority is found in the content of the gospel, Richard Lischer states.[46] Manfred Josuttis reminds us that through the centuries the perspective has shifted back and forth. In the past, he says, the authority was connected to the origin of the Scriptures: it was thought that God inspired the authors. When this approach ran into difficulties because of historical-critical research, the idea emerged that the content of the Scriptures (and, eventually, the person of Jesus Christ) guaranteed its authority. Today this approach is destroyed by postmodern thinking, and the authority is now thought to reside in the hermeneutical interaction between textual fragments and a concrete situation.[47] But John McClure thinks that in the late-modern context the authority of the biblical text has been completely lost. Ministers no longer use clear-cut exegetical methods and hardly consider the text as canonical.[48]

---

45. Calvin, *Institutes of the Christian Religion,* Book I.7.5, p. 80.
46. Richard Lischer, *A Theology of Preaching* (Eugene, Ore.: Wipf & Stock, 1992), p. 58.
47. Manfred Josuttis, *Die Einführung in das Leben. Pastoraltheologie zwischen Phänomenologie und Spiritualität* (Gütersloh: Kaiser Verlag, 1996), pp. 51-53.
48. John S. McClure, *Otherwise Preaching: A Postmodern Ethic for Homiletics* (St. Louis: Chalice Press, 2001), pp. 13-26.

Backgrounds and Dilemmas

Modern Preaching

When the church meets on Sunday morning, the Bible is read and a prayer is offered for the active presence of the Holy Spirit. The believers trust that the words of the Bible that are read will have a wholesome effect and that in the preaching the *word of God* will be heard. But as the authority of the Scriptures has come under debate, the term "word of God" is not as unequivocal as before. The focus has shifted from the *word of God* to *religious experience*. We find a good example of these developments in the view of the German practical theologian Friedrich Niebergall regarding the nature of the sermon. In 1904 he gave a presentation entitled "Die Moderne Predigt." "How should we preach," he asks, "if we are to do justice to our time?" He notes two important factors: our understanding of the *gospel,* and our understanding of the *spirit of the time* in which we live.[49]

With regard to the modern approach to the gospel, Niebergall sees three positive developments. First, he notes, critical scholarship has not halted before the door of theology. Had that been the case, theology would have been locked into academic isolation. Second, because of this development we pay more attention to the *religious personality.* This is where we find the origin of all doctrines (as time-related expressions of Christian piety) and of the Scriptures (as a collection of testimonies of a developing religiosity). Third, there is a growing interest in *other* religions. Christianity and religion, faith and piety — we must always connect these two dimensions, even when one group values faith as a personal walk with God, and the other group sees it as a pantheistic-mystical state of mind.[50]

In his day, Niebergall saw a shift in preaching. It occurred because believers became less focused on the Scriptures as such, and more focused on life. The sermon was not just about explaining Scripture, but also about how Christians were to live their lives. In addition to this shift, there was also a focus on the personality of the minister and on the situation of the congregation. So, what is the concrete gain of the modern approach to the gospel? With regard to the critical dimension of historical-critical scholarship, I want to point to two of Niebergall's views that seem relevant to me. The first is leaving behind us the idea of a *literal inspiration* of the Scriptures. We cannot simply say of every section of Scripture "It says so

---

49. Friedrich Niebergall, "Die Moderne Predigt," in *Die Aufgabe der Predigt,* ed. Gert Hummel (Darmstadt: Wissenschaftliche Buchgesellschaft, 1971), pp. 9-74.

50. Niebergall, "Die Moderne Predigt," pp. 13-17, 51-55.

in God's Word." We will have to dig deeper. We will have to ask ourselves what people were thinking when they expressed themselves in a particular way. The Bible is a book from another era, with shifting backgrounds and ideals. This means that the Bible is a collection of documents that, as Niebergall points out, "contains an ascending line of expressions of religious life." The second is recognizing the *legendary* and *mythical* traits of the Bible. If we regard the Scriptures as "expressions of the embrace, in faith, of God's gift and help," it does not make much difference whether the content of this faith is expressed in historical accounts or in myths. As Niebergall points out, "The history of man's fall into sin remains an expression of the power of sin, whether or not we see it as a historical event or view it as *Dichtung*."[51]

Niebergall thus presents a positive view of the critical side of scholarship that some might see as a threat to preaching. The idea of literal inspiration has proven to be untenable, but when we approach the Scriptures a little more from "the bottom up," the faith in God evident from ancient times can still inspire us. Moreover, not everything has to be historical in order to be relevant. Niebergall, however, goes one step further when he points to the positive effect of historical-critical scholarship. We already noted his interest in the religious personality. In this connection he finds the view that the Scriptures express the *people's personal trust in God* a liberating perspective. This helps us in the sermon as far as the psychology of religion is concerned, for it enables us to deal with all kinds of analogies between then and now. In addition, Niebergall argues, in the past we often subconsciously projected our own religious ideals back into the Bible. This danger of projection increases when we limit revelation to a particular period in history. We then run the risk of identifying our own opinions with this revelation and of creating our own Jesus. But, according to Niebergall, the ideals of life keep shifting, and we are entitled, "in continuity with the foundational period of our religion," to always shape our ideals and needs in new ways. Each era adds a new ring around the tree of Christian life. But we must not sanction this by an appeal to revelation.[52]

Niebergall thus defines preaching in the following way:

> Preaching is an activity of a religious personality who has been called to do so, and who, on the basis of his own understanding of the gospel, helps

---

51. Niebergall, "Die Moderne Predigt," pp. 47, 50.
52. Niebergall, "Die Moderne Predigt," pp. 54-55.

Backgrounds and Dilemmas

the religious community to find answers to their questions and needs, or offers assistance.

Remarkably, Niebergall emphasizes the *religious personality* of the minister, not the ecclesial or apostolic dimension of the proclamation of the Word. And this minister has a particular *understanding* of the *gospel*. The minister operates within a *religious community* and tries to respond to the *questions* of the members of that community and to assist with their *needs*.[53]

Niebergall's position is characteristic of the modernist approach of the early twentieth century. In his views, some of the main themes of nineteenth-century theology converge. But we also note that some of his emphases have exerted a lasting influence on the understanding of the sermon in Protestant worship. I will mention four of these.

First, as the authority of the Scriptures became more problematic, a shift occurred, with the result that the message of the gospel was to a greater extent approached from "the bottom up." This does not mean that the mystery of faith was now completely reduced to human imagination or projection. But it does point to a growing awareness that the biblical stories and images were conditioned by context and culture. In the emerging nineteenth-century liberal Protestantism, the Holy Scriptures and the doctrines were regarded as human expressions of religious experiences in the encounter with God. In Chapter 3 we saw how the resurrection of Christ and his appearances were interpreted as visions of the disciples and the early church.

Second, with regard to the worship service as religious praxis, human experience not only became what the gospel addressed, or the embodiment of the faith that had been awakened by the Holy Spirit; it also began to function as the place where salvation originated.[54] This led to a growing interest in religiosity and psychology. Ministers were instructed in "religiöse *Volkskunde*" (religious ethnology).[55] There was a developing interest in the hearer. This shift towards the hearer and towards the *Gelebte Religion* (religion as it is lived) of the last quarter of the twentieth century (as a reaction to revelation theology) occurred together with a renewed interest in the theological roots of the nineteenth century.

---

53. Niebergall, "Die Moderne Predigt," p. 11.

54. Mary Catherine Hilkert, *Naming Grace: Preaching and the Sacramental Imagination* (New York: Continuum, 1997).

55. Paul Drews, "'Religiöse' Volkskunde: eine Aufgabe der Praktischen Theologie," in *Seelsorge. Texte zum gewandelten Verständnis und zur Praxis der Seelsorge in der Neuzeit*, ed. F. Wintzer (Munich: Gütersloher Verlagshaus, 1978).

Third, less attention was paid to the promise and the *kerygma* as *verbum externum*. Calvin wanted to place the Word of Scripture in the spotlight, so that the hearers would find therein the will and promise of God. In the theology of revelation, the word-event received a strong eschatological focus: there is a tension between the promise of salvation and what we see in the world around us. Niebergall and other nineteenth-century theologians speak of eschatology as a human *ideal*. We see the same trend in American sermons of the nineteenth century.[56]

Fourth, a greater awareness of the historical context of the Scriptures led to relativizing its truth. We are not bound to what was linked to a particular time, and there is more room for diversity.

Dialectical theology was vehemently opposed to the kind of liberal preaching just described. In a presentation in 1921, Eduard Thurneysen — a friend and supporter of Karl Barth — spoke in fiery language against this so-called eloquence, against these so-called needs of the people, and against the role of the minister. According to Thurneysen, the relationship between God and us is much less smooth than we are told and cannot be simply characterized in terms of religious interest:

> Therefore, do not concern yourself any longer with the *psychology* of the hearers and the so-called understanding of the *human psyche*. There should be no speaking from the pulpit about life experiences, nor about the pious lives of people (neither of others nor of ourselves), in an attempt to awaken similar experiences in others. It should be all about the *knowledge of God*, the *proclamation of God!*[57]

When human beings and their life experiences become the focal point, the divine is reduced to a perspective on reality — in fact, it becomes an idol. For Thurneysen it is important that we are the object of discussion. Where can the personal and societal dimension be better challenged than where there is nothing but the *new and totally different word of God* that breaks in and comes to us? Thurneysen sees *the Word in the words* as the secret of the sermon. I will return to this dilemma in Chapter 6.

---

56. See *The Consolations of God: Great Sermons of Phillips Brooks*, ed. Ellen Wilbur (Grand Rapids: Wm. B. Eerdmans, 2003).

57. Eduard Thurneysen, "Die Aufgabe der Predigt," in *Die Aufgabe der Predigt*, ed. Hummel, pp. 110-17.

Backgrounds and Dilemmas

Eloquence in the Pulpit

Gert Otto claims that placing too much emphasis on the sermon as the administering of the Word of God can result in the proclamation of the Word becoming somewhat like the telling of a myth. The particular religious impact may receive so much emphasis that the aspect of interhuman communication is not given its due. The sermon is in fact nothing but a discourse. Otto thinks that dialectical theology, with its stress on the Word of God, has not done enough justice to the element of eloquence:

> The sermon is a rhetorical task. Therefore we must develop a theory of preaching within the context of rhetoric. Theological reflection, with its exegetical, historical, and systematic concerns, has its place within the framework of rhetoric. The rhetorical aspect is not to be subjugated to theology. Rhetoric rather than theology is the dominant factor in our reflection on questions of homiletics.[58]

This emphasis has consequences, both for sermon preparation and for preaching. It is not just a matter of *what* is being said, but also of *how* it is said. A discourse is constructed in a certain way, and its effective execution depends on the right formulation and its order. A good sermon will convince, but will not catch worshippers off-guard. To this end, homiletics should pay attention to the sermon as discourse. "If the sermon may be seen as a sub-genre of 'discourse,'" Albrecht Grözinger says, "the science that reflects on this particular genre, rhetoric, has homiletical relevance."[59] That is why we should look at the sermon not only from a theological perspective, but also from a non-theological point of view. This is important because preaching has to do with a communication process between unequal partners. When he preaches, the person in the pulpit is in a position of power. What role do the elements of power play in the sermon? What space is there for the hearer? What role does the personality of the minister play? We will make a serious mistake if we only discuss these things theologically.

In the last quarter of the twentieth century, we saw important renewals with regard to the rhetorical dimension of preaching. The narrative form of the sermon, as it developed in the United States in the so-called New

---

58. Gert Otto, *Rhetorische Predigtlehre. Ein Grundriss* (Mainz: Matthias Grünewald Verlag, 1999), p. 7.
59. Albrecht Grözinger, *Homiletik* (Gütersloh: Gütersloher Verlagshaus, 2008), p. 194.

Homiletic, is a good example. The traditional sermon style was seen as too static and too cognitive. Listeners no longer appreciated a static model with a number of points, because this too strongly presupposed a logical sequence and tended to make the sermon too much like a lecture. Eugene Lowry, who has written a book on the narrative sermon, says that the "plot," not the underlying idea, should determine the form of the sermon. The sermon, like a good movie or a good novel, should have an effective plot. A sermon is an "event-in-time" that has a narrative art form resembling that of a play or a novel.[60] A sermon should not be a construction of a series of ideas, but a movement in time that maintains the tension until its dénouement. It is a dramatic performance.

From ancient times onward, preachers have used rhetoric in the worship service. Church fathers such as Chrysostom and Augustine were well known for their eloquence. Chrysostom excelled in his "lively," concrete use of language, his use of examples from the political and social life of his day, his preference for moral and practical matters over speculative theology, and his emphasis on pastoral aspects; above all, he was superbly eloquent.[61] Augustine was well schooled in classical rhetoric and made ample use of it in his sermons. Likewise, in manuals that appear in the early Reformation period, the art of rhetoric is strongly encouraged. Hyperius provides a prominent example.[62] In one of his treatises he asserts that the worship service should offer an approach to the Scriptures that will be easily accessible to a broad, general public. "I do not know why this is so," he says, "but it is clear that its teachings bring more profit, in particular for the great masses, if it deals with things that nurture the *faith,* that call people to *love* and good works and strengthen *hope.*" These three elements, he maintains, represent the core of spiritual life. Referring to concepts from rhetoric, he indicates how the minister may use these various aspects in a sermon. When dealing with matters that relate to *statements of faith,* for example, he can employ methods of *confirmation* and *rebuttal.* When dealing with the *walk through life,* he can focus on instruction towards righteousness *(institutio in iustitia)* or the *improvement (correctio)* of immorality. When dealing with things that bring

---

60. Eugene Lowry, *The Homiletical Plot: The Sermon as Narrative Art Form,* expanded edition (Louisville: Westminster John Knox Press, 2001), p. xx.

61. O. C. Edwards Jr., *A History of Preaching* (Nashville: Abingdon Press, 2004), p. 85.

62. Andreas Hyperius, *De Formandis Concionibus Sacris, Sive de Interpretatione Scripturam Populari* (Basel, 1579). The first edition was published in 1553; a new, enlarged edition was published in 1562. In 1901 (in Berlin) a German translation was published by E. Chr. Achelis and Eugen Sachsse, *Die Homiletik und die Katechetik des Andreas Hyperius.*

comfort, he can emphasize *hope.* For Hyperius, rhetoric is particularly useful for bringing the right formulation and structure to the sermon material.[63]

In the eighteenth and nineteenth centuries, homiletics was affected by a new emphasis on rhetorical eloquence. In this period, eloquence became more popular, not just in continental Europe, but also in England and in the United States. In the eighteenth century, John Witherspoon, president of Princeton College, gave a series of lectures about rhetoric. He used the term "eloquence" as his title, and referred in that connection also to eloquence in the pulpit.[64] This new eloquence, rooted in the emerging Enlightenment, focused on the speaker, the public, and linguistic skills. Moreover, there was, more than before, an interest in the psychological dimension of communication, as well as in the literary form and style of the presentation. The term "eloquence" was broadly applied to the "art or the talent to execute a presentation in its totality." In public presentations, care was given to the enlightening of the mind, the stimulating of the imagination, the moving of the passions, and the influencing of the will. The main intention of the sermon was "the *reformation of mankind."* In this context, conviction and persuasion were important. The aim was to effect *change.* The essential thing was to convince worshippers that they should love God and lead a good and righteous life.[65]

From earlier times until today, there has been a difference of opinion in homiletics as to whether rhetoric may be enlisted as a means of convincing people.[66] For opponents of rhetoric in preaching, the term "persuasion" has a negative connotation. Could listeners be led astray by inappropriate arguments? Is there not an excessive amount of rational debate and of one-directional communication? Is there the danger of an authoritarian attitude, of abuse of power and manipulation? Behind these questions is the strong belief that people should be able to make choices in freedom and based on their own views. Moreover, the content of a speech or a sermon ought to be decisive, not the human technique of delivery. But those who have an opposite view maintain that in recent studies of rhetoric, "speech" and "communication" are linked with the creation of community, and with change and growth. Proponents of rhetoric believe that the act of persuasion does

---

63. Hyperius, *De Formandis Concionibus Sacris, Sive de Interpretatione Scripturam Populari,* i.5.

64. James F. Kay, *Preaching and Theology* (St. Louis: Chalice Press, 2007), p. 49.

65. Kay, *Preaching and Theology,* pp. 50, 51.

66. See the discussion between Lucy Hogan and Richard Lischer: Lucy Hogan, "Rethinking Persuasion," and Richard Lischer, "Why I Am Not Persuasive," in *Homiletic: A Review of Publications in Religious Communication* (Winter 1999).

not belong in the sphere of power and manipulation, but is directed towards the voluntary assent of the other. The speaker is interested in the other and wants to share something with him. This view presupposes, of course, that the speaker is honest and acts responsibly.

A good example of the use of eloquence in preaching is found in the *Homilétique, ou théorie de la prédication* (1853) of the influential Swiss theologian Alexander Vinet. This book was immediately translated into Dutch, German, and English. In his preface, Vinet states unequivocally that the *word* is the basic element of the Christian religion. Christianity is a religion of mind and thought, and must be *spoken*. The *word* occupies a primary place in the work of a minister. However, Vinet immediately adds that it is not just a matter "of *words* that must be selected and repeated, but rather of sharing the substance of *life*. For the truths from which the gospel is composed must become alive and must become a reality in living persons." It is clear, however, that in this line of thinking the word has a prominent place in Christian worship. The minister speaks to God on behalf of the people — that is the prayer; and on behalf of God to the people — that is the sermon. It is noteworthy that, from the outset, this word-event is characterized by *mutuality*. The word ensures that we are connected to each other. And instruction means that we explain the gospel to each other.[67]

Vinet pleads with passion for eloquence as a *method* of preaching. To preach a sermon requires not just a *talent* for public speaking, but also a *method* that a minister can practice and develop. The discipline for this is homiletics, the *theory of preaching*. Since the sermon is a public address, eloquence is a self-evident part of homiletics. Even though eloquence in the pulpit has a character of its own, it nonetheless falls under the umbrella of *public eloquence*. As Vinet explains, "Eloquence, certainly, is always the same; it is not one thing in the pulpit and another in the senate or at the bar."[68]

Vinet pays a significant amount of attention to the imagination of the hearers. Eloquence presupposes an intense study of the human heart, so that one knows all its motives. In the end, eloquence consists in a mutual correspondence between the spirit and the heart of the audience and the thoughts and the expressions that the preacher uses. Vinet says,

> Eloquence rests upon sympathy. One is never eloquent, except on condition of speaking or writing under the dictation of those he is addressing:

---

67. A. Vinet, *Homiletics; Or, The Theory of Preaching* (Edinburgh: T&T Clark, 1853), p. 2.
68. Vinet, *Homiletics*, p. 22.

Backgrounds and Dilemmas

it is our hearers who inspire us, and if this condition is not fulfilled, we may be profound and agreeable, but we shall not be eloquent.[69]

It goes without saying that a speaker wants to achieve something when he speaks. *Persuasion* is part of the equation, and so is *drama,* since motivations and intentions are involved. Oratory is like wrestling, like a struggle, Vinet says. The orator speaks to the mind as well as to the heart, and eventually he appeals to the will. He struggles to bring forth what is good, and he accomplishes this by touching the hearts of his listeners. This also applies to preaching. The purpose of eloquence in the pulpit is most definitely to touch the *will.* But that purpose is united with that of instruction; the preacher is a teacher in the form of an orator.[70]

Here we see in outline a new development that will be typical for the formation of a new theory of worship in the nineteenth century. There are four key points to mention here. First, the influence of Schleiermacher is noticeable in the terminology. The word *darstellen* is often used in the sense of "presenting something," and this reminds us of Schleiermacher's *Darstellende Mitteilung.* For Schleiermacher, *Darstellung* is artistic expression, and aesthetical and rhetorical elements always play a role in the presentation. Second, as a result of the emphasis on the word as the basic element of worship, the Lord's Supper disappears into the background. With Schleiermacher also the word-event is central: sermon, hymn, and prayer are the essential aspects of the worship service.[71] Third, a strong sense of mutuality and circular movement emerge as basic concepts of communication. The worship service is a communal event that seeks to nurture and build up the people. Preaching as proclaiming the Word of God moves to the background. The sermon is primarily understood as a speech act in the gathering of the congregation. And fourth, there is a focus on the anthropological dimension of religious communication, with the speaker as person and subject in the spotlight.

This attention on the personality of the speaker is also evident in J. J. van Oosterzee's *Practische Theologie,* a handbook published in 1877 for young theologians. Van Oosterzee explains, "Both a knowledge of other human beings as well as self-knowledge is essential if the speaker wants to reach his

---

69. Vinet, *Homiletics,* p. 5.
70. Vinet, *Homiletics,* p. 12.
71. Friedrich Schleiermacher, *Die Praktische Theologie nach den Grundsätzen der Evangelischen Kirche im Zusammenhang Dargestellt* (Berlin: Jacob Frerich, 1850; photographic reprint, Berlin/New York: De Gruyter, 1983), p. 75: "What are the essential elements of worship? We can only reply to this question in a matter-of-fact way: sermon, hymn, and prayer."

goal. He must not be ignorant about the strong and weak aspects of his own personality, nor of the peculiarities of his audience that he seeks to reach."[72] Van Oosterzee also emphasizes that "a sermon will not be understood unless it transmits the heartbeat of spiritual life."[73] Only what comes from the heart will reach the heart. Faith comes from hearing, and, as a rule, spiritual life is enriched not by vowels and consonants, but by gifted personalities. "We see this personality as the individuality of the minister — not to be confused with mere subjectivity — that permeates through his way of seeing and of his being in general, and through his view of the gospel in particular."[74] The more the sermon is an expression of the speaker's personality, the more *originality* it will exhibit. Van Oosterzee does have a sanctified individuality in mind, which means that the personality has been shaped by the Christian faith.

We have noted that the subjective element was strongly emphasized in nineteenth-century theology. It is important for us to see this against the background of the criticism of the traditional emphasis on abstract and formal discourse patterns. It is a plea for an existential form of faith that relates to concrete life. In an article in *De Gids,* Van Oosterzee expresses his criticism of traditional preaching this way:

> The purpose of this kind of discourse is not edification, nor the arousing of the emotions, nor the creation of enthusiasm, but a mere instruction of the hearers. It is in all aspects the old rationalistic or semi-rationalistic approach, via the intellect to the heart, as if the heart does not have its own access! . . . Nowhere do we detect the subjectivity of the speaker in an attractive manner, so that it finds an echo in the heart of the hearers. Nowhere do we detect any attempt to *individualize* the situations of the human and the Christian life, thereby giving color and life to the presentation, and pulling the admonitions away from the uninteresting sphere of generality. Nowhere a finer chord of the soul is touched, or a positive impulse given to the easily inflamed soul. Nowhere is there any aesthetic predominance over the form of reason, and logical order is always preferred over a structure built on oratory or psychological elements. The religious feelings that have been aroused require something more subjective . . . ; the religious knowledge requires more *depth* in the understanding of the

---

72. J. J. van Oosterzee, *Practische Theologie. Een Handboek voor Jeugdige Godgeleerden* (Utrecht: Kemink, 1877), p. 221.

73. Van Oosterzee, *Practische Theologie,* p. 245.

74. Van Oosterzee, *Practische Theologie,* p. 244.

Backgrounds and Dilemmas

biblical characters. A delicate taste also has its rights and demands a more dramatic stylistic form. (*De Gids*, 1844)[75]

A type of preaching emerges in which doctrinal content (theological teachings) recedes into the background, and in which practical piety and concrete acts ("moral" aspects) are deemed more important. A sermon must strike the right chords and be characterized by eloquence. In Chapter 6 I will deal at greater length with the form of the sermon.

Baptism and Confession

Backgrounds

Baptism is in itself a simple ritual: a sprinkling with water (or immersion in water), accompanied by a statement (a script): "I baptize you in the name of the Father, and of the Son, and of the Holy Spirit." In order to qualify as Christian baptism, the ritual should involve the use of water and an invocation of the Triune God. This tradition dates back to the early church. We read this in the *Didache* (a document from the end of the first century):

> Now about baptism: this is how to baptize. Give public instruction on all these points, and then "baptize" in running water, "in the name of the Father, and of the Son, and of the Holy Spirit." If you do not have running water, baptize in some other water. If you cannot in cold, then in warm. If you have neither, then pour water on the head three times, "in the name of the Father, Son, and Holy Spirit." Before the baptism, moreover, the one who baptizes and the one being baptized must fast, and any other who can. And you must tell the one being baptized to fast for one or two days beforehand.[76]

Both the invocation of the Triune God and the use of water (preferably cold, streaming water) are explicitly mentioned. Justin, another church father, writes,

---

75. J. Hartog, *Geschiedenis van de predikkunde in de protestantse kerk van Nederland* (Utrecht: K. H. Schadd, 1887), p. 392.
76. See James F. White, *Documents of Christian Worship: Descriptive and Interpretive Sources* (Louisville: Westminster John Knox Press, 1992), p. 147.

> Those who are persuaded and believe that the things we teach and say are true, and promise that they can live accordingly, are instructed to pray and beseech God with fasting for the remission of their past sins, while we pray and fast along with them. Then they are brought by us where there is water, and are reborn by the same manner of rebirth with which we ourselves were reborn; for they are then washed in the water in the name of God the Father and Master of all, and of our Savior Jesus Christ, and of the Holy Spirit. . . .[77]

Baptism is here regarded symbolically as a new birth. The pure water washes away the dirt from the soul, as is suggested in the letter to the Hebrews: "Let us draw near with a true heart in full assurance of faith, with our hearts sprinkled clean from an evil conscience and our bodies washed with pure water" (Heb. 10:22). In the early church the newly baptized person was clothed in a white garment (a symbol of the new person).

The liturgy of baptism encompasses more than just the baptismal act. It is an act that follows a script, which means that there are prescribed texts and prayers. These texts express the beliefs that baptism creates a communion with Christ and makes us a part of the church. Calvin says, "Baptism is the sign of the initiation by which we are received into the society of the church, in order that, engrafted in Christ, we may be reckoned among God's children."[78] This process of becoming one body with Christ is referred to in the New Testament as participating in the death and resurrection of Christ: "We were buried therefore with him by baptism into death, so that as Christ was raised from the dead by the glory of the Father, we too might walk in newness of life" (Rom. 6:4). Baptism therefore means going down, immersion, death. Jesus pointed to his future death with this question: "Are you able to drink the cup that I drink, or to be baptized with the baptism with which I am baptized?" (Mark 10:38). In the so-called Flood Prayer, which is prayed at a baptism, we are carried along in the symbolism of the waters as a token of judgment and of the transition to a new life:

> According to Your strict judgment
> You condemned the unbelieving world through the flood,
> yet according to Your great mercy
> You preserved believing Noah and his family,

---

77. Quoted in White, *Documents of Christian Worship*, pp. 147, 148.
78. Calvin, *Institutes of the Christian Religion*, Book IV.15.1, p. 1303.

Backgrounds and Dilemmas

eight souls in all.
You drowned hard-hearted Pharaoh and all his host in the Red Sea,
yet led Your people Israel through the water on dry ground,
foreshadowing this washing of Your Holy Baptism.[79]

The baptismal liturgy is based on a few references to baptism that we find in the New Testament and on some traditions from the early church. For the baptismal liturgy of the Dutch Reformation, we must go back to the second half of the sixteenth century. In that period, the documents originated that for centuries have served as guides in the Protestant Reformed tradition (both in the Dutch Reformed Church and in the separated Christian Reformed Churches). It is significant to note that the earliest liturgical models came not from Dutch soil but from the refugee churches abroad — namely, England and Germany. According to J. A. M. Mensinga, "Only from the middle of the sixteenth century onwards do we find an established congregation of Dutch Reformed people, but outside the Netherlands, with its own liturgy. Partly inspired by commercial interests, but in part also as the result of persecutions because of their faith, groups of Dutch people — mostly from Flanders, Zeeland, and Wallonia — moved to England. Most of them established themselves in London."[80] King Edward VI gave them permission to freely exercise their religion. There was both a Dutch-speaking and a French-speaking church. In 1553 the congregations had some four thousand members. The Wallonians worshipped in accordance with the liturgy of Pollanus (a Flemish nobleman who learned about the Reformed Reformation in Strasbourg).[81] John à Lasco, who had come from Poland, developed a liturgy for the Dutch congregation. But when King Edward died and their freedom of worship came to an end, they had to find another place of refuge. Many of them went, via Denmark, to Germany. From Hamburg they went deeper into Germany and established a church in Frankfurt am Main. When they once again met intolerance, the Elector of Paltz offered them the monastery Great Frankenthal (near Worms) as a place to stay. Here, in 1566, the basis was laid for the Dutch liturgy.

The origin of the Dutch liturgy was rather complex, since the liturgical forms were derived from various sources. (See Chapter 7 for the celebration

---

79. "Flood Prayer," *Lutheran Service Book*, pp. 268-69.
80. Mensinga, *Verhandeling over de liturgische schriften der Nederlandse Hervormde Kerk*, p. 15.
81. Valerandus Pollanus, *Liturgia Sacra (1551-1555)*, newly published and edited by A. C. Honders (Leiden: Brill, 1970).

of the Lord's Supper.) The London liturgy of à Lasco, *Forma ac Ratio,* was published in 1555 in Frankfurt. But it must already have been in use in London before that date. Johannes Utenhove, an elder in London, had possibly made a translation of the manuscript, and in 1534 Marten Micron (an elder in the London congregation from Flanders) published the *Forme des Nachtmaels.* This was to a large extent derived from à Lasco's liturgy.[82] In any case, it is clear that the leaders of the church had a strong international orientation and were in close contact with circles around Calvin. But the immediate birthing place of the Dutch liturgy was the Dutch church in the German Frankenthal. The Dutch refugee congregation utilized the Reformed liturgy that was in use in the Paltz (and that was strongly influenced by Calvin). In 1566 Petrus Dathenus (a minister of the Dutch church in Frankenthal) published a Dutch psalter which also contained the Heidelberg Catechism and forms for the sacraments and prayers. In his introduction Dathenus says that these "are in use with us." The liturgy from the Paltz offered the main content, but one can also detect influences from the liturgies of Geneva and London.

The form for baptism is a literal translation of the text used in the Paltz. In 1574 the provincial synod of Dordrecht decided on an abbreviated version that came into general use in the Netherlands. This classical document for baptism is characterized by the fact that it begins with an instruction regarding baptism: "The main aspects of the teaching of holy baptism are threefold: . . . ." It does not begin with texts from Scripture — for instance, the mission mandate of Matthew 28:19. We find the Bible texts when we come to the arguments in favor of infant baptism at the end of the instruction. Following the instruction is the liturgical part that follows this pattern: (1) the prayer (the Flood Prayer and invocation of the Holy Spirit), (2) the baptismal promise of the parents, (3) the actual baptism, and (4) a prayer of thanksgiving.

This baptismal liturgy remained in use for a long period, even though in the eighteenth and nineteenth centuries there was increasing criticism regarding the content of the instruction and the questions accompanying the promise by the parents. In the twentieth century the synod initiated some new baptismal liturgies. In the *Dienstboek in ontwerp* (1955), four new liturgical orders are proposed in addition to the classical Reformed order. This new approach has mostly to do with the instructional part and the bap-

---

82. A. F. N. Lekkerkerker, *Kanttekeningen bij het Hervormde Dienstboek,* vol. 3 (The Hague: Boekencentrum, 1952), p. 136; W. F. Dankbaar in his introduction to Marten Micron, *De Christlicke Ordinancien der Nederlantscher Ghemeinten te Londen (1554),* re-edited by Dr. W. F. Dankbaar (The Hague: M. Nijhof, 1956), pp. 6-12.

tismal questions. One of the new orders (ii) is arranged in such a way that the didactic element recedes into the background and the baptismal liturgy is given a predominantly responsive character.

Under the influence of the liturgical movement and growing ecumenical interest, this tendency continued, and in 1993 the synods of the Dutch Reformed, Christian Reformed, and Lutheran churches published a booklet with some new liturgies for the baptismal service and the public confession of faith: *Doop en belijdenis: Proeven voor de Eredienst, aflevering 3* ("Baptism and Confession: A Proposal for Worship, Section 3"). In this baptismal liturgy, adult baptism comes first. The confession is, however, not primarily a personal confession by the person who is baptized but a corporate act of the congregation that confesses the Credo. An important aspect of this baptismal liturgy is *the remembrance of baptism* that is, in particular, celebrated the night prior to Easter:

And so,
as the time of preparation comes to an end,
and Easter has come,
we want to renew the promise of our baptism.

Also, in the ordinary baptismal service the remembrance of baptism has a regular place, prior to the baptism and in connection with the confession of faith by the person who is baptized. We refer to this baptismal liturgy as part of the Protestant ecumenical order, since it is closely linked to the Lima Report of the World Council of Churches (1982).

Infant Baptism?

Should children, as members of the body of Christ, be baptized? This is most definitely affirmed in the second question of the classical Reformed baptismal form. Should we base our understanding of the rite of baptism on infant baptism, or rather on the baptism of adults (faith baptism)? This matter continually comes up for discussion. In the classical Reformed baptismal form, infant baptism remains undisputed. The Reformers did not relinquish the Roman Catholic baptism of newborn children; they opposed the Anabaptists who defended baptism upon the confession of one's faith. Remarkably enough, however, in the classical Reformed baptismal text the baptismal rite for adults is almost identical to that for infant baptism, the sole difference being that the baptismal candidate himself/herself responds to the baptismal questions. Apparently, in a correct understanding of the essence of baptism, there is no distinction between the baptism of infants and the baptism of adults. Moreover, there is no denial that there is a link between *baptism* and *faith*. When an infant is baptized, the parents respond to the baptismal questions, while, when an adult is baptized, he or she responds. Looking at it from a broader perspective, we should recognize that in the early church the new believers were mostly adults. However, the entire household was then also baptized. We read in the New Testament that the guard of the prison where Paul and Peter were kept became a believer: "He was baptized at once, with all his family" (Acts 16:33). This is also mentioned about the household of Crispus (Acts 18:8), and that of Stephanas (1 Cor. 1:14-16). Yet, these passages do not provide proof for the practice of infant baptism as we now know it. Jeremias pointed out that in the earliest centuries of the Christian era, baptism was mostly a baptism of transition. Jews and non-Jews believed in Jesus Christ and were baptized with their household. We may suppose that those around them (children, family members, and help) were also baptized.[83] In these cases we are dealing with the transition to the Christian faith. That in itself does not prove that children of Christian parents were baptized as infants. K. Aland has defended the position that infant baptism, as we now know it, became a common practice around A.D. 200, as only then did the generational growth of the church begin to become important.[84] It does appear that neither supporters nor opponents of infant baptism can simply appeal to the Bible to prove their point. But, at the same time, there are no clear arguments against infant baptism.

In the early church, people were baptized on the night prior to Easter, after they had been instructed in the Christian faith during the period leading up to Easter. On that night they confessed their faith and were baptized. In *Doop en belijdenis* we read, "Through the centuries the rite of baptism has been closely tied to the celebration of Easter. There have been periods in the history of the churches in the East and the West when baptism was almost totally restricted to the Easter night. In these periods the catechumens received their final instructions just before Easter."[85]

---

83. J. Jeremias, *Die Kindertaufe in den Ersten Vier Jahrhunderten* (Göttingen: Vandenhoeck & Ruprecht, 1958), p. 23.

84. K. Aland, *Die Säuglingstaufe im Neuen Testament und in der Alten Kirche* (Munich: Kaiser Verlag, 1961).

85. "Kanttekeningen," in *Doop en belijdenis: Proeven voor de eredienst, aflevering 3* (Zoetermeer: Boekencentrum, 1993), p. 1.

Following this ancient tradition, the Protestant ecumenical liturgy takes faith baptism as its basis (confession and baptism of adults). However, the personal confession of the baptismal candidate is embedded in the Credo of the congregation:

> You who will today receive baptism,
> and all of you who will remember your baptism,
> raise your voice and answer me:
>
> Will you serve the Lord your God
> and only listen to His voice?
> *Yes, I will.*
>
> Will you resist all powers that want to rule as gods over you?
> *Yes, I will.*
>
> Will you throw off every yoke of slavery and live in the freedom of
>   God's children?
> *Yes, I will.*
>
> Then, do not be ashamed to confess the Christ,
> for the gospel is a power of God
> for the salvation of all who believe;
> so respond in community with the church of all ages:
>
> [then follows the *Credo (Apostolicum)*][86]

So, with regard to the sacrament of baptism, we cannot make an absolute separation between infant baptism and adult baptism. It concerns one and the same bath of water, for adults and for children. The discussion in the church is about whether infant baptism has a *legitimate* place. The Reformed tradition maintains that God seals children as well as adults with the same promise of grace. Two aspects are important to emphasize here. First, the sacraments seal not what we are but *what God promises*. As the Heidelberg Cathechism states, "Sacraments are holy, visible signs and seals, given by God, so that we by using them may better understand the promises of the gospel, and seal what He has, in the unique sacrifice of Christ, accomplished

---

86. Liturgy for Baptism, in *Doop en belijdenis*, pp. 24-25.

at the cross: forgiveness of sins and eternal life through grace."[87] In baptism the emphasis is on what God does in Christ, on the grace that he gives, and on the renewal that the Holy Spirit works in us. In other words, God is the acting subject. The classical Reformed texts for baptism are based on the gracious promise of God, on the righteousness by faith and the actual incorporation in Christ. And then we may, on this basis, also speak of the human factor of the believer's assent. "Since all covenants comprise two parts, so we are admonished by God through baptism, and are called to a new obedience. . . ." Baptism thus calls us to a new life, to faith and conversion, but, as a sacrament, it is not based on a human response. It is, and remains, based on God's atoning and redeeming work in Jesus Christ. Admittedly, however, there has been a continuous tension in the Reformed tradition between God's promise, on the one hand, and, on the other, the realization of God's salvation in a human life. Over time, that tension has led to controversy over the first baptismal question — the confession that *in Christ* the children are *sanctified*. What does this mean with regard to infant baptism? One who emphasizes the new birth and the sanctification may have difficulty with regard to this unequivocal confession. For that reason some ministers in Utrecht made a few alterations in the baptismal questions, changing the language to say "the children *may* be sanctified in Christ" or "*should* be sanctified in Christ."[88] In the Christian Reformed churches, the baptismal question has also led to theological controversies. Should we, on the basis of the first baptismal question, *consider our children as born again and as sanctified in Christ until their way of life shows differently?* Even though the *Proeve* of 1993 gives priority to the baptism upon confession, this does not mean, according to M. Barnard, that the confession of the person who is baptized becomes the foundation of the baptism: "The confession may be the point of departure for the baptism, but it does not define the essence of the baptism; the church baptizes because of God's grace that precedes every act of faith."[89] The following comment is found in the *Proeve:* "The grace of God, that culminated as a salvific act in the death and resurrection of Jesus Christ, precedes every act of faith. This grace comes to us in the form of the promise."[90]

The second aspect to emphasize regarding the legitimizing of infant

---

87. Heidelberg Catechism, Sunday 25.
88. Lekkerkerker, *Kanttekeningen bij het Hervormde Dienstboek,* vol. 3, p. 82.
89. Marcel Barnard, "Doop en belijdenis," in *De weg van de liturgie. Tradities, achtergronden, praktijk,* ed. M. Barnard and F. G. Immink (Zoetermeer: Meinema, 2008), pp. 245-56.
90. *Proeve van een oecumenisch ordinarium,* p. 94.

baptism is the covenant concept. This plays a particular role in the classical Reformed form for baptism. The form does not begin with this point, but in its comments on the obedience of faith it is said that the baptism "is a seal and undeniable testimony of the fact that we have *an eternal covenant of grace with God.*" This statement is followed by a few Bible texts (Gen. 17:7 and Acts 2:39) that support this idea. Young children must not be excluded from baptism, since they are accepted in Christ through grace. "As God says to Abraham, the father of all believers, and therefore also to us and our children, saying: I will establish my covenant between Me and you and your descendants after you throughout their generations for an everlasting covenant, to be God to you and to your descendants after you. And Peter likewise testifies, with these words: For the promise is to you and to your children and to all that are far off, every one whom the Lord our God calls to him." In this connection we find a link to the circumcision as a seal of the covenant.[91] It also refers to Jesus Christ, who laid his hand on the children and blessed them. It is in this context that we find the statement that "baptism has replaced circumcision."[92] This passage is often heavily criticized because it appears to suggest the idea of an exchange: the church supposedly took the place of Israel. I do not want to expand on this, but I do not think that this criticism is totally valid. For neither do we say that Sunday, as a Christian day of celebration and rest, has taken the place of the Jewish Sabbath, even though Sunday has certainly absorbed some traits of the Sabbath. With regard to baptism, there is a reference to Colossians 2:11-12: "In him also you were circumcised with a circumcision made without hands, by putting off the body of flesh in the circumcision of Christ; and you were buried with him in baptism, in which you were also raised with him through faith in the working of God, who raised him from the dead." Here, being circumcised in Christ is referred to, in one and the same breath, as being buried with him in baptism. This suggests that baptism serves as a new rite of initiation. Yet, we must not simply put baptism on a par with circumcision, since the reference is to a circumcision "made without hands."

A discussion has arisen in the praxis of church life about the so-called *remembrance of baptism* and the *renewal of baptism*. This matter is related to that of infant baptism. I will mention a few situations that may lead to some rethinking of this issue. First, it happens that some people who were

---

91. *Dienstboek voor de Nederlandse Hervormde Kerk in ontwerp* (The Hague: Boekencentrum, 1955), pp. 46-47.

92. "Reformed Form for the Administration of Baptism," p. 56.

baptized at one time have become estranged from the church, but return to faith later in life. Somehow they want to mark this change in their lives. The fact that they were baptized as small children does not mean much to them — at least not to the extent that they consider their faith to be the confirmation of a sealing of the promises that were made at their baptism. If it were up to them, they would prefer to be baptized at this point. However, the Protestant churches of the Lutheran and Reformed tradition (as well as the Roman Catholic Church) expressly state that baptism is a non-repeatable salvific event. These churches do not allow for rebaptism. It is also clearly stated that the remembrance of baptism and the renewal of baptism are not to be regarded as a baptism, and that there should be great reticence with regard to any kind of "water ritual." However, a newly converted person often desires to connect this "dying and being resurrected with Christ" (as expressed in baptism) with his recent faith experience.

A second development regarding infant baptism (to some extent connected with the previous point) is that some young parents no longer see the need to have young children baptized. Although they are active church members, they do not have their children baptized. Yet, they do hope that their children will, once they have reached the age of decision, embrace the faith. So, it is not a lack of willingness to give their children a religious education. Apparently, the significance of infant baptism is no longer self-evident. On the one hand, this has to do with the influence of the evangelical movement, which closely links baptism with faith. On the other hand, this has to do with a new generation of young parents that sees how many of their baptized contemporaries have left the church. Because personal confessions of faith by those who were baptized as infants don't happen as often as they once did, the meaning of infant baptism is seen in a new light. What meaning can baptism have when so many, who were once baptized, no longer attach any significance to this and turn their backs on the church? Was their baptism just an empty ritual? Was it a beautiful custom as long as the Christian faith was still common? Those who were baptized were listed in the baptismal records of the church. Many, however, became dormant members — members on paper only. Does this kind of baptism have any spiritual meaning? As a result of questions like these, some young parents ask for a blessing for their children rather than for baptism. I believe that two kinds of queries are relevant in this context. Did the church adequately portray baptism (as becoming incorporated *in Christ, in the church* as the body of Christ)? Was there sufficient sacramental awareness? Was the baptismal catechesis inadequate? And, second, if we are incorporated through baptism,

Backgrounds and Dilemmas

what is the status of the children of believing parents who have received a children's blessing? Are they, or are they not, part of the church of Christ? Does this not create a strange gray area?

Characteristics of Christian Baptism

The baptismal ritual must meet a number of secondary requirements if it is to be recognized as a Christian baptism. In 1982 the World Council of Churches published a report, the Lima Report, in which the constituent parts of the baptismal rite were listed:

> Within any comprehensive order of baptism at least the following elements should find a place: the proclamation of the Scriptures referring to baptism; an invocation of the Holy Spirit; a renunciation of evil; a profession of faith in Christ and the Holy Trinity; the use of water; a declaration that the persons baptized have acquired a new identity as sons and daughters of God, and, as members of the Church, [have been] called to be witnesses of the Gospel. Some churches consider that Christian initiation is not complete without the sealing of the baptized with the gift of the Holy Spirit and participation in Holy Communion.[93]

Let us now stop to look at how these various aspects figure in the baptismal liturgies.

The renunciation of the devil. In the Lima Report, the renunciation of the devil is seen as a characteristic of Christian baptism. We already saw that the Protestant order, before 1993, asked the baptismal candidate to make this renunciation:

> Will you resist all powers that want to rule as gods over you?
> *Yes, I will.*

This custom of the so-called *renunciation of the devil* dates from the early church. Renunciation means "turning away from, no longer relying on." We meet this custom already with Tertullian (b. 160). Through this renunciation, the adult baptismal candidate distanced himself from evil, sin,

---

93. *Baptism, Eucharist, and Ministry, 1982-1990* (Geneva: World Council of Churches, 1982), p. 6.

Satan, and the world as he turned to Christ the Lord. After this renunciation (sometimes accompanied by an anointing), the baptismal candidate confessed his faith and descended into the water. Thus, renunciation and confession were linked. Ambrose made the baptismal candidate respond to the following questions:

> Do you renounce the devil and his works?
> *I renounce.*
> Do you renounce the world and its desires?
> *I renounce.*
>
> (Following this the candidate is asked whether he believes in the triune God.)[94]

Does this renunciation also occur in the classical Reformed form? Yes, in three places. First, it occurs in the instruction, at the point where we are called to a new obedience — to "forsake the world, crucify our old nature, and walk in a new and holy life." Second, the prayer after the infants have been baptized asks that they may "increase and grow up in the Lord Jesus Christ, that they then . . . live in all righteousness . . . and manfully fight against and overcome sin, the devil and his whole dominion. . . ." And, third, the renunciation occurs in the baptismal promise when adults are baptized. The baptismal candidate is asked whether he intends to lead a Christian life and "to forsake the world and its evil lusts."[95] Thus, we conclude that the renunciation is present in the response of the adult who is baptized and in the instruction and prayer that accompany infant baptism.

The invocation of the Holy Spirit and the laying on of hands. In the Lima Report, the invocation of the Holy Spirit is an inalienable part of baptism, while, strictly speaking, the sealing with the gift of the Spirit (through the laying on of hands) is not. Some churches maintain that baptism is incomplete "without the sealing of the baptized with the gift of the Holy Spirit. . . ." In the classical Reformed liturgical texts as well as in the more recent Protestant ecumenical tradition, the invocation of the Holy Spirit is a part of the "Flood Prayer." After the flood metaphor, the Holy Spirit is invoked in order to incorporate the baptismal candidate in communion with Jesus Christ.

---

94. See Lekkerkerker, *Kanttekeningen bij het Hervormde Dienstboek,* vol. 2 (The Hague: Boekencentrum, 1952), p. 100.

95. "Form for the Administration of Baptism," *The Psalter,* pp. 55, 56, 58.

Backgrounds and Dilemmas

This prayer precedes the act of baptism. In the liturgy of 1993, the person who is baptized gives a promise, and then, after his (adult) baptism, the laying on of hands takes place. The script offers two possibilities:

> Receive the Holy Spirit.
> *Amen.*

Or:

> Be blessed with the gift of the Holy Spirit.
> *Amen.*

The classical Reformed liturgical order does not include this laying on of hands. Calvin was critical of it, and his approach was decisive for the later Reformed tradition.

> But those miraculous powers and manifest workings, which were dispensed by the laying on of hands, have ceased; and they have rightly lasted only for a time. For it was fitting that the new preaching of the gospel and the new Kingdom of Christ should be illumined and magnified by unheard-of and extraordinary miracles. When the Lord ceased from these, he did not utterly forsake his church, but declared that the magnificence of his Kingdom and the dignity of his word had been excellently enough disclosed.[96]

The instruction. The Lima Report states that "the proclamation of the Scriptures regarding baptism" is an essential aspect of baptism. But the question remains what form this must be given. In the classical Reformed liturgical order, the instruction takes place during the baptismal service. In more recent baptismal liturgies, such as the one from 1993, there is no instruction during the baptismal service. In the comments we are referred to the baptismal catechesis, in preparation for the baptismal service: "We must return to this clear preparation for the administration of baptism, even though this preparation should be given a contemporary form, possibly on the basis of the baptismal liturgy."[97] The classical Reformed baptismal form begins with these words:

---

96. Calvin, *Institutes of the Christian Religion,* Book IV.19.6, p. 1454.
97. *Doop en belijdenis,* p. 8.

The principal parts of the doctrine of holy baptism are these three:

First. That we with our children are conceived and born in sin, and therefore are children of wrath, in so much that we cannot enter into the kingdom of God, except we are born again. This, the dipping in, or sprinkling with water, teaches us . . .

Secondly. Holy baptism witnesseth and sealeth unto us the washing away of our sins through Jesus Christ. Therefore we are baptized in the name of the Father, and of the Son, and of the Holy Ghost. For when we are baptized in the name of the Father . . .

Thirdly. Whereas in all covenants there are contained two parts: therefore are we by God, through baptism, admonished of and obliged unto new obedience . . .[98]

The Theology of Baptism

Through baptism God allows us to share in the salvation that is found in Jesus Christ. Three theological aspects play a role in the sacrament of baptism: (1) in our baptism we are buried with Christ in his death and resurrected to a new life; (2) through the water of baptism we are purified of our sins; and (3) through our baptism we are called to a life of faith and renewal. Let us look at each of these in turn.

Burial and resurrection. The New Testament connects the baptismal rite with the suffering and death of Jesus. Baptism is like going down, dying, being buried. As noted earlier, Jesus refers to this when he says, "Are you able to drink the cup that I drink, or to be baptized with the baptism with which I am baptized?" (Mark 10:38). Likewise, in Luke's Gospel, baptism is compared with Christ's suffering: "I have a baptism to be baptized with; and how I am constrained until it is accomplished!" (Luke 12:50). It is about being baptized into the suffering of death. It may be compared to the Old Testament picture of the waters that close above someone's head: "Let not the flood sweep over me, or the deep swallow me up, or the pit close its mouth over me" (Ps. 69:15). In Romans 6, Paul describes baptism in terms of a burial in death with Christ: "Do you not know that all of us who have been baptized into Christ Jesus were baptized into his death? We were buried therefore with him by baptism into death, so that as Christ was raised from the dead by the glory of the Father, we too might walk in newness of life" (6:3-4). Baptism expresses

---

98. "Form for the Administration of Baptism," *The Psalter*, p. 55.

a participation in the death and resurrection of Christ. The immersion in the water symbolizes death. Baptizing is dipping, bringing down, sinking in the water — hence the association with the passage of the Israelites through the sea. In 1 Peter 3, baptism is associated with the Flood. The water of the Flood "corresponds" with it (v. 21). Baptism speaks of disaster and salvation, of life and death, but always in close connection with the cross and the resurrection of Christ.

Washing and cleansing. The water is associated not just with "dipping" and "immersing" but also with "washing." The water cleanses. G. van der Leeuw explains how the cleansing is not just a matter of the removal of dirt, but also of a renewal of life: the old, the dirty, the worn out is renewed, and there is a new beginning.[99] The cleansing is about participating in what is good and rejecting what is bad. The bath of water thus is a sign of inner renewal. The Christian is born again from the water. In his night-time conversation with Nicodemus, Jesus said, "Unless one is born of water and the Spirit, he cannot enter the kingdom of God" (John 3:5). "Water" points to the cleansing from sin, while the term "Spirit" points to a miraculous event that comes from God, to something that has an inner impact on one. Ananias says to Paul, "And now why do you wait? Rise and be baptized, and wash away your sins, calling on his name" (Acts 22:16).

Baptism washes away the impurity of our sins. Christ cleansed the church through the bath of water (Eph. 5:26). In the letter to Titus we read, "He saved us, not because of deeds done by us in righteousness, but in virtue of his own mercy, by the washing of regeneration and renewal in the Holy Spirit" (Tit. 3:5). These are all indirect references to baptism. From these texts we can infer that a connection is postulated between the bath of water and the work of the Holy Spirit. In the classical Reformed baptismal form, the water functions foremost as an image of cleansing. Through the sprinkling with water, we are alerted to "the impurity of our souls." Baptism testifies to, and seals, "the washing away of the sins through Jesus Christ." The Heidelberg Catechism places the same emphasis on cleansing in baptism:

> Q. 69. How art thou admonished and assured by holy baptism that the one sacrifice of Christ upon the cross is of real advantage to thee?
>
> A. Thus: That Christ appointed this external washing with water, adding thereto this promise, that I am as certainly washed by his blood and Spirit

---

99. G. van der Leeuw, *Sacramentstheologie* (Nijkerk: Callenbach, 1949), p. 171.

from all the pollution of my soul, that is, from all my sins, as I am washed externally with water, by which the filthiness of the body is commonly washed away.[100]

The sacrament of the church and personal faith. The Reformers were afraid that sacramental acts as such were considered to be means of salvation. This led to a radical reformation in the celebration of the Eucharist in those days. The change with regard to baptism was less radical. However, the Reformation did have to deal with a new area of tension — namely, its position somewhere between the Roman Catholic emphasis on baptism as a sacrament of the church and the Anabaptist emphasis on the faith of the individual as prerequisite for baptism. The Reformers very definitely maintained the sacramental character of baptism, but emphasized two dimensions: (1) the effect of the sacrament is, in the final analysis, the effect of the *promise of God* that is expressed in the sacrament, and (2) this effect cannot be separated from the *faith* (of *the one who is baptized* and of the *community*). This is a rather ambiguous position, since it attempts to ensure that the sacrament in itself does not offer salvation, while at the same time not robbing the sacrament of its power. Baptism is an act in which God is definitely at work. Christ is just as much present in baptism as in communion.[101] "And you were buried with him in baptism, in which you were also raised with him through faith in the working of God, who raised him from the dead" (Col. 2:12).

When there is such a strong emphasis on what God does in the act of baptism, what is the value of infant baptism? What power does baptism have when there is no faith, or when faith does not arise at all? This question was also posed to Calvin. In this debate he placed the emphasis on the promise of Christ's atonement and on the value of the (Old Testament) covenant. According to Calvin, the truth and the reality of forgiveness in Christ cannot, in the final analysis, be measured according to the status of our faith. Even when the baptized person lives and perseveres in unbelief, we should not conclude that his baptism evidently was an empty and meaningless (invalid) event. Rather, we should emphasize its reality and pay attention to the appeal that emerges from it. Calvin prioritized what God gives in the sacrament:

> Even if all men are liars and faithless, still God does not cease to be trustworthy. Even if all men are lost, still Christ remains salvation. We there-

---

100. "Heidelberg Catechism," *The Psalter*, p. 9.
101. Van der Leeuw, *Sacramentstheologie*, p. 305.

fore confess that for that time baptism benefited us not at all, inasmuch as the promise offered us in it — without which baptism is nothing — lay neglected. Now when, by God's grace, we begin to repent, we accuse our blindness and hardness of heart — we who were for so long ungrateful toward His great goodness. But we believe that the promise itself did not vanish. Rather, we consider that God through baptism promises us forgiveness of sins, and He will doubtless fulfill His promise for all believers. This promise was offered to us in baptism; therefore, let us embrace it by faith. Indeed, on account of our unfaithfulness it lay long buried from us; now, therefore, let us receive it through faith.[102]

Thus, baptism issues an appeal. In our baptism we are put on the solid foundation of God's promises. This applies to infant baptism as well as to the believer's baptism of an adult. In spite of inner turmoil and doubt, the person who is baptized may call upon God's promises. And even when those who have been baptized at some point in time turn their backs on God, their baptism continues to issue an appeal. Children are baptized with the intention that they will gradually develop an independent faith and will come to a personal confession. For that reason, during the baptismal service the question is asked of the parents (and of the witnesses and of the church), "Do you promise to be an example for him/her in the way that has been prepared for us in Jesus Christ?" or "Do you promise to educate your child in such a way that he/she will learn to understand the meaning of his/her baptism?" When viewed from that perspective, the public confession of one's faith as a liturgical event naturally follows baptism. It is a personal "amen" to the communion with Christ of which baptism is the seal.

---

102. Calvin, *Institutes of the Christian Religion*, Book IV.5.17, p. 1317.

CHAPTER 5

Prayer

Prayer as a Religious Praxis

Prayer in Real Life

We must continuously deal with the events that we encounter on our journey through life: in our daily work, in our families, in our immediate social networks, and in all kinds of social and economic situations. We have an *intentional* involvement — mentally, emotionally, spiritually — with the reality that surrounds us. In our hearts and in our minds, we lay plans, we deal with disappointments, we celebrate health and worry about disease, we experience joy and sorrow. When we pray, we come to God with all kinds of considerations and concerns. In our prayers we express the inner life (the life of the spirit) as well as the concrete context in which we live. These aspects are indissolubly connected with the praying human being.

In praying and seeking to address God, we live in the awareness that the world is more than a mechanical order, that the history of the world is more than blind fate, and that human life is more than a biological-neurological process. We realize that we participate in life in a feeling, thinking, and willing mode, and that this is how we have an influence on life and on the world. This influence primarily grows out of our ability to want something — for instance, when we make plans, we desire something or want to achieve something (the volitive orientation). When we accentuate this dimension of the will, the *petitionary* element of prayer comes into focus. P. T. Forsyth says, "Prayer is not merely wishing. It is asking — with a will. Our will is involved. It is energy.... We turn to an active Giver; therefore, we go in action."[1] When

---

1. P. T. Forsyth, *The Soul of Prayer: A Christian Interpretation of the Old Testament* (1916; reprint: London, 1998), p. 12.

we ask things in prayer, we not only put a question before God; we are also prepared to act accordingly.

When we pray to God, we not only draw on our capacity to will something, but we also draw on what we think and feel. Prayer can, for instance, be an expression of thankfulness — or of remorse or distress. In our prayers we can also be focused on particular events or situations, and we can consider these and recall them; thus our more thoughtful and reflective abilities are engaged. We can imagine God, talk to him, and call upon his virtues. In other words: In addition to petitionary prayer, there are other kinds of prayer: prayers of thanksgiving, of praise, of confession of guilt, and of remembrance.

In praying we turn to God on the presupposition that God turns to the world. When we pray, we trust in God as a force of love, as One who can change the world; we trust that the world in which we live can be trusted, since it is God's creation; and we believe that the world, in the final analysis, is subject to God's loving will. It is true that these presuppositions often show a certain vagueness (also on the part of those who pray), and may be subject to doubt. But as soon as people pray, these aspects play a role — with varying intensity, depending on whether there is only a vestige of faith or rather a firm conviction. Friedrich Heiler states that prayer is based on two major presuppositions: (1) the belief in the personhood of God, and (2) the certainty of his presence. As a result, prayer is structured as interaction, as communication. In prayer our vivid relationship to God finds expression. It is a personal relationship, a finding of refuge, a discourse, a communion.[2] This vivid communication is anchored in God's *personhood, which also implies that God as a person is interested in the world, and is actively involved in it.* "Through the act of prayer," Manfred Josuttis says, "the human need for help and the divine preparedness to provide that help are connected. What was miles apart is linked together with a few sentences."[3]

The practice of prayer is associated with some basic religious and anthropological presuppositions. Prayer is deeply anchored in the human desire for happiness. People who pray do not simply accept what is given, as if what is can never change. They seek beyond the border of what is seemingly impossible, without giving up hope. In the act of prayer, those who pray recognize that they are expressing their own vulnerability and dependence.

---

2. Friedrich Heiler, *Prayer: A Study in the History and Psychology of Religion* (New York: Oxford University Press, 1958), p. 357.

3. Manfred Josuttis, *Zur Handlungslogik Spiritueller Methoden* (Gütersloh: Kaiser Verlag, 2002), p. 117.

Simultaneously, however, prayer is an expression of flexibility and lust for life, and those who pray appeal to the God of life. Prayer, Gert Otto states, is located somewhere between complaint and desire. It often gives expression to people's deepest hopes and longings. People long for happiness, for instance, but often this happiness remains distant; it frequently is a receding perspective. People also express their sorrows and complaints concerning the suffering in this world, but they hope to rise above them. And people long for a better life; it has not yet arrived, but it may come.[4]

People talk with God about their concrete experiences of life and of the world around them. "Prayer," Otto says, "means: giving words to the world and to life."[5] We may pray a quick prayer quite spontaneously. We may be prompted to pray because of severe experiences. But inexpressible joy may also cause us to pray. According to George Arthur Buttrick, the praxis of prayer carries with it a unique view of life:

> Prayer is in its essence neither fear, nor social control, nor autosuggestion, nor rationalization. The certitude abides that it is comradeship with God. We turn, then, to the vast assumptions which Jesus made in prayer — God, man, and the world: the "personality" of God, the real freedom of man, and the faithfulness yet flexibility of the world.[6]

However, the personhood of God, the freedom of humankind, and the faithfulness of the world are not self-evident. Those who do not share in these presuppositions will have another view of prayer. Prayer may also be seen as a way to deal with the insurmountable things of life, as a way to "master" them. Thus prayer can function as a coping mechanism. Josuttis suggests that some people may resort to prayer when other methods and techniques fail.[7] Even those who pray faithfully may know temptation and doubt in their hearts. If I am right, in our current Western culture the absence of prayer is strengthened by three things. First, it is reinforced by the scientific approach to life, which leaves little space for active divine involvement. The space for spirituality tends to be limited to the soft, subjective dimensions of life. Second, it is reinforced by a secular climate in which the human spirit does not so easily find the way to God. The

---

4. Gert Otto, *Sprache als Hoffnung* (Munich: Kaiser Verlag, 1989), pp. 11-12.
5. Otto, *Sprache als Hoffnung*, p. 14.
6. George Arthur Buttrick, *Prayer* (Nashville/New York: Abingdon-Cokesbury Press, 1941), p. 53.
7. Manfred Josuttis, *Die Einführung in das Leben. Pastoraltheologie zwischen Phänomenologie und Spiritualität* (Gütersloh: Kaiser Verlag, 1996), p. 96.

connection with God is not naturally embedded in common cultural or societal value patterns. And third, the absence of prayer is reinforced by the terrors of natural disasters and human tragedies, of political and societal disintegration. These undermine the trust that God is actively involved with the world.

The Tradition of Prayer in Worship

When people come to church, they enter a house of prayer. The liturgical prayers are related to the questions and desires of the worshippers. In its prayers the worshipping congregation gives expression to its life in the presence of God. This is the *quest* aspect of the liturgical prayers. But at the same time, the church also has *religious capital* at its disposal. There is a tradition of prayer that includes an agenda (an order for the prayers) and a script (established texts for the prayers). In the midst of emotional turmoil, the church offers the comfort of language, structure, and content. The liturgy (the script) ensures that emotions do not fully take over, but can be expressed in a controlled manner. The hymns in particular have this channeling function as prayers that are sung. But non-scripted prayers also express a confessional pattern. Peter Brunner righty affirms that the issue of whether the minister prays with the church in the right way is just as important as whether she preaches well.[8] In hymns and prayers, the congregation approaches God. In hymns and prayers, the congregation enters the presence of God. The Dutch hymn below expresses this progression:

> In silent awe
> we have come before You.
> Lend Your ears to our pleading,
> watch with Your eyes, day and night!
>
> You speak to us,
> You have chosen us
> to hear Your words in this place.
> You are here, for here dwells Your name.[9]

---

8. Peter Brunner, "Zur Lehre vom Gottesdienst der im Namen Jesu Versammelten Gemeinde," in *Leiturgia*, vol. 1, ed. Karl Ferdinand Müller and Walter Blankenburg (Kassel: Stauda, 1954), p. 257.

9. *Liedboek voor de Kerken*, hymn 322, verses 4 and 5; Dutch text by E. E. Smelik. The translation does not match the poetic quality of the original text.

Sometimes there is a smooth transition between personal prayer and the communal prayers of worship. But it may also be that worshippers hardly have a private prayer life, or that their prayers are very one-sided and mostly limited to petitions. This may make the transition to liturgical prayer more challenging; worshippers may suddenly have to change gears. In church they meet a wider variety of modes of prayer that all have their own backgrounds. Thanksgiving in the Eucharistic prayer, for instance, always has a Christological focus:

> To you, Lord our God,
> always and everywhere,
> be thanks,
> through Jesus Christ our Lord.

Taking part in the Eucharistic prayer means being carried along in the remembrance of Christ. It is through such liturgical means that worshippers are confronted with hymns and prayers and texts that have been shaped by the *language* and the *tradition* of the church. This does not necessarily imply that there will be a chasm between personal prayer and the liturgical prayers in church, since liturgical prayers and traditional hymns and texts also express the life and faith experiences of real people. This is particularly true of the Psalms:

> Hearken to the sound of my cry,
>   my King and my God, for to thee do I pray.
> O LORD, in the morning thou dost hear my voice;
>   in the morning I prepare a sacrifice for thee, and watch.
>
> (Psalm 5:3)

> O LORD, my God, I call for help by day;
> I cry out in the night before thee.
> Let my prayer come before thee,
>   incline thy ear to my cry!
> For my soul is full of troubles,
>   and my life draws near to Sheol.
>
> (Psalm 88:1-3)

However deeply the Psalms may be anchored in the lives of men and women, they also attune worshippers to God; they call upon him, praise his name, and find a stronghold in his loving majesty.

In the worship service the people are carried along in the *thanksgiving*. At that very moment it becomes clear that the congregation turns towards God because of his self-revelation. "Whenever a Christian gives thanks," Rainer Volp says, "it is *anamnesis*, that is to say, it is orientated towards the life and suffering of Jesus." That is, in fact, the ultimate concept for expressing how the congregation *responds* to the Word of God. Volp continues, "In giving thanks, we pull all situations of life — including the sad and tragic experiences — towards the horizon of the goodness of God that we may enjoy. The model for giving prayerful thanks is the remembrance of Him who, during the night when He was betrayed, broke the bread and gave thanks."[10] K. H. Miskotte expresses it this way:

> The church of Christ is a praying church; in its prayers its response to the word of God, that has created her, is expressed. For that reason prayer as thanksgiving and adoration, as confession and intercession, as repeatedly asking and calling in times of need, as a silent story and as a cry from the deep, is the most *inalienable* aspect of being-church.[11]

Seen from this perspective, giving thanks ought to be the core of our practice of prayer. Yet, this is often not the case. The natural inclination to give *petition* the primary place is simply too great. In our distress we call upon God. Perhaps this element of asking will survive longer than any other in our secularized lives. Petition is indeed an important aspect of prayer in our worship, albeit with a special content: it is directed towards the reign of God. As Miskotte explains, "All genuine prayers for the small and large, personal or general things, about living, working, serving, and helping, are related to the *coming of the reign of God*, as the fulfillment of God's promise."[12] This demands a continuous re-thinking of our state of mind and a continuous turning towards God's revelation.

In addition to the doxology and the prayer of petition, the aspects of *humbling ourselves* and *confessing our guilt* have a regular place in the worship service. Anyone who dares to speak to God, Calvin says, should begin by confessing his guilt. This implies the awareness that we can only speak to God if he shows his grace towards us. That is why the confession of our sins

---

10. Rainer Volp, *Liturgik. Die Kunst, Gott zu Feiern*, vol. 2: *Theorien und Gestaltung* (Gütersloh: Gütersloher Verlagshaus Gerd Mohn, 1994), p. 1112.
11. K. H. Miskotte, *De weg van het gebed* (The Hague: Boekencentrum, 1962), p. 7.
12. Miskotte, *De weg van het gebed*, p. 32.

has a prominent place at the beginning of the service. This opening scene of the worship performance is not intended to make worshippers preoccupied with guilt, but is meant to highlight the new reality of God's reign and the radical nature of grace. This confession is not only typical of the Reformed worship service; Roman Catholic worship also has such a confession in the first part of its service. In the Protestant ecumenical liturgy the confession of sin usually is part of the so-called threshold prayer.

Liturgical Prayer

According to Friedrich Heiler, prayer, in essence, "is something purely spiritual, the direct expression of an ultra-strong experience of the soul. With inner force it breaks through, to the outside, in prayer."[13] Prayer originates in human subjectivity and is an expression of a subjective and very powerful state of mind. Heiler differentiates between various types of prayer: besides the primitive type, he recognizes the mythical type and the prophetic type. He sees the prophetic type in particular in the Jewish and Christian tradition. In the prophetic tradition, he says, God has the traits of a human person: thinking, willing, feeling, and self-consciousness.[14] Heiler goes on to further distinguish prophetic prayer: "Contrary to mythical prayer, prophetic prayer is a naïve way of pouring out one's heart, the direct outpouring of great need and relentless desire. It is a prayer that asks to be heard; it is a prayer for help, for grace and salvation for oneself and the other. In this form of prayer, the primitive prayer is revived, but with a religious inner strength, and in a morally enlightened way, but not weakened in its concrete awareness of reality."[15] In this prayer type, the attention is centered on the great religious personalities, on the major prophetic figures in the Bible. This prayer "is the free, spontaneous expression of experiences which emerges on the heights of the devotional life and which deeply stirs the soul.... Its deepest motive is the burning desire of the heart which finds its rest in blissful union with God or in assured trust with Him."[16]

We find this same approach — albeit in other terms — in the Pietistic sentiments of the "Second Reformation." Wilhelmus à Brakel describes

---

13. Heiler, *Prayer*, p. 354.
14. Heiler, *Prayer*, p. 105.
15. Heiler, *Prayer*, p. 352.
16. Heiler, *Prayer*, p. 104.

prayer as "an expression of one's holy desires towards God, in the name of Christ, that through the workings of the Holy Spirit emerge from a born again heart, with the request to receive these."[17] The "expression of one's desires" refers to the activity of the soul. Everything is involved: the intellect, the will and the passions, the body — eyes, mouth, hands, knees. From the description of the effects, we may deduce that the state of mind plays an important role. Brakel says, "The soul that wants to pray can often find no words; all words are too shallow and prove inadequate to express the desire and the intense condition of the soul."[18]

Inner Life and Emotions in Prayer

The approach to prayer so far described has consequences for prayer in worship. Often the impression is created that personal prayer is the most genuine kind of prayer. When someone is personally and subjectively touched, authentic prayer is the result. The stylizing and the institutionalization of prayers are secondary processes and may easily be described as "decline." Heiler refers to the phenomenon of formalized and depersonalized forms of prayer. He maintains that these secondary types of prayer do not express any original, personal experience, but have become a kind of mimic, a surrogate or formal echo of something that was once very alive.[19] However, Heiler does not mean to say that therefore by definition all collective expressions are of the secondary type. He notes that in the Christian congregation the focus originally was on the direct expression of its inner life. Heiler typifies it as follows:

> The common prayer is also originally not the intentional creation of a more or less pious individual, but the fervent necessary utterance of the common religious experience of a group closely bound together. In times of great religious excitement . . . the spirit of religious devotion does not remain limited to individuals of creative genius but is poured out upon all the members of the congregation. . . . One great experience dominates the primitive church: the assurance of salvation bestowed in Christ and the yearning for the speedy fulfillment of the Kingdom of God. This common

---

17. Wilhelmus à Brakel, *Redelijke Godsdienst*, vol. 2 (Nijkerk: n.p., 1870), p. 363.
18. Brakel, *Redelijke Godsdienst*, p. 364.
19. Heiler, *Prayer*, p. 354.

experience spontaneously urges us to expression in prayer just as every emotional religious experience of an individual longs for relief through prayer.[20]

Heiler does regard congregational prayer, in its original form, as an expression of original spontaneity. "At the heart of liturgical prayer," he says, "is *praise* of God's greatness and power, and *thanksgiving* for the salvation bestowed by Him." Heiler bases his views on the Bible. In Acts 2:47 we read that the early church was "praising God." And in 1 Corinthians 1:4 Paul states, "I give thanks to God always for you because of the grace of God which was given you in Christ Jesus." This sounds like liturgical prayer. But Heiler points out that as the consciousness of salvation diminishes, the prayer that asks for salvation becomes more pronounced.[21]

With this background in mind, it is understandable that the prayers in the worship service with prescribed texts are regarded with suspicion. Such formulas and ever-returning phrases, in fact, are seen as forms of spiritual decline. Heiler calls such prayers legalistic. No longer is there any free and spontaneous expression; only officially approved texts are recited. The Pietistic wing of the Protestant churches, in which the subjective way of expressing oneself plays an important role, has looked from a similarly critical perspective on the tradition of prescribed prayers. In the nineteenth century, the emerging liberal criticism shared this view of liturgical prayers. In 1817 the synod of the Dutch Reformed Church declared, "The liturgical prayers were useful for the ministers who were not yet fully trained in all aspects of their holy ministry, who therefore needed certain rules, so that they might become accustomed to leading in a suitable and unified manner. Now this need no longer exists."[22] This criticism resulted particularly from the liberal opposition to the traditional emphasis on doctrine.

Even though the subjective inner life is an important foundation for the religious life, this does not imply that an established script and liturgical order are of secondary importance. Established formulas and the repetition of traditional texts should not automatically be regarded as the enemy of spontaneity. Instead, we should recognize that they may give us a grip on things in situations of distress and temptation. There are circumstances in

---

20. Heiler, *Prayer*, p. 305.
21. Heiler, *Prayer*, p. 317.
22. J. A. M. Mensinga, *Verhandeling over de liturgische schriften der Nederlandse Hervormde Kerk* (The Hague: Thierry en Mensing, 1851), p. 435.

which we can rely only on traditional texts. They can express the emotions for which, at such moments, we fail to find adequate words. The Psalms often function in this manner. They provide a voice for our deepest emotions and strongest desires, our fiercest distress and greatest gratitude. What has been "pre-thought" is not inferior to spontaneous expressions. Indeed, Willem Barnard claimed, "No prayer in our public worship should be unprepared. Improvisation as a 'method' when we face God is often rather risky, and often impolite and bold. Our intercession needs to be carefully considered, and the way in which we formulate our prayers of confession or petition — if we want the church to join in these prayers — must be classical rather than romantic in form."[23]

The heart and the emotions profit not only from a well-defined script, but also from clarity of mind. We should not play emotion and understanding off against each other; we should bring them together. In his liturgical deliberations, Romano Guardini says that "careful thought" does not impede emotional expression:

> Prayer is, without a doubt, "a raising of the heart to God." But the heart must be guided, supported, and purified by the mind. If prayer in common, therefore, is to prove beneficial to the majority, it must be primarily directed by thought, and not by feeling. It is only when prayer is sustained by and steeped in clear and fruitful religious thought that it can be of service to a corporate body, composed of distinct elements, all actuated by varying emotions. . . . Dogmatic thought brings release from the thralldom of individual caprice, and from the uncertainty and sluggishness which follow in the wake of emotion. It makes prayer intelligible, and causes it to rank as a potent factor in life.[24]

To express one's thoughts requires adequate formulations. That is why the right words and forms are important in liturgy. Wilhelm Stählin believes that any form of spiritual life, if it is to be more than a fleeting idea, needs specific forms.[25] G. van der Leeuw likewise underlines the importance of establishing forms:

---

23. A. F. Troost, *Dichter bij het geheim. Leven en werk van Willem Barnard/Guillaume van der Graft* (Zoetermeer: Boekencentrum, 1998), p. 279.

24. Romano Guardini, *The Spirit of the Liturgy* (New York: Crossroad, 1998), pp. 94, 95.

25. Wilhelm Stählin, "Der Wille zur Form" (1921), in *Evangelischer Gottesdienst. Quellen zu seiner Geschichte*, ed. Wolfgang Herbst (Göttingen: Vandenhoeck & Ruprecht, 1992), p. 231.

> God has come to us in a certain shape; His revelation has not come to us as an indefinable inner light, or as an inaudible inner voice. God comes to us as word, as an activity, as a person. The liturgy is such a shape, and the ecclesial affirmation of the liturgical form is a confession of faith.[26]

Kuyper had a good sense of the tension with regard to this issue in the Reformed tradition. Because of the emphasis on the work of the Holy Spirit, he says, there is a constant tension between freedom and form. J. H. Gunning also refers to this element of tension. He believes that freedom is a characteristic of the Reformed Church, but he insists that this is not to be understood as arbitrariness. "Nothing is greater nonsense than to continue to cry out: 'We must have the Spirit, and, therefore, away with all forms!' The form is something indescribably exalted and beautiful."[27]

A Communal Confession

In addition to the structures of script and liturgical agenda, the community is also an important factor in our prayer life. The community is not a secondary element for liturgical prayer; it is, in fact, *constitutive* of it. Charles Taylor is critical of Western individualized spirituality and maintains that in our modern society the holy continues to be mediated in collective settings. Yet, when we compare our times with earlier centuries, we note more diversity. Spiritual and political communities no longer coincide, although many will continue to look for a spiritual home in churches. "Many people will join strong religious communities," says Taylor, "because their interest [in] spiritual matters will lead them there." Taylor also points out that religious life may find its starting point in a moment of sudden insight, but that it can often develop further only within the bonds of a community. For many, in the end, a fleeting sentiment is not sufficient. They want to develop their experience further and are looking for something deeper.[28]

In exploring community, we also touch on the confessional character of liturgical prayer. The prayers that are spoken during worship breathe the confession of the church. Worshippers are presented with a framework (a

---

26. G. van der Leeuw, *Liturgiek* (Nijkerk: Callenbach, 1946), p. 14.

27. J. H. Gunning, *Onze eredienst. Opmerkingen over het liturgisch element in den gereformeerden cultus* (Groningen: Wolters, 1890), p. 25.

28. Charles Taylor, *Wat betekent religie vandaag?* (Kapellen/Kampen: Pelckmans, 2003), p. 98.

system of religious symbols) within which their everyday experiences and thoughts, their worries and desires, can find a place. The ministers and the worshippers do not face the challenge of suddenly needing to find the right words; these are found in the existing structures and traditions. The prayers of the church provide language and images that are derived from the Bible. These prayers follow the *lex credenda*. Does that restrict us or enrich us? At times we will find it challenging to join in the words with all our heart, because the language and the images may be in tension with our own state of mind. But at other times these things may provide enrichment, since they can lead us to new thoughts because of the variation in the prayers. They may help us get closer to our own experience.

The praying community addresses God and dares to talk to him directly. Addressing God always implies an element of *defining* him. In a certain way God is *invoked* and is *asked* for help. These aspects are related, because what we expect from God is related to the manner in which we address him. In the way in which it approaches God, the praying community takes a position with regard to God, and this determines in what manner it calls upon him. "Loving God," "Almighty God," and "Holy God" — these kinds of appellations express something of our religious pattern of expectation. Precisely this point deserves close attention in a communal prayer. We have become aware of the connotations that accompany such words as "Father" and "Lord." But when we also use such terms such as "eternal," we refer to particular aspects of God. These words also have associations and connotations.

The way in which we call upon God in the Christian church is directly related to God's salvific work in the history of Israel and in Jesus Christ. In those deeds the church finds the basis for its longing for salvation and its trust in God's faithfulness and mercy. The mystery of Jesus Christ is safeguarded in the church. "No one comes to the Father, but by me" (John 14:6). Prayer is rooted in the salvation that comes from God. This notion of remembering the great acts of God as the foundation for our prayers is also found in the Old Testament — for instance, in the lengthy prayer of Ezra (Neh. 9:5-33). After ample praises for the creation, the calling of Abraham, the Exodus from Egypt, the journey through the desert, and the entry into the Promised Land, there follows this entreaty: "Now therefore, our God, the great and mighty and terrible God, who keepest covenant and steadfast love, let not all the hardship seem little to thee that has come upon us. . . ." And then Ezra adds, "Yet thou hast been just in all that has come upon us, for thou hast dealt faithfully and we have acted wickedly" (Neh. 9:32-33). In Christian worship this reference to the salvific acts of God is explicitly present in the "Flood Prayer" in the baptismal service:

> ... merciful God, who through the destructive water of the Flood saved Noah and his family; You, who through the waters of the Red Sea have delivered Your people Israel; who through the waters of baptism allows us and our children, as heirs of Your covenant, to share in Your kingdom; we pray to You, recognizing Your unfathomable mercy....[29]

In addition to this reference to salvation history, there is another motif in communal prayer. In many biblical stories humility is an important attitude for prayer. For example, the recognition that one stands before the Holy and Most High is mentioned in the story of the theophany to Moses at the burning bush. In the vision of his calling, Isaiah cries out, "Woe is me! For I am lost; for I am a man of unclean lips, and I dwell in the midst of a people of unclean lips" (Isa. 6:5). Abraham says, "Behold, I have taken upon myself to speak to the Lord, I who am but dust and ashes" (Gen. 18:27). This attitude reveals the *condition humaine*. In itself, this awareness that one is a created being does not lead to an inability to speak. But it implies the recognition that we are not all-powerful, that there are weakness and failure in our lives. This awareness of creatureliness, however, becomes a reason for prayer. In one of the first chapters of the Bible we read, "At that time men began to call upon the name of the LORD" (Gen. 4:26). We find this statement in the context of the story of Cain and Abel — a story about crime and revenge, about the building of cities and the development of culture and craft. After Abel is murdered, Adam and Eve have another son named Seth, who takes the place of Abel. Seth in turn has a son and calls him Enosh. This name means "human being" and expresses weakness and vulnerability. And it is in this context that people begin to call upon God.

The Prayers in the Worship Service

Opening Prayers

The liturgy of Sunday morning worship lists several kinds of prayer. The votum and the greetings are usually regarded as the opening scene of the wor-

---

29. *Dienstboek voor de Nederlandse Hervormde Kerk in ontwerp* (The Hague: Boekencentrum, 1955), p. 66.

Prayer

ship service. However, this opening scene is often preceded by a few preparatory prayers. A short prayer is offered in the consistory, and before the service begins there is usually the opportunity for a silent prayer of dedication.

First I will picture the Reformed tradition of expressing our humility, followed by our confession. The prayer of confession is usually followed by the proclamation of grace and then by the reading of the Commandments.

> We confess before You, almighty Father,
> before Your entire church and before each other,
> that we have sinned in thoughts, words, and works.
> . . .
> Have mercy upon us,
> forgive us our sins, and lead us to eternal life.
> Through Jesus Christ, our Lord.[30]

> Almighty and gracious God,
> we have wandered like sheep,
> turning to our own ways.
> We have followed the desires of our heart
> and have been disobedient to Your voice.
> We have not done what we should have done
> and have done what You had forbidden,
> and have no power in us for healing.
> But You, O Lord, have mercy upon us. . . . [31]

In these prayers, God is asked to show mercy and the congregation expects to receive forgiveness. This raises a number of questions. Is this forgiveness given at this very moment? Or is it rather an expression of the religious recognition of the state of affairs between God and us? Or does the liturgy indeed provide the kind of illumination that makes believers at that very moment experience God's pardon?

Where the sequence in the liturgy is concerned, there has been considerable discussion about the proclamation of grace following the confession of sin. Is this an absolution given by the minister? The Reformed *Dienstboek* of 1955 contains a number of different wordings for the proclamation of grace:

---

30. *Dienstboek een proeve: Schrift, maaltijd, gebed* (Zoetermeer: Boekencentrum, 1998), p. 159.
31. *Dienstboek* (1955), p. 15.

THE TOUCH OF THE SACRED

> Because of your confession and humiliation before God, we, as servants of Jesus Christ, proclaim the forgiveness of your sins in the name of the Father, and of the Son, and of the Holy Spirit. (Order IV)
>
> To all those among you who have confessed their sins with shame and sorrow, and who in faith rely on the merits of Christ alone, I proclaim that your sins have been forgiven in heaven through the name of the Lord Jesus Christ, who be praised in all eternity. (Order I)
>
> You, brothers and sisters, if any of you have sinned, we have an Advocate with the Father, Jesus Christ, the Righteous One. And He is the atonement for our sins, and not only for ours, but for those of the entire world. Believe this gospel and live in peace. Amen. (Order III)[32]

In 1955 the point at issue was whether the minister had the right to proclaim the forgiveness of sins with an authority vested in him by the church. If so, would this tie forgiveness too much to ecclesial authority? In the formulations given above, we notice that in the first version this aspect of ecclesial authority is strongly emphasized, while there is no such reference in the third version, but rather an appeal to believe in our acquittal. Whether or not there should be a separate proclamation of forgiveness proved to be a topic of discussion already for the Synod of Middelburg in 1581. A delegate from Gelderland asked whether it would not be a good thing to proclaim the forgiveness of their sins every Sunday, after the sermon, to those who have been converted, and to the unconverted the binding by their sins. The synod replied, "Since the binding and unbinding of sins is adequately provided for in the preaching of the Word, there is no need to introduce a special formula to do so."[33]

Is it by accident that the Synod of Middelburg spoke of the proclamation of grace after the sermon? To answer that question, one must look at the history of the origin of Reformed liturgy. In medieval worship (as we saw in Chapter 4), the sermon led to the *penance*. The confession of sins thus logically followed the sermon. Zwingli also placed the *Offene Schuld* after the sermon. We see the same in the earliest Reformed liturgy in the Dutch tradition (in the refugee church in London). The liturgy of Marten Micron has, immediately following the sermon, a prayer for the continued impact of the Holy Spirit

---

32. *Dienstboek* (1955), pp. 20, 8, 16.
33. Synod of Middelburg, 1581, in A. F. N. Lekkerkerker, *Kanttekeningen bij het Hervormde Dienstboek*, vol. 1 (The Hague: Boekencentrum, 1952), p. 70.

Prayer

(based on the image of the parable of the sower); then the Ten Commandments are read. Subsequently the minister may admonish the church and call for a confession of sins. The liturgy is concluded with these words:

> We see, in this divine law as in a mirror, in what grand manner and in what manifold ways we have angered God with our trespasses. Let us then therefore desire with all our heart that He will forgive us. We do so with these words:

> O, eternal and most merciful God, we humble ourselves from the bottom of our hearts before Your divine majesty, against whom we have sinned so atrociously, and we confess publicly and without guile, that we are not worthy....[34]

This confession is, in its formulation and approach, inspired by the confession of the prodigal son (Luke 15:21). We encounter this motif quite frequently in the late medieval and early Reformation tradition. Leo Jud (1523), a precursor of the Swiss Reformation, used these words: "O Father, I have sinned against heaven and against You. I am not worthy to be called Your son. Have mercy on me, poor sinner."[35]

How, then, did this confession find its way into the introductory part of the service? That is Calvin's work. Both in Strasbourg and in Geneva, Calvin places the confession immediately after the votum. He calls for the church's attention with these words:

> *My brethren, let each of you present himself before the face of the Lord, and confess his faults and sins, following my words in his heart:* O Lord God, eternal and almighty Father, we confess and sincerely acknowledge before Your holy Majesty that we are poor sinners, conceived and born in iniquity and corruption, prone to do evil, incapable of any good, and that in our depravity we transgress Your holy commandments without end or ceasing; therefore we purchase for ourselves, through Your righteous judgment, our ruin and perdition....[36]

---

34. Marten Micron, *De Christlicke Ordinancien der Nederlantscher Ghemeinten te Londen (1554)*, re-edited by Dr. W. F. Dankbaar (The Hague: M. Nijhof, 1956), p. 61.

35. Leo Jud, "Confession of Sin," quoted by J. Schweitzer, *Zur Ordnung des Gottesdienstes in den nach Gottes Wort reformierten Gemeinden der deutschsprachigen Schweiz* (Zürich: Zwingli Verlag Zürich, 1944), p. 53.

36. John Calvin, "Confession of Sin," in *La Manyere de faire prieres* (1542).

This is a public confession of sin by the entire congregation and no longer the *confiteor* of the priest.

With regard to the prayer for humility, we must undoubtedly face the question whether the dark tones that were so predominant in Reformation times find any echo in our contemporary world. People realize that they have shortcomings and make mistakes. And it is not denied that we live in a broken world, and that this brokenness is to a large extent due to human failure, human hubris, and all kinds of egoism. Moreover, the idea that people must be challenged to accept their responsibilities and face up to their mistakes is increasingly accepted. But can this be compared with the way in which men like Calvin and Micron spoke about the need to humble ourselves and to confess our sins?

Let me respond to this question by making two points. First of all, our view of man has changed. In our Western European culture, a much more optimistic view has gained the upper hand — in the sense that more attention is paid to human autonomy and freedom, which ensures that people are more positive rather than negative about themselves. Given this mind-set, humbling oneself is easily understood as belittling a person or as placing too much emphasis on guilt. People may feel and know that they are guilty in many respects, but without losing their human dignity.

Second, the emphasis in the church today is not so much on atonement as on redemption. In other words, the thoroughgoing secularization of today's society leads to questions about the way in which God is active in the world. The resurrection of Christ thus becomes a greater "problem" than the crucifixion and death of Jesus. Everything that has to do with the resurrection — namely, the victory over death and the deliverance from evil — does not fit in a closed, modern, naturalistic worldview. It seems that Christian faith and Christian theology are more concerned about this challenge, and thus focus their attention on it rather than on guilt and atonement.

It is therefore not so strange that the Protestant ecumenical tradition of the Kyrie and the Gloria has so quickly become very commonly emphasized in Protestant worship. Giving expression to the needs of the world (which are unmistakably enormous) fits better with our current cultural climate. It is a cry to God without the notion of intervention. The concepts of guilt and penitence are addressed only in passing.

Does this mean, then, that the prayer for humility and the confession of guilt are no more than relics? No, because they are a very classic part of Christian worship. They also have a place in Anglican and Roman Catholic worship, as well as in the Protestant ecumenical tradition, but in this case as the "threshold prayer":

Prayer

> We confess before You, almighty God,
> before Your entire church and before each other,
> that we have sinned,
> in thought, word, and work. Have mercy on us.
> Forgive our sins,
> through Jesus Christ, our Lord. Amen.[37]

The Presbyterian Church also frequently has a fixed place for the confession, followed by the assurance of forgiveness, in the early part of the worship service.

> **Prayer of Confession**
>
> Eternal God, our Judge and Redeemer,
> we confess that we have tried to hide from You,
> for we have done wrong.
> We have lived for ourselves and apart from You.
> We have turned from our neighbors
> and refused to bear the burdens of others.
> We have ignored the pain of the world
> and passed by the hungry, the poor, and the oppressed.
> In Your great mercy forgive our sins,
> and free us from selfishness,
> that we may choose Your will and obey Your commandments;
> through Jesus Christ our Savior. Amen.
>
> **Assurance of Forgiveness:**
>
> Sisters and brothers in Christ,
> Hear and believe the good news of the gospel:
> In Jesus Christ, we are forgiven.
> Thanks be to God.[38]

Sin and grace, atonement and forgiveness are key concepts in the Christian praxis of faith. These concepts are not totally foreign to this world as long as they are discussed in their relationship to the concrete life situations of

---

37. Threshold Prayer, "Confession of Sin," in *Onze hulp. Een gemeenteboekje* (Amsterdam: Prof. Dr. G. van der Leeuw Stichting, 1978), p. 51.

38. "Confession of Sin," *Book of Common Worship* (Louisville: Westminster John Knox Press, 1994), p. 54; "Assurance of Forgiveness."

contemporary people. But to be intelligible and relevant, these ideas must be explored in proper relation to our situational brokenness and our human failings. Even the contemporary person can experience a sense of being lost, and the dark side of life is not to be minimalized. The script of the liturgy — and this most definitely applies to the biblical metaphors — can help worshippers to place human shortcomings and guilt in the light of divine mercy. That will do us much good.

Intercessory Prayers

In church we pray to God. Besides the prayer of praise, the prayer for humility, and the *anamnesis*, there are intercessory prayers. These pose other questions. What should we ask God? And are there things we should not ask God?[39] Do we really expect a divine intervention, or rather a somewhat hidden divine cooperation in processes that are taking place, or God's influence on the more spiritual processes in our human world? Or is intercessory prayer in fact an extrapolation of our concerns, and is the main purpose that, through such prayer, we ourselves may gain new insights? Is intercessory prayer, in the final analysis, therapeutic in nature, in the sense that it helps us to deal with the situation in which we find ourselves? If so, prayer will further the process of acceptance, and we pray, in fact, for the power to persevere. "The most immediate effect of prayer is not the satisfaction of our needs or the solution of our problems," R. Nauta argues, "but the change in the person who prays; he may change the ways in which he asks the questions, and thus needs may seem to be fulfilled."[40] The fact that prayer may change the person who prays is obviously part of the praxis of Christian prayer. But that does not provide a full theological justification for petitionary prayer. Do we ask God to do something so that the situation in which we find ourselves changes? Or is this too simplistic an idea?

Even though this kind of prayer arises directly from human need and our desire for salvation, we should bear in mind that we call upon the God who has revealed himself in the history of Israel and in the person of Jesus Christ. This conviction guides the church when asking things from God.

---

39. F. Gerrit Immink, "Kun je alles aan God vragen? Praktisch-theologische notities bij het vraaggebed," in *Praktische Theologie* 4 (2004): 449-63.

40. R. Nauta, *Ik geloof het wel. Godsdienstpsychologische studies over mens en religie* (Assen: Van Gorcum, 1995), p. 89.

"Before the face of this God," Hendrikus Berkhof says, "we dare to voice our deepest motives and all the shortcomings we sense in our life and in the world. Even the most superstitious who came to Jesus, asking for bread or healing, he did not send away unanswered. On the contrary, in fellowship with him they learned to ask for *more* than they had begun with, and to ask differently: no longer only from the standpoint of their own needs, but much more from the perspective of God's purposes of which their cares were a part."[41] Here we notice that prayer to this God may indeed result in a process of change in the praying person. He or she comes to a more profound insight or begins to pray in a different manner. In this contact with God, the concrete, existential situation is brought before him. The praying person allows God to shed his light upon it — the light of atonement and redemption. K. H. Miskotte reminds us that "all correct prayers for small or large personal things, or things that go beyond us, that we may live, work, serve, help, are related to the coming of the kingdom as a fulfillment of God's promise."[42] In turning to God, the person who prays and communes with God will be aware of God's promise: the coming of the kingdom, the redemption of the world. This clearly shows that the so-called therapeutic effect of prayer is a dimension of the Christian praxis of prayer.

In petitionary prayer we are aware of the *kyrie eleison,* of the cry of the heart, because of the many terrible events in this world and in our own lives. But we turn the complaint into a positive request for a meaningful life, for satisfying growth in our existence and joy in our daily situation. As praying people, we ask for health, communion, love, and justice. In our petitions we acknowledge that we have a *transcending* and *transforming* ability. Being made in the image of God, we address God as the Creator of heaven and earth, and because of the promise of salvation, we look forward to the future. Because of this expectation of salvation, we do not simply accept a broken existence; we want to find healing and restoration. In the Christian church lives a sacred longing for renewal and victory beyond the border of hopelessness. "This desire," Miskotte says, "is necessary. There is need of a deep, continuous desire, if the pure petitionary prayer is to reach maturity and simplicity. The Holy Spirit must teach us to pray, in particular when it concerns petitionary prayer, which is the deepest, most childlike yet most powerful prayer that exists."[43]

---

41. Hendrikus Berkhof, *Christian Faith,* rev. ed. (Grand Rapids: Wm. B. Eerdmans, 1986), p. 497.
42. Miskotte, *De weg van het gebed,* p. 32.
43. Miskotte, *De weg van het gebed,* p. 31.

The prayer of intercession that is part of the Sunday worship service is a petitionary prayer. Every minister knows that the wording of these prayers is important. The congregation is alert. Unfortunately, there has been far less theological attention paid to petitionary prayer than to other categories of prayer.[44] Is this because at one time the liturgical discussion regarding the Kyrie or the confession of sin absorbed most of the attention, while currently the discussion about praise and worship takes center stage? Or do we have to conclude that the issues surrounding the divine providence of God have so many theological and philosophical dimensions that the more pastorally inclined theologians shy away from them? Whatever the answer may be, it is true that in actual practice the intercession tends to resemble a shopping list that is transmitted to God. And at times, church members must have the feeling during prayer that they are simply being informed about all the serious health problems of their fellow church members. In some cases the congregation is taken along on a voyage around the world to situations of war and places of disasters.

In Chapter 3 we concluded that faith in the resurrection opens a new perspective on everyday life. It is because of the resurrection of Christ that the church has a solid reason to expect a genuine transformation of this world. The resurrection of Christ did indeed change reality: the evil powers have been restrained. The intercessory prayer of the church presupposes this faith and confidence. But how do we connect this faith with the concrete ups and downs, large and small, of the world around us? Two theological restrictions must be considered here. In the first place, we minimalize the effectuation of salvation if we see the resurrection and the reign of God in purely *eschatological* terms and fail to see where these beliefs touch real life in the here and now. If we do so, salvation in Christ receives a *docetic* character with respect to life on earth. It remains limited to a forensic judgment or to a purely spiritual influence. The petitionary prayer almost ceases to ask for concrete things. It is clear that there may be moments in life when our prayer approaches this boundary. At such points we must recognize that what we ask for in the here and now is not realistic. But that does not snuff out the passion of the petitionary prayer. We reach a second boundary when we accept the world in which we live as fully identical with the laws of nature and the course of history. In this case, we don't ask for change anymore. When that happens, the petitionary prayer is completely absorbed into the

---

44. Philip Clements-Jewery, *Intercessory Prayer: Modern Theology, Biblical Teaching, and Philosophical Thought* (Aldershot/Burlington: Ashgate, 2005).

"world of providence." According to Miskotte, "Nothing ties believers and non-believers in these days of spiritual decline so closely together as operating with this 'Providence' that is totally separated from other aspects of the Christian message."[45] Then salvation in Christ no longer has any impact on the renewal and restoration in the here and now, and the petitionary prayer changes into a premature plea for resignation.

What may we properly pray for? Because of its public character, liturgical prayer differs from private prayer and from prayer offered during a pastoral visit. These latter situations offer the possibility to deal more concretely with a particular situation than a worship service does. Still, in the context of public worship, the minister and the congregation pray against the background of their personal and social circumstances. The prayer is offered in the space of public worship, in the awareness that the church members fully participate in this prayer. In addition to the theological restrictions just mentioned, the level of involvement is important. When we pray to God, an existential involvement manifests itself. In our prayer our affections are activated; our passion and our emotions are not secondary but primary "conduits" in this communion with God. As a result, we will in that moment approach our world not by seeing it primarily as a closed system that operates with fixed rules, but with a degree of openness — an openness in which God is actively present as a power of love. In our intercessory prayer we presuppose that God, as a living personality, is somehow actively involved with the things of his creation. And in our prayer we realize that we, like God, are also an *active part* of the totality of things. Precisely because our talking with God is an interpersonal encounter, the notion of involvement prevails. When formulating a public prayer, one has the responsibility to ensure the right kind of balance between two things: the affective intensity and the factual circumstances. These dimensions should not be played off against each other, as this may result in a short-circuiting. At times there are factual circumstances that must be respected. Someone with an incurable disease will remain incurable, and a handicapped child will remain handicapped. This does not immediately destroy all hope for healing and every desire for new possibilities for our lives, but it does mean that our emotions at that moment should be attuned to the soberness of the facts. The petitionary prayer should not block the process of dealing with problems. The intercessory prayer in the worship service must leave room to accept disappointments and adjust expectations. That is true for the personal and the pastoral prayer, but also

---

45. Miskotte, *De weg van het gebed*, p. 15.

for the prayer of public worship. This is why formulating a public prayer of intercession is so difficult. A prayer on behalf of someone who is seriously ill may sound as if the congregation has given up on this person — or it may sound like a surrender to hope and trust, which is very different.

Intercessory prayers may be characterized by notions of restoration, healing, and wholeness, of real peace and justice in the world. This can only be seen as a spiritual truth in Christ Jesus. That, in itself, can be a great comfort. But the petitionary prayer reaches further. It has to do with the things we see, touch, and feel in this life. Even though it may remain fragmentary and preliminary, the petitionary prayer is directed towards the realization of God's plan in this life. It is an anticipation of the *parousia*.[46] In our prayer we ask God to do what he has not yet done. Faith demands to see *signs* in this world. "When praying for God's salvation in and around us," J. H. Gunning says, "we pray for everything that is part of the preparation for the new heaven and the new earth."[47] And the congregation responds with these words: "Lord, our God, we pray: hear our prayers."

---

46. Peter Baelz, *Does God Answer Prayers?* (London: Darton, Longman & Todd, 1982), p. 86.

47. J. H. Gunning Jr., *Blikken in de openbaring*, vol. 3 (Rotterdam: Höveker, 1929), p. 380.

CHAPTER 6

Preaching

This chapter will deal with the sermon as *performance:* the actual preaching event as an interaction of speaking and hearing. The sermon as performance is more than a language event and a rhetorical act. The life and faith of the worshippers are at issue. And even these things are not independent of other aspects. They will be dealt with in connection with the Holy Scriptures. The Scripture readings that are heard in the liturgy play an important role in the sermon, and not just in an expository way. For in the liturgy, prayers are offered for the enlightenment by the Holy Spirit. This implies that for the congregation the Scriptures are no dead letter, but the living word of God — a Word that creates salvation. The sermon as performance has a saving effect.

The actual preaching event is a complex religious practice. In an attempt to deal with this complexity in a somewhat orderly and comprehensible fashion, I have chosen three points of departure that have a more or less empirical basis. First, I will look at the worshippers as the hearers of the sermon. What role do they have in this process? Second, I will speak about the Holy Scriptures. What happens to the Bible when it is preached? In what way does the minister use the Bible, and what impact does that have on the actual sermon? Third, what is the *rhetorical* format of the sermon? How is the sermon put together?

The Act of Participation

We have seen that, according to nineteenth-century liberal theology, the religious personality of the minister and the real piety of the listener constitute important factors in the preaching event (see Chapter 4). This emphasis started with Schleiermacher: "In the worship service we are concerned about the *Darstellung* of the Christian life as it manifests itself *in reality*."[1] This interest in faith as it is lived has contributed to the development of theology and homiletics as anthropologically oriented disciplines. In the first issue of the *Monatsschrift für Kirchliche Praxis* (1901), Paul Drews offered a plea for scientific research in popular religiosity. He began his article by saying, "We believe that practical theology should be approached in a descriptive-inductive rather than in a systematic-deductive manner." The focus should be on the knowledge of the "present religious life in and outside the church."[2] In full agreement with the spirit of the nineteenth century, Drews placed the religious and moral life of the people at the center. If one wanted to preach the gospel, he said, one should not address the audience in a haphazard way; one should know about the actual forms of piety of the people and their needs. Decades later, in 1971, American homiletician Fred Craddock confronted the preaching of his day with the publication of his book called *As One without Authority* — and launched what became known as "the New Homiletic" in America. In this book Craddock pleads for an inductive type of preaching. In the old style of preaching, he says, "there is no democracy, no dialogue, no listening by the speaker, no contribution by the hearer." This traditional approach to preaching cultivates a passive audience and obstructs the participation of the worshippers. Craddock refers to the traditional style as "three points and a poem." More often then not, the traditional sermon is made up of three mini-sermons that show little connection. The style is argumentative and deductive. An inductive approach, however, emphasizes identification with the hearers and makes creative use of analogies. Analogies are important, Craddock argues, not only because they help our imagination to stay alive, but also because they ensure that we can integrate our experiences into a learning process.[3] The inductive style brings the hearers to the forefront; the sermon becomes an *experiential event*. The faith and life of the hearers become part of the *performance*. The inductive character points to the fact that not only the Scriptures but also the concrete faith and life of the hearers must be heard in the sermon.[4]

---

1. Friedrich Schleiermacher, *Die Praktische Theologie nach den Grundsätzen der Evangelischen Kirche im Zusammenhang Dargestellt* (Berlin: Jacob Frerich, 1850; photographic reprint, Berlin/New York: De Gruyter, 1983), p. 156.

2. Paul Drews, "'Religiöse' Volkskunde: eine Aufgabe der Praktischen Theologie," in *Seelsorge, Texte zum gewandelten Verständnis und zur Praxis der Seelsorge in der Neuzeit*, ed. F. Wintzer (Munich: Gütersloher Verlagshaus, 1978), pp. 54-61.

3. Fred B. Craddock, *As One without Authority: Essays on Inductive Preaching* (Nashville: Chalice Press, 1971), p. 55.

4. F. Gerrit Immink, "In gesprek met de 'New Homiletic'. Literatuurbericht Homiletiek,"

At first, this debate about the hearers sounds somewhat strange. How could it be that homiletic theories would relegate attention to hearers to a secondary place? How could it be that someone like Rudolf Thurneysen would fulminate so strongly against the so-called insight into human character and the pious experiences of the people, while hammering away at only one theme: the *proclamation of God!* It would seem that dialectical theology plays God and humans off against each other, to the extent that the hearers take second place.

However, we must bring some nuance to this picture. The important thing is not whether hearers are sufficiently recognized, but the perspective from which people hear comes into play. Barth emphatically speaks of the *Gemeindemässigkeit* of the sermon. He even suggests that the congregation is the measure of the sermon. But he is referring to the church under the dome of Jesus Christ, those who have been called by the liberating Word. A minister cannot open his mouth, Barth says, without realizing that Jesus Christ died and was resurrected for these people.[5] The sermon is an act of the congregation that exercises the ministry of the Word. From that angle, an anthropological or social analysis can never be the most important factor. The congregation may expect to be addressed on the basis of the atonement in Christ, and to hear the proclamation of salvation. Hearers must be addressed on the basis of God's revelation in Jesus Christ. The proclamation comes to them as human beings, as sinners, and it comes "right from above: *senkrecht von oben*." Barth does not say this in order to put the minister on a pedestal. On the contrary: the minister as well as the congregation live from this liberating Word.

Yet, some misunderstandings may easily arise at this point. It may be true that the Christological perspective is the pivotal point here, in the sense that the church is to be considered the redeemed community in Christ, but this is not the only perspective that characterizes the truth of the church. The being-in-Christ is also expressed in faith, hope, and love, in human strivings and desires, in the human heart and in everyday life. This growing together with Christ is not just something incidental, "senkrecht *von oben*"; it is characterized by its lasting effect and its impact in time and space. The struggle to live in Christ and to put off the old nature and to put on the new

---

in *Praktische Theologie* 3 (2001): 370-93. See also Charles L. Campbell, *Preaching Jesus: New Directions for Homiletics in Hans Frei's Postliberal Theology* (Grand Rapids: Wm. B. Eerdmans, 1997), pp. 117-45.

5. Karl Barth, "Die Gemeindemässigkeit der Predigt," in Gert Hummel, *Aufgabe der Predigt* (Darmstadt: Wissenschaftliche Buchgesellschaft, 1971), p. 168.

nature (Eph. 4:22-24) is a concrete form of faith as it is lived. This faith may express itself in devotion and moral renewal — not just inside the church, but also outside the church. Not just in terms of a confessed faith, but also in human searching and striving.

Theological and Anthropological Perspectives

The contrast between inductive and deductive is rather confusing, so it is important to discuss this further. The term "inductive" presupposes that we can describe the real religious and moral situation, and that we can draw certain conclusions from this. The question is this: What exactly may we conclude? Should the sermon connect with the actual experiences of the people? Should the sermon expand on the experiences of the worshippers in their faith and life? Can the Bible be a source that enables us to talk effectively about existential and religious themes? The other term — "deductive" — suggests that the sermon will deal with matters that are derived from the confession of the church, from its tradition, or from the Scriptures. The term suggests that the sermon applies objective truths from the Christian tradition to the present hearers as if they are objects that must receive fixed truths. In addition, the term seems to suggest that these abstract truths have no existential relevancy in themselves.

This contrast may have some relevancy, but it is too simplistic. Paying attention to the situational circumstances of the hearers is a crucial element in the preaching event, but the contrast of inductive and deductive creates a false dilemma. During a sermon there are plenty of moments when the experiences of actual life and faith are touched upon. Worshippers affirm that this is helpful for them, because it allows them to identify with the sermon. These moments may be experienced as comforting and encouraging, but may also cause worshippers to take a critical look at their lives.[6] However, the attention to and the participation of the hearers must not be played off against their *receptivity*. This is what I mean: Insofar as the sermon is proclamation *(kerygma)*, or exhortation and education, there is a movement in and from revelation history (and the Scriptures) to the present. Or, in other words, a movement from Christ and the *pneuma* to the present hearers. Seen from the point of view of the hearers, this has to do with openness and

---

6. Theo Pleizier, *Religious Involvement in Hearing Sermons: A Grounded Theory Study in Empirical Theology and Homiletics* (Delft: Eburon, 2010), pp. 265-67.

Preaching

receptivity. Seen from the angle of tradition, this is a matter of transmission, *paradosis*. This is part of the sermon as a religious practice. This dimension points to a movement other than the inductive approach. However, this facet is totally misunderstood when we refer to it as deductive, as if it were just a matter of applying confessional truths, as if it were a deduction from abstract principles. The *kerygma* of the gospel that is heard in the sermon, on the one hand, and the role of the hearers, on the other hand, may not be played off against each other in these two contrasting concepts of deductive and inductive. Their relationship is quite complex, but not contradictory.

I think that Albrecht Grözinger deals with this topic in a better way. He points to the fact that the biblical stories are simultaneously theological *and* anthropological.[7] The Bible, he says, is a storybook. It is about a God who gets involved with people and their stories. Anyone who wants to tell stories about God "cannot avoid [dealing] with the people and their individual life stories, and their individual values. Why? Because God is a God who gets involved with humans, not for His own sake but for the benefit of humanity." Grözinger thus underlines that the hearers of the sermon are not just addressees; hearers make their own contribution.[8] During the week, the minister is in contact with church members in various ways. As she works on her sermon, she carries with her all kinds of experiences and ideas from pastoral conversations, group meetings, and incidental encounters. Research has shown that, when listening to a sermon, the hearers likewise connect what is being said with situations they experienced and conversations about faith.[9] Thus, many factors play a role in the background — in particular, hearers' existential deliberations and reflections on their worldview, besides attitudes that are anchored in the immediate situations of their lives. Worshippers place what they hear against that background. The biblical stories and images enable them to do so — indeed, they stimulate this process. The Gospel stories, for example, describe Jesus as he heals the sick, visits with those who have been ostracized from society, and puts those who have lost their way back on the right path. In this way the human arena of life is addressed in all its aspects — misery included. This happens by means of concrete events, but also through images and metaphors that make the deeper dimensions visible. Biblical stories thus express both the theological and the anthropological dimension.

---

7. Albrecht Grözinger, *Homiletik* (Gütersloh: Gütersloher Verlagshaus, 2008), p. 120.
8. Grözinger, *Homiletik*, p. 119.
9. Pleizier, *Religious Involvement in Hearing Sermons*, pp. 233-36.

The stories about the raising of Lazarus and of the only son of the widow of Nain make this abundantly clear. In the story of the widow, Jesus approaches the city gate with a group of followers. He sees that a dead body is being carried from the city. It is the only son of a widow, and a multitude of weeping people accompanies her. "And when the Lord saw her, he had compassion on her and said to her, 'Do not weep'" (Luke 7:13). In this story Jesus, the Messiah, who proclaims the kingdom of God and brings it closer, meets a funeral procession near the city gate. In the worship service, aspects of this story may be expressed in words and images — in hymns and prayers and in the sermon. In this story we see conflicting worlds — significantly, at the city gate, where justice is dispensed. There is the personal dimension of Jesus seeing the woman and taking pity on her. There is the social dimension of this death: the only son of a widow has died, and Jesus approaches and touches the bier. And there is the religious dimension: Jesus commands, "Young man, I say to you, arise" (Luke 7:14). The personal, the social, the religious — it is all there. Worshippers are reminded of their own sorrow; they become aware of the brokenness of the world in which they live. The story echoes their own faith and hope, their own doubt and disbelief. Precisely because these stories can evoke so many sentiments on the part of worshippers, it is important that the sermon touches both the theological as well as the anthropological dimension.

Both Barth and Thurneysen have often been accused of putting real-life situations on the back burner. But that was not true for Barth. To make my point, I will quote some sermon fragments of the young Barth that show how he developed the dialectic between the actual situation and God's Word. The first two fragments are from October 1914 and discuss the situation that resulted from the breaking out of World War I. It is significant that Barth uses most of his sermon to analyze the cultural-political situation. In his analysis, the thought from the first sentence of the sermon keeps re-occurring: *as if* the war has awakened something great and good in the world of nations. In those nations that participate (Germany, France, England, and Austria), a passion has been awakened. In that passion they think they defend the highest values and the most sacred good. Barth does not support that idea — in fact, he bluntly rejects it.

> Dear Friends,
> So far we have hardly, or not at all, discussed the great and *beautiful virtues* and qualities that the war has brought to light for the people, and with good reason. For in the newspaper reports, in particular abroad,

we can read enough about patriotism, courage, a spirit of sacrifice of the soldiers who fight in this war. Try as I may, I cannot agree with these. . . .

Aber! *Meine Freunde*, for us it is essential that we are more and more convinced that the war, and everything that goes with it, is an unmentionable injustice and, in all respects, a terrible misery; that the wild animal has been unleashed in the people and causes, to the dismay and mockery of the people, the most terrible destruction. This clear insight, that obliges us through our conscience and through the gospel of Jesus Christ, must be the firm foundation on which we unwaveringly stand. . . .

War is sin, and guilt and punishment — and the will to declare war on the war and on all that is part of it, is ultimately obedience to the God of peace and love.

Barth wonders how it can be that people can speak positively about this passion. How can the German newspapers laud the heroism of their soldiers, while the French do the same for theirs? "What in the world may be those *terrible* and *hellish* forces, that have succeeded to suddenly evoke all positive powers, and to put them just as suddenly in the service of evil?" Barth is perplexed that these hellish forces have annihilated the impact of all teaching and preaching. He is utterly amazed that men of science and *Bildung* are in support of the war machinery. "How you are fallen from heaven, O Day Star!" (Isa. 14:12). Only towards the end does Barth refer to the text for his sermon: "[Nothing] will be able to separate us from the love of God in Christ Jesus our Lord" (Rom. 8:38-39).

> For us Jesus is now the light of certainty in the midst of a dark world. We trust in Him. We look up to Him. From Him powers, that are stronger than the powers of evil, stream towards us. He has battled against them. They put on their hypocritical garment of truth and justice for Him. He has been in the midst of them, in the darkness of the night. The "angels, powers, and principalities" took all people around Him prisoner, even the best, the dearest friends. But not Him! His light has not ceased to shine. Easter followed Good Friday. Now a worldwide Good Friday has come about. But it will not kill the spirit of Jesus. He lives in all who do not let themselves be taken prisoner by the spirits that rule the air; in all who recognize the lies and the injustice, and will not be led astray by any magnificent disguise.[10]

10. Karl Barth, from a sermon preached on October 18, 1914, in *Predigten 1914*, republished by Ursula and Jochen Fähler (Zurich: Theologischer Verlag, 1974), pp. 518-32.

We may characterize his analysis of the world as critical and anti-ideological. As far as humankind is concerned, Barth states that the good is in the grip of evil powers. God is a judging God, and humankind has turned against God; thus guilt and punishment will result. At the end of the sermon, hearers are urged to choose another way. Barth as preacher does not use big words but is searching for the right response. He concentrates on Jesus himself (the cross) and on living in the *spirit* of Jesus. In that way the hope for a new world is not lost. This is also apparent in a fragment of a sermon that he preached a month later:

> Now we have already entered the time of Advent and soon we will celebrate Christmas. But this year it will be a *strange Christmas.* Our thoughts will turn to the millions of people who, also during this Christmas Eve, will be in the trenches, facing the enemy, equipped for battle. And to the thousands, yes, tens of thousands of families who will celebrate Christmas without their father, especially those who know that he will never return. This time our joy cannot be an innocent, undisturbed joy. Too much suffering is pressing upon us. And the question arises in us: Does it make sense under these circumstances to listen to the Christmas message: Glory to God in the highest and peace on earth, among the people of good will! Is the picture of the world as we now see it not a mockery in the face of these words? . . . I can well imagine that someone says: This year, really, we do not want to celebrate Christmas, and maybe we will also skip it next year. For, in our present situation it seems hypocrisy. . . . [However,] is God's *will* not in contrast with the things that occupy the world in all its corners? If we had been obedient to Him, there would not have been any war. We should enter a plea against ourselves and not against Him. . . .
>
> There is comfort for those who are now weeping in this dark night. Salvation will come for the humanity that now has lost all sense in this unparalleled storm of foolishness and dismay. Why would we reject this light, that in a rare fashion stands out against the present state of the world, but that precisely for that reason, and at this moment, has the promise: something else is coming! There is a way out from this dark world. There is victory over sin and guilt and death. There is a world of truth and peace that one day will triumph over this present world.[11]

---

11. Karl Barth, from a sermon preached on First Advent, November 29, 1914, in *Predigten 1914*, pp. 588-600.

Preaching

In an Easter sermon from 1917, based on Colossians 2:15, Barth highlights this contrast between the human situation and God's victorious power in an even more powerful way. God, Barth says, "disarmed the principalities and powers and made a public example of them, triumphing over them in Christ." God appeals to us:

> Look at what I have done and completed, while you were looking at the figures and were studying, arguing together and fighting, or were getting drunk, and while you were concocting wise stories and clever sayings, and were leading your insignificant life with grim seriousness.

While we were going our own ways, Barth says — while we were worshipping Mammon, were waging war, and were suffering in this dark world full of questions, riddles, and problems — Jesus Christ rose from the dead on the third day. What is wrong with this world? It seems that it possesses everything, but it lacks the most beautiful and the most crucial things. There is no intelligence, no love, no hope. The more seriously a person looks at his life, the more miserable it gets:

> We want to work, want to earn money, use our powers, have things for ourselves (without God!). Behold, modern capitalism. King Mammon is at the door. He puts his claws around us and turns us into his miserable slaves that are being chased along.

Barth believes that we are constantly being caught in a trap. And while we try to free ourselves, we walk from one trap into the next. But, he says, a new world has arrived, as on the first day of creation. What then is the new thing that Jesus brought?

> The only new element that Jesus brought was this word, this power, this hope: God! . . . There is only one explanation. That He fought for God. That He only had one goal: God's justice and rule and kingdom.

That is what Jesus stood for, and that is why, in fact, Easter began already on Good Friday. In the darkest hour, He called out: I am forsaken, but You are God! God was stronger than all human iniquities, stronger than Mammon, stronger than the powers of the devil and of death. Here Barth speaks of God as being present in everyday life. But a distance remains; God is spoken of in a critical tone. Gradually he becomes visible in the death and resurrection of Jesus.[12]

To end this section, I want to focus on two important post-war German homileticians who try to do justice to the critical opinion of Barth, but also pay due attention to the hearer: Rudolf Bohren and Ernst Lange. Bohren points out that it is not enough to refer only to the hearer in his or her actual circumstances. Also required is the power of imagination to put the hearer in a particular light. "The important thing is to know about the possibilities of the hearer and not only about his present position and his past. What counts is that we find out — 'discover' — his potential for the future." This discovery, this imagining of the situation of the hearer, is linked not only to a healthy view of the concrete situation, but also to the imaginative creativity of faith. Imagining the hearer means that we see the person whom we encounter as "standing before God, that is: as standing in the *Gnadenwahl*." Suddenly we see him from a different perspective. "I discover the hearer," Bohren says, "when I see him in his worth and esteem, which he has in Christ Jesus."[13] But how does this being-in-Christ relate to the real situation in which the worshipper finds himself? How can this be experienced as truth, without trivializing the other: the actual conditions?

Ernst Lange positions himself more on the side of the concrete hearer, with emphasis on the actual situation. At the beginning of the sermon, we do not have the text, he says, but we have the worshippers, the people with their contradictions, their problems, their questions, and their needs. They have come with their hope and their awareness of the Christian tradition — and, simultaneously, with their doubts. Lange wants to take the actual hearer seriously, in her life situation, and not immediately in the beam of Christ's light. This light is a mystery that must yet be discovered. The point of departure is the concrete human being with her frustrations and expectations:

> Preaching is: I speak with the hearer about her life. I speak with her about her experiences and opinions, her hope and disappointment, her success and her failure, her duty and her destiny. I talk with her about her world and her responsibility for this world, about the threats and the possibilities in life. The hearer is my theme, and nothing else. But note: The hearer

---

12. Karl Barth, from a sermon preached on Easter 1917, quoted and discussed in A. W. Velema, *God ter sprake. Een homiletisch onderzoek naar de vooronderstellingen van de prediking bij Karl Barth in vergelijking met Hans Joachim Iwand, Ernst Lange en Rudolf Bohren* (The Hague: Boekencentrum, 1991), pp. 56-63.

13. Rudolf Bohren, *Predigtlehre* (Munich: Kaiser Verlag, 1971), p. 466.

stands before God. That, however, does not add anything to the reality of her life, which is my actual theme, but it does help to discover the ultimate truth of that reality.[14]

Nonetheless, Lange wants to descend to a deeper, existential layer. The ultimate reality of human existence is living before God. That, however, requires discovery.

What Do the Worshippers Say?

The empirical research by Theo Pleizier has shown that the involvement of worshippers in the sermon is directly related to the aspect of *recognition*. They realize "This is about me" or "This touches me." As soon as worshippers recognize something of their own life or their own faith experience in the sermon, Pleizier concludes, they become more intensely involved and will more consciously participate.[15] This pertains not only to their everyday life but also to the world of faith.

It is clear from Pleizier's study that the personality of the minister plays a significant role in the listening process. In her sermon, the minister offers hearers a concrete presentation, and she is a living example of what she preaches. The religious personality of the minister appears to have a greater relevancy for hearers than is generally assumed.[16] This concerns not only how she communicates with them but also how they perceive her faith. The *ethos* of the minister also plays a role. In the sermon the minister reveals something of her own faith. This offers hearers the possibility of identifying with her. Two aspects come to the forefront. First, the minister is viewed as a *fellow believer*. That happens, for instance, when she does not hide that she struggles with the same problems that the church members do. But it may also happen through confrontation — when hearers cannot identify with her or have an opinion totally different from hers. Second, the *pastoral* and *empathetic* side of the minister is also laid bare in this relational identification. Does she care for her hearers? It also becomes clear that worshippers do not just listen for things that concern themselves.

---

14. Ernst Lange, *Die Verbesserliche Welt: Möglichkeiten Christlicher Rede Erprobt an der Geschichte vom Propheten Jona* (Berlin: Kreuz Verlag, 1968), p. 84.
15. Pleizier, *Religious Involvement in Hearing Sermons*, pp. 233-51.
16. Pleizier, *Religious Involvement in Hearing Sermons*, p. 243.

They sense whether the minister also cares about others, about those who face serious problems. This means that hearers may get involved when the sermon does not directly touch them but touches the life of others. Accordingly, the ideas of Friedrich Niebergall and J. J. van Oosterzee (see Chapter 4) are not total fantasy. The sermons of the young Barth clearly show that he presents himself as a fellow believer. He takes a position in the political arena and refers to his own faith. Even though his position on the war is a critical one, he expresses his deep concern for the atrocities the soldiers and their families must experience.

How is it that, from a religious perspective, worshippers are able to identify with the world of the sermon? It appears that participation in the liturgy in the preceding part of the service constitutes an important link by which worshippers can become involved with the sermon — existentially and with regard to their faith. Active participation in the sermon would be difficult without the prior phase in which the framework of the common faith is laid out as the basis. In the liturgy the congregation experiences communion with God, and the same occurs in the sermon. However, the sermon adds a dimension: it offers opportunity for reflection, consideration, and meditation. It offers moments of critical assessment and thought. David Buttrick refers to this as the "symbolic-reflective" modus.[17] In various ways worshippers are actively concerned with their own sphere of faith.

The sermon *cultivates* worshippers' faith. The word "cultivate" has several meanings. First, it may be linked to nature: it may refer to working the land and caring for what is planted. The second meaning follows from this: civilizing, forming, developing. Words like "civilization" and "culture" are related terms. The dictionary tells us that these words may also be used in a more figurative sense: to indicate raising or breeding — that is, diligently caring for, with the intent of increasing. In that sense one may cultivate certain feelings. "Cultivate" is therefore a fitting word to describe the effect of the sermon, since it points to a *formative* and *developmental* activity. Richard Lischer rightly remarks that the term "event" as a metaphor for the sermon is one-sided and fails to do justice to the *formative* effect. In the New Testament, he says, it is important that the congregation receives guidance and support. A sermon is more than information about a new way of being before God, more than making people aware of vague similarities between religion and meaningful experiences. It points believers to the implications of their

---

17. David Buttrick, *Homiletic: Moves and Structures* (Philadelphia: Fortress Press, 1987), p. 13.

atonement in Christ.[18] Cultivating has to do with development. It implies progress and growth. A sermon will help hearers to acquire deeper insight. If we may describe "civilization" as "refinement of the spiritual and moral life," we may justly state that the sermon contributes to spiritual civilization.

Worshippers indicate that attending church regularly and listening to sermons helps them to maintain their faith. Listening to a sermon on a regular basis helps to ensure that the gospel of Christ and the Bible continue to play a role in worshippers' lives. The sermon helps them to keep and renew their faith. It is part of a spiritual routine that helps them stay on track. Some say that it helps them to cope with the week ahead. Others say that the sermon stimulates their awareness that faith is something that people have in common. By participating in a worship service, worshippers broaden their outlook in the domain of faith. Pleizier includes this in the *anamnetic* effect of the sermon.[19] The sermon keeps the remembrance of Christ alive. In addition, worshippers speak of special moments of insight, of comfort, of deep joy; they also speak of moments of intense involvement, of renewed commitment, and of a strong intention to become part of social and missional activities. These are moments of special enlightenment, or, if one prefers, of special revelation. They offer a precious awareness, a new understanding or intense desire. These are moments of *illumination*.[20] Regular churchgoers tell us that those moments of illumination are relatively rare. The sermon cultivates faith, but keeping the faith is mostly a cumulative and communal process. Moments of illumination do occur, but being focused too exclusively on these will bring disappointment. If, however, they do not occur, or they seldom occur, the dynamic of the sermon may disappear, and its cultivating effect may weaken. In short, cultivation demands moments of illumination.

Local Theology

When Jesus proclaims the kingdom of God, he does so with images and incidents from daily life — with the image of a farmer who sows his seed, of a son who sets off for faraway lands, of wedding guests who are looking for the arrival of the bridegroom, and so on. No wonder that stories and

---

18. Richard Lischer, *A Theology of Preaching* (Eugene, Ore.: Wipf & Stock, 1992), p. 89.
19. Pleizier, *Religious Involvement in Hearing Sermons*, pp. 257-61.
20. Pleizier, *Religious Involvement in Hearing Sermons*, pp. 255-57.

experiences play a major role in Christian preaching. But behind this simple fact we find a great complexity. As Thomas Long explains,

> Stories, images, analogies, and experiences are not mere decorations in sermons; they are active ingredients of communication. They cause certain things to happen in the minds of the hearers and are thus powerful, but also potentially disruptive, poetic elements. An image can clarify, and it can also mislead. An example can ground the truth of the gospel in the actual experience, but it can also make the gospel seem merely mundane. A story can be richly evocative or insipid and cloying. A well-chosen experience can enable people to envision new possibilities for discipleship, but a contrived one can manipulate them and be a form of verbal entrapment.[21]

We may discover some implicit theological ideas in the way in which stories, examples, and life experiences function in sermons, since these are employed to establish the connection between everyday life and the message of the gospel. For example, if a minister refers repeatedly to miraculous escapes that God has provided, it may suggest that providing such escapes is typical of the way in which God acts, and thus offers a particular concept of God. If a minister emphasizes the difficulties in life and the examples of continuing struggles in the life of the believers, it suggests that full joy will continue to wither under a bell jar of doubt. These examples point to the fact that concrete statements about God in relationship to the daily life of worshippers fit into a broader framework — which is far from simple to define. From the perspective of the congregation, the *theology of the congregation* is part of that broader framework. From the perspective of the minister, we may speak of a *personal* theology that is related to the office he holds.[22] This theology is inspired not only by official church documents and confessional statements, but also by a local faith perspective that takes the concrete community into account. It is a form of communal theology that is "lived," and the questions, insights, and struggles of the members are part of it. Leonora Tubbs Tisdale refers to this as a "local

---

21. Thomas G. Long, *The Witness of Preaching* (Louisville: Westminster John Knox Press, 1989), p. 157.

22. Paul Wilson thinks that a minister works with a particular theological pattern in sermon preparation. In his view, it is based on the tension between "trouble and grace." See Paul Scott Wilson, *The Four Pages of the Sermon: A Guide to Biblical Preaching* (Nashville: Abingdon Press, 1999).

theology."²³ We may also call it a religious subculture. The framework has a social dimension: it belongs to the congregation as a social community. And because it has a social dimension, it fits into a broader framework of a religious tradition. Over time, it receives its shape, and it is subject to continuous change.

What is the nature of this broader framework, of which the sermon is a part? Is it a system of values, insights, rules? Words like "frame" and "framework" and "system" sound rather closed, solid and inflexible. In reality the framework is quite flexible and more defined by the context. Examples, experiences, and stories emerge from a concrete situation; there are underlying situations, reasons, incidents, and things that "happen." On the other hand, there are broad presuppositions, accepted values and truths, and ideas based on a particular worldview. In the genesis of the sermon, these aspects play a role in the background. This is true not just of religious presuppositions but also of the (normative) ideas about how one ought to live. Of course, such a framework exerts a significant *regulatory* pressure. It involves a (developing) *set* of convictions, insights, and values concerning faith, lifestyles, attitudes, and practices. We may refer to that set as *culture*. Precisely because language is so important in the worship service, it stands to reason that we specify it as a cultural-linguistic framework. "A religion," George Lindbeck suggests, "can be viewed as a kind of cultural and/or linguistic framework or medium that shapes the entirety of life and thought."²⁴ The examples that are used in a sermon and the life experiences that are referenced are based on concrete situations in the world or the congregation, but they acquire a special significance against the background of that wider cultural-linguistic framework of a local faith community. The church's own theology and the social and ecclesial milieu are part of that cultural-linguistic framework.

A Typology of Connections

Within the framework of this local theology, connections are made between the gospel message and the world in which the believers find themselves. This may happen in different ways. Globally speaking, there are two main

---

23. Leonora Tubbs Tisdale, *Preaching as Local Theology and Folk Art* (Minneapolis: Fortress Press, 1997), pp. 31-55.
24. George A. Lindbeck, *The Nature of Doctrine: Religion and Theology in a Postliberal Age* (Philadelphia: Westminster John Knox Press, 1984), p. 33.

types of connection. Some preaching styles connect the gospel and today's world *analogically*. The emphasis is placed on the parallels between divine reality and our human world. The intent is that, when hearing the word "God," worshippers will have some ideas and some understanding of what the word means. To keep this from becoming rather arbitrary or remaining totally vague, there must be some relationship with our present world. This concerns not only noetic matters, such as knowledge and understanding, but also the discovery of *traces of God* in our lives.[25] It concerns the question *how* and *where* we might see and experience God. There are, however, also preaching styles that emphasize the contrast, the difference, the *dialectic*, the contradiction. God is the Other, an odd phenomenon that disturbs our world and turns it around.

I will now offer some excerpts of two Easter sermons that show how ministers try to make connections. In an Easter sermon in 2002 (which was published on the Internet), the minister begins by referring to a discussion in a television program between a presenter and Antoine Bodar, who is described as a conservative Roman Catholic priest. The presenter quotes the proclamation "The Lord is truly risen." She considers this to be a beautiful dogma, but it also causes her problems, because it is so far removed from the experience of everyday life. Bodar does not experience this same difficulty, and for him these words reveal a different world. Then the minister continues:

> How do you experience the resurrection of Christ in your life? Does it have meaning for you? Or do you say: That is miles away from where I am? You cannot simply decide to believe in the resurrection. There must be something else, a kind of explanation, or a similar kind of experience in your own life. Only when in your own life you have experienced a kind of resurrection from death, only when in your own life you somehow come to the point where you realize that death really means death, but that life conquers — only then you will be able to give a better place to Christ's resurrection.

Remarkably, the words above must be added as a kind of explanation or a reference to a similar experience. Apparently people sense a wide gap between the Easter message and our present situation. This gap has a noetic

---

25. Hans-Günther Heimbrock, *Spuren Gottes Wahrnehmen. Phänomenologisch Inspirierte Predigten und Texte zum Gottesdienst* (Stuttgart: Kohlhammer, 2003).

dimension (it is hard to grasp) and an experiential dimension (only when in your own life you experience something similar . . .).

Another Easter sermon first attempts to establish some intra-biblical connections, then link them to situations that the hearers recognize. Themes of victory are linked to images of light and darkness, morning and night, and the emerging spring:

> Early in the morning Israel saw the defeated Egyptians lying at the shores of the sea. When morning was breaking, in the last hour of the night, the disciples saw Jesus walking on the water. Early in the morning the women went to the tomb to care for Jesus' body. But He was no longer where they had expected to find Him. The night has been heavy, the darkness more dense than ever. But now that the morning has come, we have solid ground under our feet.
>
> The night is over, the morning is here. In several stories, in any case also in those stories about the rescue from the sea and about the resurrection of Jesus from death, this reversal of night to early morning is emphatically mentioned. . . . In our discussion in the group that assists in the sermon preparation we have talked for quite some time about this image of the morning; that image evokes so many thoughts. It reminds you of those nights that you yourself have been waking, the nights in which you felt afraid. Nights full of tension, of waiting for a message. . . . This movement of the birth of a child, this movement towards life, is propelled forth by forces that cannot be stopped. You cannot stop God's work of creation. It has such an enormous power that you cannot put a break on it. . . . This mighty stone, how would you be able to stop Him who made heaven and earth?[26]

The sermon is constructed in such a way that the image of the dawning of a new day has a clear intention. It is about a divine, unstoppable power that produces new life. Biblical images serve as analogies to our own real-life experiences. Easter is associated with the breaking through of a new day, the birth of a child. There is a flower in the bud, a mustard seed in every human life.

---

26. Easter sermon, Utrecht, 1998, in F. Gerrit Immink, "'Missio Dei' in Preaching: God Language and Human Receptivity," in *Preaching as God's Mission*, ed. Tsuneaki Kato (Tokyo: Kyo Bun Kwan, 1999), pp. 116-35. Note: This was a baptismal service. The reference to the birth of a child is perhaps meant to relate to the parents of the child.

Charles Campbell points out that in the narrative sermon style, the *experiential event* may be presented in such a manner that the uniqueness of God-in-Jesus-Christ, as it is brought to us in the biblical stories, shifts to the background. The danger exists, he says, that we dare no longer say anything about God apart from our human experiences. This may lead to reducing Jesus to a symbol of our human experience. Our own experiences become the leading theme, and the biblical stories and motifs function as representations of those profoundly human experiences. In contrast to this reduction, Campbell defends the "oddness" of the gospel.[27]

A good example of a more contrasting connection can be found in a sermon preached by Walter Brueggemann.[28] In a sermon entitled "Outrageous God, Season of Decrease," Brueggemann introduces the biblical witness as almost scandalous:

> There is something deeply outrageous about Advent, which is made clear in this poem of Isaiah 65. It is so outrageous that none of us really believes it. Nonetheless, we are the baptized people who have promised to share such a text, such a vision.

The tension between the text and the hearers is pushed to the extreme: none of us believes in the message of Advent. Yet, Brueggemann insists, the poetic text of Isaiah presents the view of a new world. A world that is called to life by God. A world in which there is no longer a place for tyranny and extortion, where children no longer die.

> I told you it was outrageous. It is outrageous because the new world of God is beyond our capacity and even beyond our imagination. It does not seem possible. In our fatigue, our self-sufficiency, and our cynicism, we deeply believe that such promises could not happen here. Such newness is only poetic fantasy, and there are the persistent realities of injustice and grief and terror, and it will never end, not in any future we can conjure.

Brueggemann says that the role of lyrical poetry allows us to step beyond the human cynicism concerning our daily life. We are cut off from it and are challenged to imagine new things. In this new world, *everything* is so

---

27. Campbell, *Preaching Jesus*, p. 142.
28. F. Gerrit Immink, "Introduction: Bearer of the Word," in Paul Scott Wilson, *The New Interpreter's Handbook of Preaching* (Nashville: Abingdon Press, 1999), pp. 433-35.

outrageous that it baffles us — and perhaps leaves us to just quietly wait? In Brueggemann's sermon the emphasis on the outrageous becomes an ethical appeal. Do away with the old and destructive, and give priority to compassion for life and forgiveness. Advent demands that we pay attention to the extraordinary things of God and that we contribute to the diminishing of everything that destroys life.[29]

In this sermon Brueggemann constructs a dialectical tension: God's new world differs completely from our world. There is a profound antithesis between our world and God's kingdom: the prophetic word is completely outrageous. Through the employment of the potential of symbolic language and poetic eloquence, God's new world almost turns into fiction. You may ask: Can this language about God's new world refer to a possible reality? Does this prophecy claim to convey the truth? Is this outrageously different reality a figure of speech that is only intended to strengthen the ethical appeal?

H. F. Kohlbrugge (1803-1875) is another example of someone who increases the tension between our world and the kingdom that was inaugurated with the resurrection of Christ. *Is it unbelievable that God raises the dead?* he asks in a sermon on 1 Corinthians 15:29. Kohlbrugge argues that it is totally wrong to look for an anchor for our Christian hope in our present reality. The kingdom of Christ cannot be seen; it is a kingdom of faith. He continues,

> Grace cannot reign, faith has no meaning, if the contrary does not exist. The church must face temptation and struggles, and must, as it were, be overpowered; for, if its situation becomes so precarious, it can no longer help itself. It must call upon its king, Jesus, so that He can help and save it.

Kohlbrugge creates the impression that any kind of visibility becomes a temptation for the believer, that every form of human piety and moral progress may have dangerous aspects, because the believer may elevate himself in his arrogance and no longer rely on Christ. Kohlbrugge thus creates a paradoxical relationship: there is no visible connection between Christ and the actual life situation of the church. Kohlbrugge says,

> What confusing ideas about the kingdom of Christ do we find with those who explain the resurrection only spiritually, or morally, or symboli-

---

29. Walter Brueggemann, *The Threat of Life: Sermons on Pain, Power, and Weakness*, ed. Charles L. Campbell (Minneapolis: Fortress Press, 1996), p. 66.

> cally. . . . Christ has a kingdom. This kingdom, however, cannot be seen, but it is a kingdom of faith. Everything about it must be believed and will only be seen at the time and in the hour of salvation.

Kohlbrugge pictures the kingdom that is revealed in the resurrection of Christ as a divine reality. However, it is a purely eschatological reality that cannot be mixed with this earthly existence as long as it is ruled by the powers of sin and death:

> What about death, if you want to have the resurrection before the second coming of Christ? No, there cannot be any resurrection until this last enemy has been disarmed and destroyed.[30]

We meet a totally different approach in a sermon by Barbara Brown Taylor. She wants to connect with everyday life and tries to find analogies between the reality of God and our present world. In a sermon on Acts 2 (the outpouring of the Holy Spirit), she introduces the Holy Spirit as a power that is at work in the ordinary things. The Holy Spirit streams in and out of us and binds us together. Her concept of the Holy Spirit is from "below" rather than from "above." The Holy Spirit is as close to us as the air that we breathe. She suggests that the air that we inhale is like a kind of blanket that envelops the earth (already from the days of creation), and she uses this image to make a connection between Jesus' last breath and the sound of the strong wind on the day of Pentecost in Jerusalem:

> When Jesus let go of his last breath — willingly, we believe, for love of us — that breath hovered in the air in front of him for a moment and then it was set loose on earth. It was such a pungent breath — so full of passion, so full of life — that it did not simply dissipate as so many breaths do. It grew in strength and in volume, until it was a mighty wind, which God sent spinning through an upper room in Jerusalem on the day of Pentecost. God wanted to make sure that Jesus' friends were the inheritors of Jesus' breath, and it worked.

According to Taylor, ordinary life is full of God's presence. The question is this: Do we recognize the active presence of the Spirit? In her sermon Taylor

---

30. H. F. Kohlbrugge, *Is het ongelooflijk dat God de doden opwekt?* (Rotterdam, 1862; reprint, Zoetermeer: Boekencentrum, 1996), pp. 38-49.

gives a few examples of such situations. Sometimes, she says, we do not know exactly how to define our experiences. "But when something happens in your life that you cannot give a name, I would like to suggest that perhaps the Holy Spirit is at work." Or suppose that someone has become estranged from a companion, and she rediscovers herself again in that relationship. "You may call it what you want, but I would call it the work of the Holy Spirit."[31]

In contrast to Brueggemann and Kohlbrugge, Taylor thinks that the holy manifests itself in everyday things. The ways in which the Spirit moves are not spectacular or ecstatic. Here the danger is that the divine presence becomes an immanent and intimate power, without the dynamic of the critical contrast.

The Scriptures in the *Performance*

In the worship service, the Bible is read aloud. At such moments the Bible is a tangible document, an open book. The human voice is loud and clear. The reading has an acoustic impact. These tangible dimensions are not unimportant. Should there be any inclination to spiritualize the salvation event or to reduce it to something that is in us, the reading of the Bible calls us to order: salvation is unfolded through a text that was transmitted to us. Ultimately, in the worship service the Holy Scriptures have the last word — not the credo, not the authentic faith, not any age-old symbolic act.

In this section I will first deal with exegesis with regard to the sermon: How does the minister treat the Bible text as she prepares her sermon? Then I will mention three dimensions of the preparatory process: (1) hearing the text when reading; (2) the use of historical-critical scholarship; and (3) the homiletical-theological construction of the message.

Homiletical Exegesis

In Protestant worship, the sermon and the Bible text are closely linked. The sermon is not an incidental discourse about a social or religious subject, but is tied to the exposition of Scripture. By connecting the sermon to the text of the Bible, the Reformation wanted to guarantee the theological content

---

31. Barbara Brown Taylor, *Home by Another Way* (Cambridge: Cowley Publications, 1999), pp. 143-49.

of the sermon. A minister cannot lose herself in all kinds of reflections but is obliged to study the part of Scripture that was read during the service. This, however, does not mean that the sermon is only an explanation of the Scriptures. Albrecht Grözinger correctly remarks that preaching has to do with the explanation of texts, and that one cannot preach without a careful exegesis. However, he adds, if we say that preaching is nothing but an explanation of Scripture, we fail to do justice to the sermon: "The explanation of a text (whatever method we might choose to use) is exegesis. But the sermon is more than that, and therefore also differs from this."[32]

In the Reformed tradition, the sermon was defined in terms of exposition and application. According to T. Hoekstra, "In accordance with the essence of the ministry of the Word as the exposition and application of God's Words, the homiletic treatment of the text requires a distinction between exposition and application."[33] However, this principle is not without problems — for two reasons. First, in the Reformed tradition this application (or appropriation) was regarded as a theological category that primarily focused on the sharing in the salvation in Christ: "The preacher must not only present the truth of salvation in an objective manner, but must also be eager to ensure that this will be appropriated subjectively," Hoekstra affirmed.[34] Our sharing in Christ is, of course, a question about the relationship between then and now, but it is not the same as the exegetical search for the meaning of historic texts. Second, the distinction between explication and application also suggests that the homiletical exegesis begins with a purely exegetical part which may subsequently be applied. Recent studies in homiletics tell us, however, that this process is more complicated and that, in any case, it is of a circular nature.[35] It is not only a matter of applying the text to a situation, for the situation already plays a part in the reading and the hearing of the text.

"When we interpret a part of Scripture for preaching," Thomas Long says, "it changes not only what we do with the results of the exegesis, but also the way we go about the exegesis in the first place."[36] The entire exercise is intended to discover what the text might have to tell us now — today. Therefore, the situation in which we find ourselves, the congregation being

---

32. Grözinger, *Homiletik*, p. 156.
33. T. Hoekstra, *Gereformeerde homiletiek* (Wageningen: Zomer & Keuning, 1926), p. 280.
34. T. Hoekstra, *Gereformeerde homiletiek*, p. 300.
35. Jan Hermelink, "Ausmahlen und Hindurchsehen. Das Diskurssemiotische Konzept des 'Mentalen Bildes' in der Predigtarbeit," in *Predigen im Plural. Homiletische Aspekte*, ed. U. Pohl-Patalong and F. Muchlinsky (Hamburg: Eb-Verlag, 2001), pp. 36-45.
36. Long, *The Witness of Preaching*, p. 60.

addressed, and the context in which the members live all play a role in the exegesis. The Bible is read aloud in the worship service, and this implies that it is a *Word directed to us*. Consequently, the homiletical exegesis must take into account the *effect* of the text as well as the religious *truth* that is expressed in the text. Those two aspects are closely related. Reading the Scriptures as the Word of God, as we saw in Chapter 4, also implies that we do not place God and humankind in quotation marks, which might have been valid when the words were written, but that we regard them as expressing a living reality that affects us today. Homiletical exegesis has the task of unfolding the texts in such a way that the *reality of God and humankind* takes center stage.

On the basis of Luther's exegesis of Romans 1:17 (about the righteousness of God), Gerd Theissen points to four aspects of what he considers to be theological exegesis. First, theological exegesis has to do with transcendence: "We use the term 'kerygma' for a word that unfolds transcendence: a message that unwraps God's reality. If it is to be a theological discipline, exegesis must first of all have a *kerygmatic* function. Theology deals with having a dialogue with God. Among the many words of the Bible, it is in search of the one word in which God Himself becomes accessible."[37] Second, theological exegesis also deals with our *human existence*, with failing or succeeding in living before the face of God. It focuses on the existential, ultimate dimension of a text. A purely philological exegesis will not have that same focus. Third, theological exegesis deals with the church — that is to say, it has a *canonical* function. It explains the text to a community which believes that these texts contain the norms and values of life and faith. Fourth, theological exegesis has a *critical* function: all authorities (even ecclesial authorities) may be subject to its criticism.

K. H. Miskotte likewise uses the term "theological exegesis." According to him, "The theological exegesis provides the direction and order that are necessary to tame the hegemony of the didactic element."[38] His point is that the sermon goes beyond a mere didactic comment. The sermon is about the *kerygma*, says Miskotte: "The full kerygma, the true counsel of God, must be 'unfolded.' From one flower, Luther says, the preacher must unfold the entire meadow full of flowers."[39] What I have called homiletical exegesis, and what Miskotte and Theissen refer to as theological exegesis, apply to the same phenomenon: in our exposition of Bible texts, we encounter the self-

---

37. Gerd Theissen, "Exegese und Theologie. Über Bedeutung und Funktion der Exegese in der Theologie," *Nederlands Theologisch Tijdschrift* 58 (2004): 293.

38. K. H. Miskotte, *Om het levende Woord. Opstellen over de praktijk der exegese* (Kampen: Kok, 1973), p. 109.

39. Miskotte, *Om het levende woord*, p. 98.

revelation of God as well as the existential layers of human existence. Both dimensions — God's revelation and the human condition — are at issue, in very different times and under very different circumstances. The homiletical exegesis enters the zone of the holy as a reality; in the texts it is in search of traces of *divine revelation* and *situational human faith.*

Homiletical exegesis is, in all respects, a theological exercise. It is a task that is directly concerned with the progress and continuance of the Christian praxis of faith. It presupposes knowledge of and involvement with the living religious practice. In that sense, theology is both a normative and a critical discipline. Theology poses this question: How can we believe, act, and live as we should? Miskotte argues that all theological subdisciplines have this same practical intent; if not, we should speak of religious studies and not of theology.[40] Theology cannot avoid the question of truth, and must reflect critically on religious practices and contexts. This implies that homiletical exegesis will also take responsibility for the practical effects of the Holy Scriptures. At times, it will mean that a critical analysis of the praxis will lead to a *renewed understanding* of the Scriptures, and at other times to a *new interpretation* of the Scriptures. It may also mean that a minister leaves a text untouched because she is unable to deal with it.

Through the homiletical-theological approach to the biblical text, the sermon will eventually acquire a *performative* religious effect. As a result, it becomes clear that the sermon is not just an exposition of the text, and not just a discussion with the hearers about the world in which they live. The unique aspect is the actualization of faith and life experiences. The worshippers get actively involved through their faith, their questions, and their expectations. In the sermon, a religious reality is evoked. *The participants experience a touch of the sacred.* The setting of the liturgy is a contributing factor: the *epiclesis,* the hymns that are sung, the confession and the praise of the entire community. The sermon also has lyrical moments: the salvation is offered and experienced. God is called upon, his presence is expected, the Word "happens," hope comes alive, and love awakens. The *kerygma* has its impact, when God is praised and the hearers are carried along in wonderment. That is why the sermon always has a doxological ring to it. David Lose emphasizes how the sermonic elements of praise and confession help to actualize the faith.[41] Rudolf Bohren underscores this dimension by pointing

---

40. Miskotte, *Om het levende woord,* p. 99.
41. David J. Lose, *Confessing Jesus Christ: Preaching in a Postmodern World* (Grand Rapids: Wm. B. Eerdmans, 2003), pp. 189-232.

to the fact that God is the first hearer of the sermon. Whether the people will come to church remains uncertain. But there is One who has promised to be there: he who neither slumbers nor sleeps. In this sense, Bohren says, each sermon has a liturgical character, and all preaching of the gospel is directed towards the doxology: giving praise to the Name.[42]

Preparing the Sermon

It is difficult to say how exegesis eventually finds its way into the sermon. Ministers have been academically trained and have learned to study the biblical text in the original languages. In their weekly sermon preparation, they approach the Bible in a professional manner. They know how to differentiate between literary genres; they are able to trace the genesis of the texts and are acquainted with the specific literary characteristics of the different biblical books, and so on. But how does this textual analysis relate to the sermon? One minister comments,

> When I have finished most of my roaming around in the text, a rather chaotic phase follows. I look at all kinds of useful and useless things, until some kind of core emerges, a kind of sermon-skeleton, to which, as I write, and as I speak in the pulpit, the flesh of the sermon may be attached.[43]

In the study of the texts, some significant things may jump out: for instance, a certain word that draws the attention, a sentence construction that seems remarkable, or an association with another part of Scripture. At the beginning of the Gospel of Mark, John the Baptist says, "The time is fulfilled, and the kingdom of God is at hand; repent, and believe in the gospel" (1:15). When the minister reads this, he realizes that the phrase "kingdom of God" will have to be looked at more closely. What does Mark intend to say? What does this tell us about the message of John and about the coming of Jesus? Through this kind of close reading of the text, the minister discovers sermon material.

A great deal has been written, especially in English, about sermon prepa-

---

42. Bohren, *Predigtlehre*, p. 455.
43. "De twee petten van de prediker," ed. Ernest Henau, Gerrit Immink, and Jaap van der Laan, in F. Gerrit Immink, *Praktische Theologie* 4 (1997): 412.

ration. The literature deals in particular with the various steps the minister must take in the process of preparing the sermon, and with the time between exegesis and the final sermon, and also with the meditation, the sermon outline, and so forth. Some manuals provide models for sermon preparation. Paul Scott Wilson suggests an approach in which the minister spends some time each day in the preparatory process.[44] On Monday, he should ask, What does the text say (understanding)? On Tuesday, What does the text mean (explanation)? On Wednesday, What does experience say (application)? On Thursday, What does the preacher say (purpose)?

Much less is known about the creative process itself, about the moment when the minister has that inspiration or insight. There is, however, quite a lot of (English) literature about sermon construction. But most of it deals with the rhetorical components rather than with the influence of the exegesis on the sermon. This is understandable, since structure and order can be discussed in more general terms. Much of the literature is prescriptive. It deals with the way in which the minister might approach the job in his study.

In her sermon preparation the minister is, in different ways, involved with the Bible as text. First, the minister must pay attention to the fact that the Bible will be read in the liturgy on Sunday morning as a Scripture lesson. This is important as she prepares the sermon. For the reading of the Scriptures already has its own performative effect. Something happens when the Scriptures are read in the liturgy prior to the sermon. The minister who sits in her study to prepare the sermon must take this into account. Second, the minister has been trained to examine Scripture as a literary and historical document. Ministers have developed academic exegetical skills that they apply every week. Third, the preparation must focus on the theological approach to the text, on the hermeneutical and pastoral insights. These are directly connected with the exegetical work, but they go beyond this: What impact does this part of Scripture have in the context in which the church assembles on Sunday morning?

In the actual work on the sermon, these three dimensions cannot be separated. Yet, it is important to distinguish between them and to pay attention to each. In that way it is possible to avoid the risk that the third dimension — the theological or pastoral approach to the text — may outflank the actual exegesis. If that occurs, the biblical text will not have its own expressive power and cannot function as a critical norm. But it is also possible that the

---

44. Paul Scott Wilson, *The Practice of Preaching* (Nashville: Abingdon Press, 1995).

Preaching

scholarly exegesis is so overpowering that the dialectic between the literary exegesis and the hermeneutical application remains inadequate. When that happens, the minister runs the risk that the sermon will offer all kinds of interesting pieces of information, but that worshippers will find it difficult to connect these with their own lives. The art of preparation is to ensure that these three dimensions are in dialogue with each other.

THE BIBLE TEXT AS LITURGICAL SCRIPT

Worshippers listen to the reading of the Scriptures, but each does so from his/her own framework of understanding. This framework is a mix of the culture of the congregation and the faith and life of the individual worshipper. Participants may experience the reading as strange or in opposition to their own world, or it may be that the reading appeals to them, evokes their curiosity, and raises their expectations. Those primary reactions and associations are the materials that the minister can work with in her study. They do not eventually appear on her desk as data when the literary exegesis is completed, but they influence the preparatory process from the very start. The *hearers' response* (the reaction of hearers to the reading) may elicit a particular insight, and thereby cause the minister to pursue a special theme. As a result, the homiletical exegesis may change gears. In listening to the miracle stories, for instance, hearers may experience a degree of understanding or estrangement. They may wonder how they should understand these stories, and whether such things also happen today. Possibly, they connect these stories with Jesus as the promised Messiah and with the expectation of peace and justice. But it is also possible that this framework is lacking, and thus a strange world of miracles causes skepticism and creates a formidable distance. On the other hand, during the reading some may be touched by the impact of a biblical story. We may, for instance, think of a text in Luke and imagine how worshippers hear in the reading how, together with a large group of disciples, Jesus approaches the town of Nain. "As he drew near to the gate of the city, behold, a man who had died was being carried out, the only son of his mother, and she was a widow; and a large crowd from the city was with her. And when the Lord saw her, he had compassion on her and said to her, 'Do not weep'" (Luke 7:12-13). The hearers may identify with some elements of this story; they may be reminded of a situation of loss or mourning in their own lives. Consciously or subconsciously these associations and considerations may continue to have an echo as they listen to the sermon.

Listening to the Scriptures as a sacred text in the concrete situation of the worship service is a contextual event. The Scriptures are connected with real-life situations. Ministers use this facet as they prepare their sermons. This shows that Scripture has an expressive power, that actual and new meanings may be evoked, and that we may speak of a "salvific effect."[45] In this way the Bible functions as sacred text. The Holy Scriptures did not just have an original meaning when the words were written; they also have a renewed meaning when they are read today. These associations and reactions may, however, point to a gap with regard to the original meaning. The impact of the text *now* is not automatically the same as the impact was *then*. The hearers may, for instance, be struck by the disparities in power, by different ideas of gender roles, and by strange customs and methods. It is important for the homiletical exegesis to make use of these elements. The time difference heightens the exegetical dynamic. Martin Nicol underscores the point that a minister can use these immediate associations in an effective manner. In so doing she can get at the underlying tensions in the biblical text much more quickly.[46]

THE BIBLE AS A HISTORICAL AND LITERARY DOCUMENT

The domain of explaining Scripture has become rather complicated. As H. G. L. Peels notes,

> The time of simplicity is past, when an exegete needed only a few tools (textus receptus, lexicon, grammar, and a few commentaries) to proceed with a text and speedily arrive at a clear meaning.... The validity, the unity, and [the] uniqueness of the biblical witness have become once again the topic of debate, because there is an increased awareness of historical and cultural distance, and a new insight in the genesis and religion-historical context of the Bible.[47]

Of course, ministers are not expected to contribute to the study of the Old and the New Testament at the level of scholarly exegesis — in any case, not in their sermon preparation. But preachers have been trained in exegetics

---

45. Manfred Josuttis, *Die Einführung in das Leben. Pastoraltheologie zwischen Phänomenologie und Spiritualität* (Gütersloh: Kaiser Verlag, 1996), p. 60.
46. Martin Nicol, *Einander ins Bild Setzen. Dramaturgische Homiletik* (Göttingen: Vandenhoeck & Ruprecht, 2002), p. 78.
47. H. G. L. Peels, "Helder en onbevangen. Een recent pleidooi voor een ambachtelijke exegese van het Oude Testament," *Theologia Reformata* 46 (2003): 46, 47.

Preaching

and use exegetical methods as they prepare their sermons.[48] This causes a considerable tension that raises many questions. I want to single out two of them: (1) How do I, as a minister, deal with a "literary product" in connection with the "biblical story" that I refer to in my sermon? and (2) How do I acquire the exegetical material that will allow me to construct my sermon? The first question is more on the macro-level and may be regarded as a background matter. Nonetheless, this question will affect the way in which the preaching takes place. The second question is more directly related to the work of exegesis and is more on the level of "juggling the text"; here, dictionaries and commentaries may be helpful.

Let me begin by sketching the background of the first question. The exegete is confronted not only with the text as we have it today, but also with the long period in which the text acquired its present form and was transmitted. Although in our worship service we can proceed from the fact that the canon has been established, we realize that the Bible is a book that originated in a long process of tradition and selection. "Secular" Bible scholarship has made an important contribution in this area. However, in the study of the Old Testament a considerable gap has grown between the "biblical Israel" and the "old Israel" as it has been reconstructed by the scholars. When ministers preach about Old Testaments texts, the biblical stories will play a role in their sermons. It is not so strange that biblical historiography has been colored by having been written from a particular religious perspective. The Bible does not provide a secular or neutral reporting of historical facts. When history is reported, there is a prophetic ring to it. The texts contain theological opinions.

The end of the Northern Kingdom serves as a fitting example. E. Noort explains, "The black and even darker than black colors that are used to picture the end of the Northern kingdom are well-known. In the eyes of the writers, Ba'al worship, idolatry, images of bulls, sacred poles, and child sacrifice were the reason for the fall in 722/721 B.C.: 'Therefore the LORD was very angry with Israel, and removed them out of his sight; none was left but the tribe of Judah only' (2 Kings 17:18)."[49] Critical biblical scholarship poses the question of whether this is an *ideological* perspective. The Northern Kingdom was taken into exile, and only Judah remained. People from other nations were transported to the towns of Samaria (2 Kings 17:24). Does the

---

48. Eep Talstra, *Oude en nieuwe lezers. Een inleiding in de methoden van uitleg van het Oude Testament* (Kampen: Kok, 2002).

49. E. Noort, "Reconstructie van de geschiedenis van Israël," *Nederlands Theologisch Tijdschrift* 58 (2004): 314.

text indeed tell us something about events that actually took place, or is it rather a reconstruction by the author, who wanted to paint a negative picture of the kings of the Northern Kingdom? In other words: Was it a construct aimed at giving Judah and Jerusalem, including their religious tradition, a preferential status?

According to Noort, the final redaction of these texts is a literary product of a rather late date. And, at the same time, the archeological and religious-historical research provides another picture of Israel and Ahab. "Gradually a different picture of the Omri Dynasty emerges in the more recent studies of biblical scholars. They cease to be the bad guys, *pur sang.*"[50] Recent studies seem to indicate that the rulers of the Northern Kingdom were competent leaders and remained, from a religious viewpoint, more or less within the confines of a Yahwistic framework. But these northern traditions received their final form as literary texts in the South (Jerusalem). This helps to create the implication that Jerusalem is the true heart of the religious tradition and puts the Northern Kingdom in a negative light. In recent research, Noort says, ecological and socio-geographical elements also play a role. It appears that Northern Israel was a more open culture, while Judah was a more inwardly oriented society. "If we add the geographic, demographic, and cultural pictures to the new respect for the Omrides, they do not only appear as strong kings, but their country also appears as an open, cultivated, multiracial, and prosperous state. The South remains more like a mini-state that legitimizes itself through its religion but has no political importance, and, while in search of an identity, is strongly inwardly oriented."[51]

Thus the implication is created that the negative view of Ahab is a construct of fanatical believers who lived at the time of the later Judean king Josiah. Some scholars are indeed inclined to view the Old Testament writings as ideological literature from the Hellenistic period.[52] The problem with preparing a sermon based on these texts is that the minister finds it difficult to place himself in opposition to the biblical text as a canonical text. However, he can decide not to preach about these texts. That also applies to the retelling of the biblical story in the sermon. If the text as a literary product is indeed written from a *theological* (a term that is in this connection more fitting than "ideological") perspective, that is an element which must be

---

50. Noort, "Reconstructie van de geschiedenis van Israël," p. 317.
51. Noort, "Reconstructie van de geschiedenis van Israël," p. 319.
52. K. van de Toorn, *Scribal Culture and the Making of the Hebrew Bible* (Cambridge: Harvard University Press, 2007), pp. 109ff.

taken into account when preparing the sermon. This perspective may be somewhat relativized, but somehow it is the basis for the message. If the minister decides to relate biblical stories — also stories that have been colored prophetically or theologically — he must be willing to take responsibility for that prophecy or that theology. In any case, he must be willing to take a position and must be willing to communicate this in the sermon.

This discussion is not meant to imply that we do away with historical-critical research, but it becomes clear that the minister uses the biblical text as a testimony of faith. As such, it is embedded in a textual tradition, and historical-critical exegesis has the important role of discovering the development of the texts and tracing the genesis of ideas. The homiletical exegesis, however, eventually must work with the theological message of the final text. This is close to Brueggemann's view that the Bible, as a canonical book, must be viewed primarily as witness. The minister is the last witness (in a series) to give voice to the text that comes to us as canonical text. "Israel's witness of the character and essence of God is accepted by the church community as a credible witness of God's true character. . . . When biblical statements are considered as trustworthy, the human witness is accepted as a revelation that unveils God's true being."[53]

Bob Becking says that periods of crisis played an important role in the development of theology: "Changes in the basic patterns of a society inflict the mechanisms of the symbol system."[54] The Exile was a crisis with an enormous impact. Becking notices the differences in Yahwism before and after the Exile. The books of Ezra and Nehemiah, for instance, breathe a form of religion that some have typified as tending towards fundamentalism. "In the book of Ezra we encounter a tight and walled-in community that regards itself as the only true continuation of the Judean community prior to the exile."[55] But when we look at Deutero-Isaiah, we encounter a tradition that does not complacently accept the Exile as a bitter pill, but that imagines an exodus in which nothing is impossible for the Creator. Deutero-Isaiah paints salvation from a broad perspective.[56] It appears that it is quite possible

---

53. Walter Brueggemann, *Theology of the Old Testament: Testimony, Dispute, Advocacy* (Minneapolis: Fortress Press, 1997), p. 121.

54. *The Crisis of Israelite Religion: Transformation of Religious Tradition in Exilic and Post-Exilic Times*, ed. Bob Becking and Marjo C. A. Korpel (Leiden: Brill, 1999), p. 4.

55. Becking, "Continuity and Community: The Belief System of the Book of Ezra," in *The Crisis of Israelite Religion*, ed. Becking and Korpel, p. 275.

56. Korpel, "Second Isaiah's Coping with the Religious Crisis: Reading Isaiah 40 and 55," in *The Crisis of Israelite Religion*, ed. Becking and Korpel, p. 104.

to construct very different theological treatments of the deep crisis of the Exile. On the one hand, we have Ezra and Nehemiah, who contribute to the formation of an orthodox and exclusive community, and, on the other hand, we have Deutero-Isaiah, which reformulates the faith with a broad view to the social and political context.

Brueggemann explains in a rather systematic way how the texts may have developed:

> In the long book of Isaiah . . . the actual words from the eighth-century prophet are judged by scholars to be relatively few; no critical scholar, moreover, believes that the book as a whole is "authored" by the eighth-century prophet. Rather, the book of Isaiah, while rooted in the person of Isaiah, has emerged only through a long, extensive, and complex traditioning process, perhaps through a continuous succession of "disciples" of Isaiah who continue to articulate the general interpretative trajectory of the person of Isaiah (see 8:1), but who in fact were themselves powerful interpreters capable of generating new articulations. To some extent the literature of the book Isaiah is simply a continued meditation upon the destiny of Jerusalem, a meditation that occurred in something like separated, random acts of responsiveness to new issues of faith in new circumstances.[57]

The minister who is preparing a sermon must take into account the way in which the texts originated. But in the sermon she must, of course, deal with the theological ideas that are found in the text. If the text provides a correction to earlier religious ideas, she must work with that view. However, that does not prevent her from letting the congregation share in the development that has taken place. This does not necessarily lead to religious relativism. Brueggemann shows that the faith community will adopt this testimony of faith and will therein recognize God's revelation. He says that the minister, like a "scribe" in biblical times, has the task of helping her audience to re-textualize — that is, to rediscover the richness of these texts.[58] The minister preparing a sermon has a responsibility that goes beyond scholarly exegesis. She takes a position with regard to the content of

---

57. Walter Brueggemann, *An Introduction to the Old Testament: The Canon and Christian Imagination* (Louisville: Westminster John Knox Press, 2003), p. 160.

58. Walter Brueggemann, "The Preacher as Scribe," in *Inscribing the Text: Sermons and Prayers of Walter Brueggemann*, ed. Anna Carter Florence (Minneapolis: Fortress Press, 2004), pp. 5-19.

the witness of faith that is expressed in the text and must, more than once, conclude that historical-critical exegesis and literary exegesis have their limitations in that regard.

The second, less controversial point that I want to highlight is the exegetical material that presents itself as ministers do the literary-historical exegesis of a text. The analysis of the various sources from which a part of Scripture is composed, the attention to different traditions, the special views of the redactor, the linguistic differences, and so on provide a wealth of data. If the minister wants to preach on the Gospel of John and consults Rudolf Bultmann's commentary, she cannot fail to be impressed by the enormous erudition it exhibits. Even though his views are one-sided, and some of his thoughts about the gnosis and the Hellenistic background are dated, the commentary is a treasury of information. Take, for instance, the address of Jesus after the miraculous feeding in John 6. Jesus told the crowd, "Do not labor for the food which perishes, but for the food which endures to eternal life, which the Son of man will give to you; for on him has God the Father set his seal" (John 6:27). Bultmann tells us that the Evangelist uses the miracle of the feeding as a symbolic image to represent the revelation of the Redeemer: Jesus is pictured as the Giver of the bread of life.[59]

The immediate result of the multiplication of the bread is that the crowd recognizes Jesus as the prophet who was to come: "When the people saw the sign which he had done, they said, 'This is indeed the prophet who is to come into the world!'" (John 6:14). We notice a similar insight, a few chapters earlier, when Jesus meets the Samaritan woman: "The woman said to him, 'Sir, I perceive that you are a prophet'" (John 4:19). In John 6 there follows a conversation about the bread that provides life. Jesus speaks in the synagogue, "as he taught at Capernaum" (John 6:59), and the text then notes the disquiet among many of his disciples: "After this many of his disciples drew back and no longer went about with him" (John 6:66). But the Twelve remain. And in response to Jesus' question "Do you also wish to go away?" Peter answers, "Lord, to whom shall we go? You have the words of eternal life" (John 6:69).

How is the conversation constructed? In the beginning (vv. 26-34), it is about manna. Will Jesus show his majesty by giving bread from heaven? Will he establish the Messianic kingdom in a miraculous way? The "true bread" is linked to the idea of the new time that is to begin. From verse 35 onward, it

---

59. Rudolf Bultmann, *Das Evangelium des Johannes* (Göttingen: Vandenhoeck & Ruprecht, 1968), pp. 161-79.

is clear that Jesus himself is the living bread. He has descended from heaven and gives life to the world. This, however, provokes protest: "Is not this Jesus, the son of Joseph, whose father and mother we know? How does he now say, 'I have come down from heaven'?" (v. 42). Jesus then replies that the One who comes from God has seen God (v. 46). From verse 51 onward, the emphasis is on Christ himself as the bread, who is also the Giver of the bread. The emphasis is now on unity with Christ: "He who eats my flesh and drinks my blood abides in me, and I in him" (v. 56).

It is fascinating to discover how the Scriptures deal with so many motifs. Bultmann points to verse 29 as a kind of connecting link between the various sources that have been used to compose this story. There Jesus says, "This is the work of God, that you believe in him whom he has sent." The crux is not the miracle in itself, but to believe in the *Offenbarer* (the One who reveals). Through faith we may share in Christ himself, Bultmann tells us.[60] It is clear, however, that in the final part of the dispute between Jesus and the Jews, the emphasis is on the eating of his flesh and the drinking of his blood (vv. 47-63). C. H. Dodd, another classical author in the domain of John's Gospel, pays special attention to this aspect. He says, "The instructed Christian reader cannot miss the reference to the sacrament of the Eucharist."[61] That thought is further enforced by the time indication in verse 4: "Now the Passover, the feast of the Jews, was at hand." Does this point to the Eucharistic practice in the church, and does it emphasize the elements of the body and blood of Christ? Or is the accent foremost on "He who believes has eternal life" (v. 47), and should we interpret the references to flesh and blood rather as anti-gnostic remarks that serve to emphasize the earthly character of Jesus?

The "Offenbarer" says — in response to the question about the food that gives eternal life, and to the answers that are usually given to such questions — "I am the bread of life." If we want to have something from him, Bultmann says, we must realize that we must have *him*. If we ask for the gift of life, we must know that he *himself* is it. If we want to receive life from him, we must believe in him — or must, as the metaphor tells us, "come to him." There is only one way in which the world may receive life; the bread from God is the "Offenbarer" himself, who comes from heaven and gives life to the world.[62]

---

60. Bultmann, *Das Evangelium des Johannes*, pp. 161-79.
61. C. H. Dodd, *The Interpretation of the Fourth Gospel* (Cambridge: Cambridge University Press, 1978), p. 338.
62. Bultmann, *Das Evangelium des Johannes*, pp. 161-79.

THE HOMILETICAL RECONSTRUCTION

On the basis of her work with the text alone, as described in the two preceding sections, the minister cannot produce a sermon. How does she make choices, and how does she determine the focus? Theissen argues that the search for the *una sanctio interpretation* is something of the past. For a considerable time it was thought that the main idea in a biblical text could be ascertained through diligent exegesis. After careful exegesis the *skopus* could be formulated. H. Jonker says, "After all these examinations the *skopus* is to be formulated, the rose to which the sermon may shoot its arrows. What is the main thought in this text? What does the Word want to say to us in the text? The *skopus* must be summarized in a few sentences."[63] Martin Nicol disagrees: "The dictatorial attitude of an exegesis that provides the homilete with a normative interpretation of the text (skopus) belongs to the past. Exegesis and homiletics meet together in the insight that the potentiality of meaning will only appear in complex processes of communication."[64] Albrecht Grözinger acknowledges that "it was part of the underlying pattern of a course in homiletics to learn how to formulate the skopus of the text, and to design a sermon, through a series of meditative steps, on the basis of the skopus."[65] However, according to Grözinger, many texts in the Bible do not lend themselves to a *skopus* approach, because they are "open" texts. When we read a poem, for instance, we encounter all kinds of images that may evoke different associations and feelings. Sentence constructions often do not have one clear meaning, and invite us to look in different directions. "In that sense," says Grözinger, "a poem is an 'open text.' We realize that quite intuitively, and therefore we treat a poem differently from the way we treat a repair manual."[66] And biblical texts are like poems, according to Gerd Theissen: "Biblical texts are open texts. Instead of complaining that exegetes do not deliver a clear and unambiguous exegesis, they should be happy about this: the greater the number of potential meanings, the more valuable a religious text is. The sermon is dependent on the richness of meaning in the Bible text."[67]

Even though as a preacher I am not looking for *the* explanation of this text, I must find a specific angle so that I can give the sermon a clear focus.

63. H. Jonker, *En tóch preken* (Nijkerk: Callenbach, 1973), p. 142.
64. Nicol, *Einander ins Bild Setzen*, p. 60.
65. Grözinger, *Homiletik*, p. 140.
66. Grözinger, *Homiletik*, p. 142.
67. Quoted in Grözinger, *Homiletik*, p. 143.

This means that I must stand at a certain distance from the exegetical material in order to have an overview and to make choices. In the homiletical literature we read about "bridging the *gap*." How do I bridge the gap between the exegesis and the script for the sermon? It is important not to lose sight of the first phase of our dealing with the Scriptures: the probable response of the hearers. Others point to the meditative involvement with the text.[68] Tom Long has provided a workable model with a statement on focus and function: What do I, on the basis of this text, want to *say*, and what do I want to *achieve*?[69] David Buttrick goes in search of "analogies *of experience*."[70] All of these are techniques to take one of the most difficult steps in the preparation of the sermon. Crucial, however, is the fact that the text can be further scrutinized for *theological* motifs and convictions of faith. What do we see from the perspective of faith? What ideas about God's salvation do we detect? What tensions or contradictions are present in the text? Does the text perhaps present an aspect of faith that runs counter to present-day convictions? Where does the text remain odd and incomprehensible?

For instance, why does Jesus, according to John 6, speak so directly and forcefully about the eating of his flesh and the drinking of his blood? Dodd argues that John uses his dramatic account of the conversation with the intent of creating a crisis. The words of Christ are "Spirit and life," but some do not believe: "This is a hard saying; who can listen to it?" (6:60). There is something offensive about it. Why? Dodd explains: "The multitude is prepared to find in him a second Moses, who will restore the gift of manna. This is set aside. Christ gives something better than manna; he gives bread of life: more than that, he *is* Bread of life. . . . Union with him is eternal life."[71]

Hans-Joachim Iwand places the emphasis on the Word *that became flesh*. The expression "flesh and blood" underscores the human nature of Christ, his earthly form and his suffering. "The Christological doctrine must be the motif for the exegesis of this text," Iwand says. "And the text asks us, asks the preacher, asks the congregation to what extent this doctrine still impacts on their daily life and the faith they confess. The Word that became flesh, the second Person of the Trinity, who is here offered and recommended as the food that gives life."[72]

---

68. Bohren, *Predigtlehre*, pp. 347-85.
69. Long, *The Witness of Preaching*, pp. 78-91.
70. Buttrick, *Homiletic*, pp. 370-72.
71. Dodd, *The Interpretation of the Fourth Gospel*, p. 344.
72. Hans-Joachim Iwand, *Predigt-Meditationen I* (Göttingen: Vandenhoeck & Ruprecht, 1977), p. 64.

Joseph Ratzinger (Pope Benedict) sees a direct connection with the Eucharist. In the Eucharist, he says, God gives us the true manna for which humankind has been waiting, the "bread from heaven" that gives us ultimate life. And, conversely, the Eucharist is the place where we meet God continuously. Because of the Lord's "bodily" giving of himself, we may join him in his "spiritual" way.[73]

As I think about the question of whether there is a reference here in John's Gospel to the early Christian Eucharistic practice, I am struck by the fact that there is, in addition to the expression "flesh and blood," a strong emphasis on the *pneuma:* "It is the spirit that gives life, the flesh is of no avail; the words that I have spoken to you are spirit and life" (6:63). In the conversation with Nicodemus in chapter 3, we meet a similar expression: "that which is born of the Spirit is spirit" (3:6). And in chapter 4, in the conversation with the Samaritan woman, we find a reference to praying to God "in spirit and truth" (4:23). What is the relationship between these expressions and the almost physical eating of flesh and blood? Might it be that the idea that Christ is the *true* bread (that descends from heaven) and has become real flesh and blood — that this idea is offensive to the people? Do we receive real life, the real bread, from him who came in the flesh? Does this sound *scandalous* in the ears of the disciples? Or does "flesh and blood" indeed refer to the practice of the Eucharist?

I am reminded of a sermon by Eberhard Jüngel on this portion of Scripture. He first points to the strangeness and, possibly, the offensiveness of these texts:

> This, dear people, is not gospel for those who have been satisfied. Neither for those who have been satisfied in a worldly sense, or for those who are spiritually satisfied. The bread of life — this is bread for the hungry, for people who have a hunger for life. These sentences have not been written for those who are satisfied with life, who have been satisfied from their youth onward, and have enough of everything.[74]

Jüngel, however, adds, "Or perhaps it might happen that the person who has been overly satisfied may have a *new desire* for this food." Apparently, a

---

73. Joseph Ratzinger (Pope Benedict XVI), *Jesus of Nazareth: From the Baptism in the Jordan to the Transfiguration* (New York: Doubleday, 2007), pp. 262-71.

74. Eberhard Jüngel, ". . . ein Bißchen Meschugge . . . ," in *Predigten und Biblische Besinnungen* (Stuttgart: Radius Verlag, 2001), pp. 119-26.

totally different kind of bread is spoken of when Jesus says about himself, "I am the bread of life." This bread seems to end all hunger. But it is a different kind of hunger — a hunger that cannot be satisfied in any other way, for it is a hunger for life itself: "The bread of life causes hunger for life. And who of us does not know about this strange kind of hunger?" This hunger has many different forms, Jüngel says, and no one should feel any shame about this. "On the contrary, for without this hunger for life, we would have to deliver ourselves to death. Therefore, those who hunger for life are blessed. They will be satisfied. The usual kind of hunger always longs for the end of this deficiency: 'Ist das Brot im Bauch, hört der Hunger auf.' ('With bread in the belly, the hunger has gone.')"[75] The hunger for life is not interested, however, in what is *lacking*; it wants *more* of what is already available. Hunger for life wants a reinforcement of life; it wants more and still more of life. And this hunger is stimulated not by the shadows of life, not by misery and woe, but by the positive elements and the beautiful aspects of this earthly existence. Jüngel makes no connection with the Lord's Supper at all. In his sermon the emphasis is on faith.

I begin my own sermon in a different way and choose the link with the celebration of the Lord's Supper:

> In this part of Scripture the people just had an extraordinary experience. A large crowd is following Jesus of Nazareth. They are fascinated by this unique person. Could He be the long-awaited Messiah? They have heard that He performs miracles. He heals the sick. He is concerned about the poor and the miserable. He puts people back on the path of life. Who does not long for this? Who does not want to live an exuberant life, without the restraints of sickness or sorrow or disappointment? It is quite understandable that many people are constantly in search of healing, peace, and salvation....
>
> Jesus has provided bread for a great multitude. Could it be that they are only curious to see this miracle worker? Yes, it could be. But it might also be that they long for the joy of life, for fulfillment.... Maybe they are looking for food that does not perish but gives eternal life?
>
> He has given bread to the people. Could that be the bread from heaven? Do the people who follow Him not know the stories of Israel on their journey through the wilderness? That was an immensely difficult journey; the people suffered, as they had no food or other necessities.

---

75. Jüngel, ". . . ein Bißchen Meschugge . . . ," pp. 119-26.

Had they never heard about Moses? Did, in his days, the manna not rain from heaven? Bread from heaven...

Here food is spoken of in rather raw terms. In terms of flesh and blood. In fact, very concrete and earthly words. He does not say: Of course, this has to do with spiritual food. "... unless you eat the flesh of the Son of man and drink His blood, you have no life in you." No wonder, therefore, that the Pharisees say: "How can this man gives us His flesh to eat?" This is impossible, unless... unless we think of the celebration of Communion. "For my flesh is food indeed, and my blood is drink indeed!"...

If you love life and are fascinated by being alive, and have a great desire to live intensely: Then come, and taste the bread that has descended from heaven: Jesus Christ. It will give you a taste for more. Your view will become widened, and you will be able to see beyond this earthly life. Eternal life comes into view. Should you have been struck in the course of your life by misery and sorrow — and this is true for many — then come, and taste the bread that has come from heaven: He comforts.... He heals the wounds that have been inflicted. He strengthens the knees that have become weak and gives force to the hands that have lost their grip. He Himself went through the depths; He traversed death and suffering. The bread was broken; the wine was poured out: He died and was buried. However, it was not a dead-end street, but it led, on Easter morning, to the message "Come and see! He lives!"

Should you be laden with worry and guilt, should you at times think that there is no pardon and redemption... Come, and taste the bread that has descended from heaven. He gives you life, true life. For He is here....[76]

The Rhetorical Form of the Sermon

In the sermon as performance, the results of the homiletic exegesis are put onstage. The minister chooses from what she has considered from an exegetical, a theological, and a pastoral angle and what she thinks may be useful in her sermon on Sunday morning. Before we discuss how that might take place, we need to spend some time on the different *speech modi* of the sermon. What kind of address is a sermon? It is often emphasized in Protestant homiletics that the sermon is proclamation — not a lecture about religious

---

76. F. Gerrit Immink, sermon on John 6, preached in Alblasserdam on June 27, 2010.

themes, but the proclamation of God's grace. No doubt this approach is characteristic of the Reformation. But there is another line of thought, also rooted in biblical concepts, which emphasizes that the sermon is a form of teaching aimed at encouragement and stimulation, exhortation and comfort. I will first describe both kinds of preaching, so that we have a better understanding of the different sermon genres.

Proclamation

Whether a sermon may be designated as proclamation depends on the degree to which it speaks of *salvation in Christ*. A sermon of proclamation unfolds and discloses God's redemptive activity in Jesus Christ. Two theological dimensions must especially be noted. First, it becomes clear that this salvation is assured through God's movement towards humankind, and, second, it becomes clear that this salvation is anchored in the historical revelation in Jesus Christ. Because the *Redeemer* has appeared, there can be salvation for the *world*.

Jesus saw himself as the One who brought salvation. That is very clear from his reply to the disciples of John the Baptist in Luke 7. They ask him, "Are you he who is to come, or shall we look for another?" (v. 20). At that very time Jesus was healing many people, freeing them from their illnesses and problems; he delivered many from evil spirits and returned the sight to many who had been blind. Jesus responds, "Go and tell John what you have seen and heard: the blind receive their sight, the lame walk, lepers are cleansed, and the deaf hear, the dead are raised up, the poor have good news preached to them" (v. 22).

Using Old Testament images, Jesus defines the time of redemption. He says that the hour has come and salvation is near. Since the *Redeemer* is now present, the new creation becomes visible in these signs and wonders. And Jesus adds, "And blessed is he who takes no offense at me" (Matt. 11:6). Marinus de Jonge is right when he comments that Jesus not only proclaimed the kingdom but also inaugurated it; he continues, "This placed Him in a unique relationship to God, and He was aware of it when He addressed God."[77] When teaching in the synagogue in Nazareth, Jesus quotes the

---

77. Marinus de Jonge, *Jesus, the Servant-Messiah* (New Haven: Yale University Press, 1991), p. 75.

prophet Isaiah: "The Spirit of the Lord is upon me. . . . Today this Scripture has been fulfilled in your hearing" (Luke 4:18-21).

Preaching as proclamation is based on the conviction that Jesus himself, in his person and work, realizes the kingdom. Seen in this light, it is not strange that Paul uses the expression "the preaching [*kerygma*] of Jesus Christ" (Rom. 16:25). The sermon is a proclamation of Jesus Christ. The ending of the Gospel of Mark tells us that the risen Lord himself commissioned his disciples to proclaim the gospel (the good news): "Go into all the world and preach the gospel to the whole creation" (Mark 16:15). And what happens next? "And they went forth and preached everywhere" (v. 20).

Paul frequently uses the word "proclaim" *(kerussein).* "For what we preach [proclaim] is not ourselves, but Jesus Christ as Lord . . ." (2 Cor. 4:5). The *kerygma* is a short message in which the gospel is summarized, as in 2 Corinthians 5:15, where we read, "And he died for all, that those who live might live no longer for themselves but for him who for their sake died and was raised." The word *kerygma* refers to the act of proclaiming, to the address. In the First Letter to the Corinthians, Paul tells them that he came to proclaim the secret of God, and that he does not possess any great amount of eloquence or wisdom: "For I decided to know nothing among you except Jesus Christ and him crucified. . . . My speech and my message were not in plausible words of wisdom, but in demonstration of the Spirit and of power" (1 Cor. 2:2, 4). In this same letter, dealing with the resurrection, Paul says, ". . . if Christ has not been raised, then our preaching is in vain and your faith is in vain" (1 Cor. 15:14). Likewise, in the letter to Titus, the *kerygma* is referred to as the act of proclamation (Tit. 1:3).

In Karl Barth's view, the *kerygma* is the heart of the sermon. He bases his opinion on an article by Gerhard Friedrich in *Kittel's Theological Dictionary of the New Testament.*[78] According to Friedrich, the sermon is not an informative presentation about the kingdom of God; it is the proclamation of the kingdom, the announcement of an event. Like a herald who precedes the carriage of the king and announces his arrival, so the preacher goes through the world and calls, "Be prepared, for the kingdom is at hand." This image of a herald has become the symbol for *kerygmatic* preaching. Because of this image, the impression has been created that the preacher should remain in the background (for the herald may only announce what has been given to

---

78. Gerhard Kittel, *Theologische Wörterbuch zum Neuen Testament,* vol. 3 (Stuttgart: Kohlhammer, 1950), pp. 683-717; *Theological Dictionary of the New Testament* (Grand Rapids: Wm. B. Eerdmans, 1985), art. "kerusso-kerugma."

him, and he has no input of his own), and that the hearers are simply the receivers, while the context is rather unimportant.[79]

The strength of this view of preaching is that it expresses that God himself provides salvation. He breaks into our sinful existence and brings redemption and salvation. He comes first and takes the initiative. Ronald Thiemann says, "God's priority can be construed in a variety of ways, but it cannot be eliminated altogether if the centrality of God's grace in the Christian life is to be given theological expression."[80] This theological thought is expressed in biblical concepts such as *promise, covenant, creation,* and *election*. But what remains rather vague in this view of preaching is that the *kerygma* is an effective power that also realizes what is being proclaimed. It is not only a matter of the priority of God, but also of the effective impact of the gospel. The *kerygma* produces faith, obedience, and renewal of life.

A correct understanding of the sermon as *kerygma* requires that what the *kerygma* produces — faith, hope, and love — is taken into account. That dimension of the *kerygma* has remained undervalued in dialectic theology. This is due to the distortion that the image of the herald has caused. For the texts that speak of the *kerygma* also indicate that it is an effective power. For your faith must "not rest in the wisdom of men but in the power of God" (1 Cor. 2:5). The *kerygma* leads people to have faith, and in faith they discover the power of God that is present in the *kerygma*. In that sense, Theissen is correct when he argues that *kerygma* is a word that discloses transcendence. A kergymatic sermon has an *illuminating* impact. The *kerygma* deals not just with the a priori dimension of the divine initiative, but also with that which God works *in us*. The *kerygma* gets hold of people so that in faith they discover that Christ brings peace and salvation. The fact that God comes first and is the One who takes the initiative does not diminish the importance of faith and obedience. Justice, peace, and salvation are not just human ideals that are cherished by believers, but are revealed in human lives as a "power of God." Paul says that he is not ashamed of this gospel because it is a saving power (Rom. 1:16). As Paul Althaus explains, "The righteousness is 'revealed,' that is to say: it manifests itself, it makes its impact felt. The term 'revelation' in the New Testament never refers to a doctrinal statement or the disclosure

---

79. Bultmann's views on preaching are also connected with the term "kerygma," but he places a stronger emphasis on the *kerygma* as an existential event. As a result, much more attention is placed on the hearers. See James F. Kay, *Christus Praesens* (Grand Rapids: Wm. B. Eerdmans, 1994), pp. 26-28.

80. Ronald F. Thiemann, *Revelation and Theology: The Gospel as Narrated Promise* (Notre Dame: University of Notre Dame Press, 1985), p. 61.

of a state of affairs, but is an act of will, the realization of the goal that God has in mind."[81]

The divine power is active in the proclamation — the same Spirit power that was active in the resurrection. Preaching, therefore, is a salvific event in which the *pneuma* of Christ is engaged — and not just in the speaking, but also in the hearing. It is a five-part event of calling upon, believing, hearing, proclaiming, and being sent. This leads Paul to the conclude, "So faith comes from what is heard, and what is heard comes by the preaching of Christ" (Rom. 10:17).[82]

The fact that Paul is so impressed by the immediate effect of the *pneuma* of the risen Christ is no doubt connected with his Damascus experience: "For I would have you know, brethren, that the gospel which was preached by me is not man's gospel. For I did not receive it from man, nor was I taught it, but it came through a revelation of Jesus Christ" (Gal. 1:11-12). I do not say this to suggest that the *kerygma* is directly linked to the self-revelation of Christ as an experience of existential disclosure, but rather that it underscores how the kerygmatic dimension cannot be detached from the insight and experience of faith. When does a sermon become kerygmatic? When the congregation discovers the richness of Christ. When an insight of faith occurs. When joy breaks through. When the desire for salvation is awakened. In such moments the *kerygma* is discovered — in spirit and truth. In the meantime, Paul does not deny the value of tradition and of the apostolic transmission. He writes to the church in Colossae that the gospel had been preached to them by a certain Epaphras. So, in a physical sense, there had to be a witness. But this proclamation resulted in the establishment of a new community, a church that lived from faith, hope, and love. Apparently they did not receive the word that was preached to them as just a message from man, "but as what it really is, the word of God, which is at work in you believers" (1 Thess. 2:13).

Comforting, Encouraging, Exhorting, Teaching

The building and developing of the life of faith plays an important role in the New Testament churches. Besides the sermon as *kerygma,* there

---

81. Paul Althaus, *Der Brief an die Römer. Das Neue Testament Deutsch* (Göttingen: Vandenhoeck & Ruprecht, 1949), p. 13.

82. Otto Michel says, "Paul constructs in this connection an intrinsic unity of 'obedience, hearing, and what has been heard' — all these terms are derived from the same verb." See Michel, *Der Brief an die Römer* (Göttingen: Vandenhoeck & Ruprecht, 1963), p. 262.

are other modes of speech that may be used. James Thompson points to the fact that the word *paraklesis* occurs quite often in Paul's letters. This word has the connotation of "friendly demand" and suggests exhortation, comfort, and encouragement. The God who has taken us into his care comforts and encourages us (2 Cor. 1:3-7).[83] Paul was concerned not just about the proclamation of the good news, but also about the in-dwelling of the good news in everyday life. *Paraklesis* implies that an appeal goes out to the church. The gospel calls for faith and renewal. Paul writes to the church in Rome, "I appeal to you therefore, brethren, by the mercies of God . . ." (Rom. 12:1). The same letter lists a number of tasks in which the church should be engaged:

> Having gifts that differ according to the grace given to us, let us use them: if prophecy, in proportion to our faith; if service, in our serving; he who teaches, in his teaching; he who exhorts, in his exhortation; he who contributes, in liberality; he who gives aid, with zeal; he who does acts of mercy, with cheerfulness. (Rom. 12:6-8)

In 1 Corinthians 12 we find another list with charismatic functions. God has appointed in the church first apostles, then prophets, and then teachers: "And his gifts were that some should be apostles, some prophets, some evangelists, some pastors and teachers, to equip the saints for the work of ministry" (Eph. 4:11-12). According to Henry Davis, besides the proclamation *(kerygma),* "teaching and therapy" are important forms of communication in the Christian church. When he uses the word "therapy," he has in mind all those terms that are associated with changing and improving the situation of the hearers. This refers not only to the ethical aspects of life, but also to the emotional and religious dimensions of faith. "Therapy, then, is clearly recognized as one function of discourse within the church," says Davis. "There are also forms of speech used for curative or corrective purposes within the church. Christians believe themselves forgiven, but know they are imperfect and sinful. Exhortation and admonition must both become corrective wherever there is fault or remissness."[84]

Speaking in a comforting and exhorting manner finds its source in the

---

83. James W. Thompson, *Preaching like Paul: Homiletical Wisdom for Today* (Louisville: Westminster John Knox Press, 2001), p. 55.

84. Henry Grady Davis, *Design for Preaching* (Philadelphia: Muhlenburg Press, 1958), p. 131.

Preaching

gospel of Jesus Christ: "Now may our Lord Jesus Christ himself, and God our Father, who loved us and gave us eternal comfort and good hope through grace, comfort your hearts and establish them in every good work and word" (2 Thess. 2:16-17). In the midst of all its needs and worries, the church finds a stronghold in Christ's salvation. In the comfort and encouragement that we may give each other, the comforting activity of God himself is revealed. For that reason, God is sometimes called "the God of all comfort" (2 Cor. 1:3). When in the book of Acts we are told that the church has peace, and is built up in faith, and increases in number, this is attributed to the "comfort [*paraklesis*] of the Holy Spirit" (Acts 9:31).

In addition to comforting and encouraging, teaching has an important place in the church. At the end of the book of Acts, we are told that Paul arrives in Rome after a long sea journey and gets permission to rent his own house, with a soldier as his guard. He stays in that house for two years, "preaching the kingdom of God and teaching about the Lord Jesus Christ quite openly and unhindered" (Acts 28:31). *Kerygma* and *teaching* are mentioned side by side. There is more emphasis on the biblical text with regards to teaching than with regards to proclamation. Through the Scriptures (the Old Testament), it is proven that Jesus is the Messiah. We are, for instance, told in Acts 18 that Apollos was an erudite person who was acquainted with the Scriptures. This Apollos "had been instructed in the way of the Lord," and "spoke and taught accurately the things concerning Jesus" (Acts 18:25). The accent was not primarily on the facts of salvation, but on the *Christocentric biblical evidence*.[85] This form of teaching is particularly prominent when the apostle deals with Jews and Jewish-Christian churches. In the later Pauline letters, teaching also has a more pastoral-ethical connotation, with the goal of leading the church to "maturity" in Christ (Col. 1:28).

We would be correct if we concluded that the early church not only knew the form of address in which the *kerygma* dominated, but also knew other forms of communicating the gospel of Jesus Christ. These speech modi put more stress on the impact of the message and on argumentation based on the Scriptures. While Barth and Bultmann are mostly referred to as the defenders of kerygmatic preaching, Calvin is the primary witness when it comes to the teaching sermon. Calvin used two images in connection with the sermon: the school and the preacher as ambassador. The first image evokes the idea of the sermon as *didache*, teaching. The second image is

---

85. Carl Heinrich Rengstorf, "Didaskoo," in Kittel, *Theological Dictionary of the New Testament*.

closer to the *kerygma* concept.⁸⁶ "Nothing is more important for God than the preaching of the gospel," Calvin says. "For that is the kingdom through which He wants to rule in this world. Preaching is the means by which people are led towards salvation. . . . For the only means by which people can be saved is by being taught in the teachings of the gospel *(enseignez en la doctrine de l'Evangile).*"⁸⁷ When Calvin uses the images of the school and the teacher, he thinks of both the professor in the university and the teacher in the elementary school. Nonetheless, we should not conclude that this makes the sermon into a purely educational exercise. For Calvin strongly emphasizes the revelation of God as well as the role of the Spirit in the preaching process.⁸⁸ When preaching takes places, God himself is present and at work. The teaching produces something in the life of the people. During the teaching process, the Scriptures are explained in a way that allows the church to know God's promises and his will. To his disappointment, Calvin has to admit that the comportment of the people in Geneva does not agree with the will of God: "Let us look for a moment at what people can see in our life. It is true that we have the gospel, but when one investigates our deeds and sees how we behave, will any change be noticeable? Not at all. For we do not stay on track." And then Calvin becomes very sharp in his comments: "The slander, the faithlessness, and the denial of God are now worse than ever. We have rules that say that we should not play with money. But things go from worse to worse. When these godless villains have lost all their money in one day, their wives and children must go hungry, because of the bad ways in which these brutes have handled their means."⁸⁹

In today's climate, which is heavily influenced by the entertainment culture and the media, the teaching form of preaching is not easily accepted. There is tension between emphasis on the exposition of the Scriptures and the hearers' desire for something with immediate relevance for daily life. But, Ronald Allen says, this does not change the fact that teaching sermons actually do justice to modern hearers by appealing to their independence and responsibility.⁹⁰ Hearers are treated as intentional persons who judge and act independently and who make their own decisions. "In a time of spiritual

---

86. T. H. L. Parker, *Calvin's Preaching* (Louisville: Westminster John Knox Press, 1992), p. 25.

87. W. H. Th. Moehn, *God roept ons tot zijn dienst* (Kampen: Kok, 1996), p. 256.

88. Parker, *Calvin's Preaching*, p. 29.

89. Moehn, *God roept ons tot zijn dienst*, p. 275.

90. F. Gerrit Immink, "Homiletics: The Current Debate," *International Journal of Practical Theology* 8, no. 1 (2004): 109.

Preaching

quest, a sermon with qualities of teaching and learning appeals to many people, as it brings together quest and Christian tradition."[91] A teaching sermon, says Allen, helps hearers to conquer their religious and theological illiteracy. Those who desire deeper insight into the mystery of faith also feel the need for explanation and reflection. Moreover, we should not underestimate the fact that, whatever is said, each sermon has a *formative* function. Whether or not the minister realizes it, every sermon has a teaching dimension. All sermons somehow make the connection between God and the world. Therefore, it would be a good thing if the minister carefully helped church members to interpret that relationship between God and the world in such a way as to make it consistent with the basic theological teachings of the church.[92] The teaching element in a sermon does not primarily aim at the transmission of knowledge. The goal is "a deeper experience of discipleship through the integration of information, feeling, and behavior." According to Allen, "Teaching sermons help the congregation to learn the content of Christian tradition, to reflect critically upon that content, and to think creatively about how to relate the tradition, the congregation's beliefs, in the contemporary setting."[93]

The Sermon as Address

The actual sermon is shaped like a speech. When a minister enters the pulpit, his preparatory work on the sermon has given it an order and a format that allow him to speak freely to the congregation. Of course, how the sermon came about is not unimportant, but in the actual preaching, the presentation is most important.[94] That is what the congregation will see and hear. Does the minister speak from a manuscript? Usually that is the case. A manuscript can, of course, be brief: a single sheet of paper containing the main points of the sermon and an "outline" that sketches its direction, with perhaps some verbatim statements. Most ministers, however, use a much more complete manuscript, ranging from elaborations on the main ideas, with some key words for digressions and illustrations, to a sermon that is completely written out. But even when the minister has a complete manuscript, he must use everyday language, because the sermon is a speech.

---

91. Ronald J. Allen, *The Teaching Sermon* (Nashville: Abingdon Press, 1995), p. 21.
92. Wilson, *The New Interpreter's Handbook of Preaching*, p. 421.
93. Ronald J. Allen, "Teaching," in Wilson, *The New Interpreter's Handbook*, p. 422.
94. For a good survey of different models of "Gestaltung" in the German tradition, see Grözinger, *Homiletik*, pp. 177-260.

The creation of such a speech takes a significant amount of work. Some ministers write the sermon (or the outline) in one sitting (sometimes even early on Saturday evening or late into Saturday night); others are less sure of themselves and write the sermon early in the week, then keep making changes in the format during the week. After analyzing the church's local culture (and its sociocultural context), and after doing the homiletical exegesis, the minister drafts the sermon — which is a new creative step. It demands much thought, meditation, creativity, and courage — yes, courage too, for choices must be made that involve the minister's personal judgment. To be aware of this, and to make choices in good conscience, is part of the minister's task in preparing the sermon. It is a condition for the minister's speaking freely from the pulpit.

Lucy Hogan points out that shaping and structuring the sermon are not just a matter of bringing order to the material. No, that involves "the judicious selection and use of the available means to the desired end."[95] During her preparatory work, the preacher has assembled a lot of material through her homiletical research of the Scriptures. Now she will have to make choices, and she will have to make them carefully. What is relevant to the sermon? At the same time, the minister is acquainted with the culture of the congregation. She knows what the people think about social and religious matters. This multitude of impressions needs a focus. What is relevant at this moment to the sermon? So, in both areas — the homiletical findings from the Scriptures and the observance of local church culture — the minister has to consider her options. These considerations influence each other. But selection is not the only concern. Preaching is *presenting* — that is, making present. There is something for the audience to hear. The material that has been collected in the preparation is now put in an orderly fashion and is presented. In her presentation of collected and selected material, the minister has a story to tell. One of the meanings of the term "material" is "data for a work of the mind." This applies, for instance, to someone who collects biographical or research material. The preacher, therefore, must consider how hearers will react to the material that she is going to present. Already in the preparatory stage, her anticipation of the encounter with the audience plays a role. She must decide what she will and will not say. Presenting is a relational event. Making a presentation is indeed entering into a relationship. The preacher shows something of herself *(self-disclosure)* and has certain

---

95. Lucy Hogan, "Creation of Form," in *Teaching Preaching as a Christian Practice*, ed. Thomas G. Long and Leonora Tubbs Tisdale (Minneapolis: Fortress Press, 1997), p. 141.

expectations or certain presuppositions with regard to her audience. We may therefore see the sermon (as speech) as a form of social interaction.[96] In the sermon the minister is in conversation with the congregation, and this conversation takes place, in part, in her study.

In the sermon an imaginary world is developed. The minister speaks and the worshippers listen. In this interaction, in which all aspects of the liturgy play a role, a world of ideas, experiences, emotions, remembrances, meditations, considerations, and so on comes into being. It is in this convergence of language and mental activity that the imaginary world is created. This "world" is more or less projected: the listening audience shares in the minister's imagination, "sees" all kinds of things, and acquires a *mental* image of them. During the service, the worshippers do not remain absorbed in the here and now. Through the Bible texts they travel back in history, or are sometimes (for instance, through eschatological texts) stimulated to move towards the future, while other cultures and people become part of the background. In the prayers they are directed to the problems and the joys of other people, and are pointed towards God. In their singing they become aware of a poetic and metaphorical way of speaking. All these elements are part of "the world of the sermon." The selection and the presentation of the material are crucial factors in the design of this world that is being created. The appearance of this world depends, to a large degree, on the choices of the minister as she drafts her sermon. These choices bring primary convictions about faith and life to light. These convictions may sometimes have a greater influence on the sermon than the minister's exegetical labor.

We should not underestimate the third and final step in the preparatory process: the construction and style of the sermon as *performance*. Traditionally, ministers have spent a great deal of time on these elements. Today, however, ministers tend to use more audiovisual media than before, and a well-thought-out structure, though increasingly important, is frequently lacking. The use of a projector adds a complicating factor to the presentation. Often, Hogan states, worshippers do not see a coherent message, but rather a chaos of fragmentary impressions or tidbits of information.[97] Usually, this does not improve the quality of the sermon.

---

96. Arthur Van Seters, *Preaching as a Social Act: Theology and Practice* (Nashville: Abingdon Press, 1988); Peter Hartly, *Interpersonal Communication* (London/New York: Routledge, 1999).

97. Hogan, "Creation of Form," in *Teaching Preaching as a Christian Practice*, ed. Long and Tisdale, p. 147.

Sermon Models

In this section I will describe the most important models that have been quite influential in American homiletics in the last half-century. We discover similar influences in Europe, but they have not resulted in the same practice-oriented, pragmatic models that we see in the United States. At times the discussion about the construction of the sermon seems like stating the obvious. And when students are asked to participate in preaching exercises, they often secretly think, *Well, this is something we already know.* But when instructors listen to and analyze their sermons, it becomes clear that the actual practice is quite difficult.

Since the American literature is to a large degree directed towards the training of students and the skill of sermon preparation, the actual practice is dominant in this literature. In the so-called New Homiletic, the emphasis is on preaching as an *event*, on the concrete sermon. It is not a static speech that follows a schedule, but a *movement in time*. This way of thinking and talking about the sermon began in the late 1950s, when H. Grady Davis published his *Design for Preaching*. According to Davis,

> The proper design of a sermon is a movement in time. It begins at a given moment, it ends at a given moment, and it moves through the intervening moments one after another.... A sermon is like music, not music in the score but in the *live performance*, where bar is heard after bar, theme after theme, and never all at once. A sermon is like a play, not the printed book but the action on a stage, which moves from a first act through a second to a third, and the drama is never seen all at once.[98]

This highlights the dynamic and interactive character of the sermon. The topic of the sermon is still important to Davis. But, he says, we cannot have thoughts without giving them a form. Thoughts receive their concrete expression in language, and it is only when we are able to clearly express ourselves that others understand what we intend to say. His book deals with this aspect of taking the sermon material and putting into it into the right words and giving it the right shape: "As there must be a plot, with character and incidents, to embody the idea of a story, so there must be a plan, a movement from thought to thought toward a goal, to give body and shape to the sermon idea."[99] Continuity is

---

98. Davis, *Design for Preaching*, p. 163.
99. Davis, *Design for Preaching*, p. 42.

key, Davis says succinctly: "To put the whole matter of continuity in one short sentence, there must be something to begin with and something to get at the end."[100] But creating a good beginning and a timely end is far from simple. Tom Long suggests that the beginning of a sermon should contain a promise without disclosing the secret.[101] This ensures that people pay attention at the start — but there must be a focus for that attention. It is more difficult to keep the attention of listeners as the sermon proceeds.

Building on the ideas of Davis, Eugene Lowry published a book in 1980 titled *The Homiletical Plot: The Sermon as Narrative Art Form*. In it he suggests a new approach that has become very influential: the narrative preaching style. Davis's idea of the "plot," which had not yet become the leading principle, now holds center stage. The sermon is a "story" with a "plot": "Plot! This is the key term for a reshaped image of the sermon. Preaching is storytelling. A sermon is a narrative art form. . . . And so I shall prefer to speak of the continuity or the movement of a sermon, rather than of its outline."[102] Lowry is opposed to the thematic sermon that follows an outline with a number of points. The old idea, Lowry says, is that we may at a certain moment have the building blocks, but if we want to build a wall, we will need to stack them properly, and we will need cement. He thinks that this creates the wrong picture. Substance matters, but it needs to have flow and good transitions. The sermon is not a presentation about a certain theme, but an event: "A sermon is not a logical assemblage; a sermon is an event-in-time which follows the logic born of the communication interaction between preacher and congregation. To organize on the basis of the logic of ideational ingredients is to miss altogether the dynamics of the communicational reality."[103]

Lowry argues that tension and dénouement, as in a thriller or a drama series on television, are the elements that need to be used in the development of a sermon. As he says very concisely, the sermon needs to go "from *itch to scratch.*" In Lowry's work, the form of the sermon is all-important: the preacher starts with sketching a person or a situation, and makes sure that there is a certain ambiguity, discrepancy, or difficulty. "The movement from problem to solution of the discrepancy," he points out, "shapes the form of the narrative." As the sermon proceeds, the complicating factors are elaborated upon and treated in depth. When the climax is reached, there

---

100. Davis, *Design for Preaching*, p. 172.

101. Long, *The Witness of Preaching*, pp. 138-47.

102. Eugene Lowry, *The Homiletical Plot: The Sermon as Narrative Art Form*, expanded ed. (Louisville: John Knox Press, 2001), pp. 12, 14.

103. Lowry, *The Homiletical Plot*, p. 8.

is a sudden turn of events (as, for instance, in the encounter between the prophet Nathan and David). At that point the tension is discharged, and worshippers enter a new situation. But also towards the end some things continue to "itch." Thus Lowry is concerned about the order in which the sermon progresses. There must be a continuous movement from problem to solution. But in order to arrive at this solution, something must be disturbed or in disarray. The homiletical plot must touch worshippers with the depths of the terrible discrepancies in their world — socially and personally. This gives the gospel a high problem-solving quality.[104]

Lowry's model has exerted a considerable influence, and still does. It is not primarily about narrative skills when a minister preaches biblical stories, but about the narrative structure of the sermon as such. In this approach, anecdotes and everyday events easily find their way into the sermon. Experiences from contemporary life are used as analogies of biblical stories. There is much room for free association, and the sermon becomes an open work of art, without confessional statements. Particularly in the American context, where the sermon is also supposed to have a considerable entertainment value, the audience expects an anecdote, or a story as illustration, or even a good joke. There are plenty of books with examples, sermon illustrations, one-liners, metaphors, and so on. Almost all handbooks on homiletics deal extensively with the use of examples, illustrations, and stories. It requires skill to use these not only as attention-grabbers but also as truly functional elements in the sermon. And this is very important, since the right choice of examples and anecdotes may be decisive for the "imaginary world" that the sermon wants to evoke.

In 1987 David Buttrick published a book titled *Homiletic: Moves and Structures* in which he gives ample attention to the structure and ordering of the sermon. He is at ease with the idea that has become quite common in the New Homiletic — namely, that the sermon is a movement, an event. Here I will focus on Buttrick's approach to the composition of the sermon. He is opposed to preaching with a list of points to be covered (as if these points are linked to fixed truths "out there"), and he describes the sermon as a "movement of language." Buttrick believes that the sermon consists of a series of rhetorical units or "moves." As Buttrick explains, "All human conversation, unless it is nothing more than a brief exchange of small talk, has structured sequence; it will happen in a series of moves. Moves are tied together by various 'natural' logics. Sermons are similarly constructed: They

---

104. Lowry, *The Homiletical Plot*, p. 24.

Preaching

will involve a series of moves — language modules — strung together in some sort of logical movement." Each module is only a few minutes long, and should have only one illustration or example, which enables the minister to keep worshippers' attention. In this unit of language the minister names an aspect of the world in which we live, so that worshippers may understand themselves in it. The sermon is thus a series of such language modules that are connected through a particular structure that creates an ongoing unity.[105]

Buttrick emphasizes that these connections are extremely important. Without such a structure, the sermon is left with loose parts that do not connect. It should be clear that one element must be rounded off before the next one begins — otherwise, everything flows together. Therefore, each rhetorical unit has a beginning and an end, and moves from one to the next. The composition of the sermon depends largely on the right sequence. The minister asks herself, *What will I say? And what structure do I need in order to produce what I am aiming for in the consciousness of my hearers?*[106]

Building a Sermon

After this survey of different models, we return to the essential question: How does a minister construct her sermon? We have seen that she needs to make selections from the material that is on the table (both the elements from Scripture and the elements of the local congregational culture), and that she will present these in a particular way in her sermon. When she preaches, she develops an "imaginary world." The survey of recent homiletics has shown that the preaching act, as interpersonal communication, is a dynamic event in which rhetorical composition and "timing" are essential. The sermon as a whole does not have to be a "story," but it does need to have narrative elements that picture the concrete world in which we live. In bringing order to the material, the minister must keep what Buttrick calls the language modules of limited length and structure them in such a way that they are attention-getting. Some listeners may be able to identify more easily with one particular module, and other listeners with another. Accordingly, variation and alternation are extremely important. From the perspective of the hearers, it is advisable to appeal to cognitive as well more emotive capacities.

---

105. Buttrick, *Homiletic*, pp. 23-24.
106. Buttrick, *Homiletic*, p. 24.

A sermon should have an uninterrupted line that provides the links between the various attention-getting moments. The beginning and the ending are the most important points when drawing this line. In the introduction, the attention of worshippers is drawn and directed; a hint is given and expectations are evoked. According to Buttrick, "introductions give focus to consciousness and provide some sort of hermeneutical orientation." The conclusion must provide a real ending, and the minister should know when to stop. Buttrick gives two important pointers: "Conclusions are directed by intention" and "Conclusions are actually meant to provide a conclusion." The intentional dimension implies that the preacher has certain objectives with the "plotting" of the attention-getting moments, and that this must also have an impact on the ending of the sermon. If the minister intends the congregation to be motivated to action, the end of the sermon should be in harmony with this. If the minister aims for wonderment or thankfulness, that should also be clear from the final short "module" of the sermon.[107] In this process of structuring, Tom Long's guiding principle is important. The minister needs to ask herself, *What do I want to say? What do I want to achieve?*[108] The order of the different foci of attention between the introduction and the conclusion are connected by the line of thought and the narrative line that is developed. It is possible to create a moment of textual attention, or a moment of reflection and meditation, or a moment of contemplation and analysis, or a moment in which amazement and adoration are central. If the links and the transitions between those moments are clearly indicated, that allows worshippers to take a short moment to relax, or to catch on again.

How are these "moments of attention" of the sermon given substance? According to Rudolf Bohren, telling a story through preaching belongs to the basic structure of the sermon.[109] The fact that the telling of a story is so central is inherent to the Christian faith. When speaking about the God of Israel and of the Father of Jesus Christ, one cannot avoid saying something about the Exodus and the Exile. Anyone who wants to explain atonement and redemption will need to tell the passion story. When in the New Testament the apostles speak to the people, they use brief stories to tell of the great deeds of God in history. The identity of Jesus is revealed in the history of his life and death. Preaching about the letters of Paul is impossible without touching on the concrete situations and the cultural context of the churches to which these are addressed.

---

107. Buttrick, *Homiletic*, p. 83.
108. Long, *The Witness of Preaching*, p. 86.
109. Bohren, *Predigtlehre*, p. 171.

A sermon has an ongoing narrative thread. But there are different attention-getting moments that must be distinguished. It is possible to limit the narrative aspects to one or two attention-getting moments. In this way, one main line of thought may be the major thread, with a few short stories in between. And since there is a fundamental relationship between the history of God and that of humanity, some stories and incidents may contain traces of God in the here and now. These may be stories that highlight contrasts or show analogies.

The sermon must clearly show that the Scriptures have been read. This gives occasion for the exposition of the text. Ask worshippers what the sermon was about, and many will respond in terms of the Scripture reading; the sermon has a certain "Scriptural *about*ness."[110]

Textual attention is essential for a Protestant sermon. But this does not mean that the entire sermon should be devoted to scriptural exposition. Textual exposition may focus on the sentence constructions and the word combinations in a portion of Scripture that was read. Historical and contextual issues may also be explored. However, these exegetical "moments of attention" must be embedded in the ongoing structural thread of the sermon and must be relevant to the total composition of the sermon. The exegesis that has been done during the sermon preparation is not to be poured out over the congregation. Still, these "moments of attention" that are devoted to textual matters can be very valuable and may help worshippers to understand the words of Scripture in a new way. Bohren points out that the Scriptures may be quoted in a number of ways.[111] A text may be quoted verbatim and then repeated at various moments during the sermon. That reinforces the effect. But a paraphrase has its own function. In that case, the minister puts the text in her own words and uses her own rhetorical style. She must do this very carefully, for her words will usually be a combination of exposition and interpretation. She must ask herself, *What picture is being painted? What suggestion is being evoked?* But a sermon is more than just "story" and "Scripture." The scriptural texts are *about* something: events, processes, persons, circumstances, and so on. In the sermon as speech, the minister alludes to noetic contents and refers to concrete situations and to divine persons: God the Creator, or Jesus Christ, or the Holy Spirit. Brevard Childs comments aptly that it is of fundamental importance for Christian theology to presuppose an extra-biblical reality — namely, the risen Christ, who is at

---

110. Pleizier, *Religious Involvement in Hearing Sermons*, p. 224.
111. Bohren, *Predigtlehre*, pp. 191-98.

the heart of the New Testament witness.[112] It is precisely this noetic content that demands a certain kind of teaching. In the sermon the minister and the congregation are in conversation about themes they have encountered in the reading of the Scriptures. This conversation may concern questions and contradictions that arise, sudden insights and links with other portions of Scripture and textual traditions, and a longing for deeper understanding. It would be strange if a sermon never reflected on the miracles of Jesus. How are we to interpret those miracles? Is the point that Jesus is the great "miracle worker," or are miracles meant to be understood as signs? If so, what does that mean? The minister will use explanations in the form of teaching that are colored by our confessional language. What is sought is not scholastic exercises, but a "faith seeking understanding." The approach is not purely cognitive, but is characterized by wonderment and adoration.

In the last quarter of the twentieth century, homiletics showed a significant reticence with regard to including a great deal of theological content in the sermon. In America the accent was on communication and *performance*, while on the European continent there grew a tendency towards a hermeneutical-narrative emphasis, in an open-aesthetic style. In both cases this was linked with severe mistrust of doctrinal content and confessional choices; instead, religious experience was highlighted. How did homileticians deal with theological content? Without much critical thought they associated it with "objective truth," using this concept in a rather negative way. And Lucy Rose points out a significant problem with this approach: "No 'truth' is objective, absolute, ontological, or archetypical."[113] A "round-table pulpit" is based on the presupposition that there is no absolute truth or gospel, and that all voices around the table ought to be heard. The preacher becomes a discussion leader who gives a voice to the various opinions, with special attention given to those who are unable to raise their own voices. In "conversational preaching," Rose maintains, the content is a proposal that is put to the community, which may be supplemented, corrected, and countered with other proposals. Openness, the group's diversity, and democratic relationships are emphasized to the extent that there is hardly any room for the preacher to "take a position" and to state her conclusion.

I believe that two things are getting mixed up here, and for clarity's sake

---

112. Brevard Childs, *Biblical Theology of the Old and New Testaments* (London: Xpress Reprints, 1993), p. 20.

113. Lucy Rose, *Sharing the Word: Preaching in the Round Table Church* (Louisville: Westminster John Knox Press, 1997), p. 5.

Preaching

we must unravel them. In one domain, the focus is on the truth of confessional statements; in the other, the focus is on the position of the minister vis-à-vis the congregation. We must distinguish between these two areas. First of all, the position of the minister in the pulpit must be relativized. She does not possess ultimate authority. After the wave of democratization in the 1960s, the professional authority of the pulpit is no longer automatic (in fact, the preacher is "as one without authority"). As a result, the emphasis in homiletics has shifted towards mutuality and communality. As Rose explains, "The preacher and the congregation gather symbolically at a round table without head or foot, where labels like 'clergy' and 'laity' disappear and where believing or wanting to believe is all that matters."[114] However, this issue — the relationship between the preacher and the congregation in the *performance* — should not in all respects be linked to the question of the truth of our faith. For it is not the case that all that is *said* or *argued for* in the sermon becomes relative. And it is not the case that the noetic content of the sermon is fully equivalent with the authority of the speaker. It seems that Rose and others are convinced that the content of our faith cannot be propositional. Apparently, faith is an *attitude* or an *experience*. It seems they hold that there are no *truths* of faith. Significantly enough, Rose connects the propositional content of truth with such prefixes as "absolute," "objective," and "ontological." In a recent article, even Tom Long criticizes Phillips Brooks, a nineteenth-century liberal preacher, because Brooks defines truth as a "fixed and stable element."[115] However, this in no way applies to this type of liberal theologian. The term "absolute truth" is used by contemporary homileticians as a pejorative epithet, which creates the suggestion that truth always parallels absolute certainty. And that certainly is not the case. It must be noted, however, that this type of suspicion towards theological content is changing. In their writings, David Lose, Paul Wilson, Charles Campbell, and Richard Lischer pay explicit attention to the theological aspects in homiletics.

Touching the Sacred

In the sermon, the dimension of content is performed as *kerygma*, encouragement, comfort, and teaching. This expresses the unique character of the

---

114. Rose, *Sharing the Word*, p. 4.
115. Long, "A New Focus for Teaching Preaching," in *Teaching Preaching as a Christian Practice*, ed. Long and Tisdale, p. 7.

Christian sermon. In the *kerygma* the focus is on the Triune God, who comes to us with his grace and redemption. The comforting and teaching sermon has a *doxological* ring to it. Even though the content of the sermon is related to God, the *kerygma* places the emphasis on the movement of God towards humankind. When listening to a comforting, exhorting, or teaching sermon, worshippers experience a deep realization that they stand before God. God's transcendental presence is disclosed. Rudolf Bohren points out that the act of remembering, the *anamnesis*, is indeed a human activity — for it is the human person who remembers — but the faith dimension in this remembering directs the attention to *what God does*. "The God who brings salvation is Himself the One who remembers," says Bohren. "The historical events do not in themselves become powerful and effective, but the essence is their validity in the eyes of God. . . . The fact that God is with us is characterized by His remembering. When He writes history, His actions are not primarily determined by history, but by His remembering of His past salvific acts."[116] The church is reminded that it is God himself who remembers his covenant. How can the people of Israel find joy in events that happened centuries ago? How can the Christian church be inspired by events that took place two thousand years ago? It has to do with the *religious* character of these events. God himself was at work in them, and now he will speak and act accordingly. It is not the past events in themselves but rather our trustworthy God that is the connecting link in salvation history. He remembers his covenant. He comes to his church as the *life-giving Spirit*. In *kerygma*, comfort, and teaching we hear a *theological* echo. The content revolves around the name of God.

Teaching moments in the sermon are intended to strengthen the insights of faith and trust in God, and to stimulate the concrete discipleship of Christ. Teaching is a speech mode that calls the congregation to reflection and contemplation. It is not primarily a matter of the transfer of knowledge but of the development of a communal awareness of the *mystery* of God's name. Teaching moments in the sermon are embedded between an awareness of God's sacredness on the one hand and a compassion for the world in which the hearers live on the other hand. Faith seeks understanding, desires God's love and justice, weeps for the peace that has not yet dawned, and moans because of the difficulties of life. Biblical texts and themes are not topics for theoretical reflection, but become fluid in the lives of ordinary people. Precisely because faith is a mystery, seeking and questioning characterize the way that Christian faith is practiced. *How do I get on with my life?*

---

116. Bohren, *Predigtlehre*, p. 161.

How do I deal with disappointments? How do I value my daily blessings? Do I dare to fully enjoy creation, the relationships that I have, my work? And the questions continue. The sermon offers space for such considerations, and teaching moments in a sermon can be helpful to that end. Take, for instance, the miracles and signs that we encounter in the Bible. "Behold," Jesus says, "I cast out demons and perform cures today and tomorrow, and the third day I finish my course" (Luke 13:32). Peter says in a sermon, "He [Jesus] went about doing good and healing all that were oppressed by the devil, for God was with him" (Acts 10:38). Contemporary Westerners are not familiar with that kind of world. Some will be inclined to refer to this worldview as mythical or outdated, while others still embrace it with a faith that believes in miracles. On the one hand, we see a closed, secular worldview from which God has disappeared, and on the other hand, a kind of piety that is not of this world and believes that anything is possible. The sermon is not the occasion to give a lecture about the miracles in the Bible. But miracles do raise questions that cannot be ignored. The following sermon excerpt from Christoph Blumhardt is a good example of a teaching moment. If we are unable to assign miracles a place in God's kingdom, then what meaning, he wonders, can concrete renewal and change have in our life?

> Signs and wonders can only be adequately appreciated by those who long for the coming of Christ, for the end of this world, for the final fulfillment. Without this faith, we do not care whether or not signs and wonders occur. But we believe in the Savior and we say to Him: "Yes, dear Lord, it is true, we must see signs and wonders . . . until one day everything is sign and wonder, until everything on earth is ready to help mankind, until those who suffer are truly relieved — in this time of struggle, however, we need signs and wonders."[117]

Blumhardt sees a sign as a signal, a flash of light that illuminates the path of life for us, a sign of what is to come and has already been given in Christ. Jesus restored sight and healed infectious diseases. Those are signs of God's kingdom and of his power, including his power over earthly relationships. When God comes again, all things will be under the power of the divine kingdom. This must be announced — that there is a divine kingdom that will change, improve, and purify all earthly situations from top to bottom. Blumhardt realizes that many preachers find it difficult to speak about this.

---

117. Quoted in Bohren, *Predigtlehre*, p. 328.

But if they do not, we remain caught in the status quo. We will no longer experience spiritual growth, and will become disillusioned. "That is why," Blumhardt says, "we need such new signs that clearly say: Here is Christ! Here is the pathway to peace! Here is the road to the kingdom of God! So that we will together become one in our adoration of God, through Jesus Christ our Lord." Blumhardt places the teaching element in a confessional setting: "For we confess our faith in the Savior . . ."[118]

The sermon as *performance* has an actualizing effect. During the sermon, worshippers get involved. "In listening," says Theo Pleizier, "the hearer *perceives* the world of the sermon; he becomes aware of the religious realities presented in the world of the sermon."[119] Thus, according to Pleizier, this performative, actualizing effect also relates to a religious reality: "The listener becomes oriented towards the presence of God and the reality of Christ. Even if this presence and reality is particularly problematic and listeners feel abandoned by God or they find themselves in a situation of questioned faith. In either way does the sermon direct the mind of the listener towards a religious reality. How clear or obscure, vivid or vague this might be, the sermon arouses *religious* attention."[120] When our *attention* is drawn towards a particular point, it implies that we also become intentionally involved. Something may touch us because it latches on to latent feelings or to questions that we may have at that very moment. Our attention may also be caught by something that the sermon presents or offers. Listeners often tell the minister that the sermon caused them to start thinking about certain things or that they enjoyed particular ideas that were proposed.

As we listen, we may experience a moment of "sacred impact." It can be a moment of spiritual insight. The sacred touches us. It can be connected with an emotional stimulus. It can be a strong awareness of truth. We may experience a decisive preparedness to act as Christ did. A sense of urgency. Or a moment of sudden clarity: This is how it is!

Religious experiences often are a confirmation or an intensification of what we already believe. They can give us joy. For instance, we may experience joy in our faith that Christ has conquered death, that God is truly merciful, that there is grace for people who have made a mess of things. That is why a sermon does not just provide clarification when new points of view are offered. Like the liturgy and the sacrament, the sermon has elements

---

118. Quoted in Bohren, *Predigtlehre*, p. 329.
119. Pleizier, *Religious Involvement in Hearing Sermons*, p. 212.
120. Pleizier, *Religious Involvement in Hearing Sermons*, p. 216.

of *repetition*. "It makes me happy just to hear about Jesus," one worshipper said.[121] Apparently this is not a moment of transfer of information, but a moment that helps to put one's spiritual experience into words. The sermon also offers a vocalization of the faith that we, as a community, confess. This means not that the minister must make sure that she says what we like to hear (as a form of local theology), but that the sermon expresses the faith that we have in common. The spoken words become a vehicle for an *experience of truth* that in itself has a religious character. A sense of interconnectedness and the recognition of a common faith are important experiences during a sermon. A sense of sharing insights, emotions, convictions, desires. . . . The teaching element in this case has to do with knowledge and understanding — not giving information but rather providing a catalyst for communion with God. When we become consciously involved and listen attentively, we will come into the radius of the Triune God: the cross and the resurrection become effective realities, and the Spirit provides illumination. *The sacred touches us.*

---

121. Pleizier, *Religious Involvement in Hearing Sermons*, p. 196.

CHAPTER 7

Celebrating the Lord's Supper

Protestant Communion Practices

The celebration of the Lord's Supper in Protestant churches shows a great diversity. The differences are not only visible in the liturgical format, but are also found in the way in which communion is celebrated. In the second half of the twentieth century, many local churches introduced the ecumenical formula for the celebration. The Table Prayer became the dominant feature in the liturgy, and the participants walked to the table to receive the bread and the wine from the servants at the table. The traditional Calvinistic practice — with its emphasis on the instruction by means of the "Form for the Administration of the Lord's Supper," and the partaking in communion while seated around the table — became less common. This tradition succeeded in maintaining itself in the more conservative wings of the Protestant churches. We must also note that mixed forms have emerged. In some congregations, the Protestant ecumenical form was introduced only in part. One of the issues was, for instance, the place of the Words of Institution in the liturgy. Should these words be part of the Table Prayer, or should they be read as a scriptural text to the congregation? On the basis of the Reformed tradition, there are some reasons why the Words of Institution should not be part of the Table Prayer.

Recently some practices reveal a new area of tension — not the old opposition between ecumenical and classical Reformed, but the tension between a prescribed form and free, spontaneous expression. There is a tendency towards a minimum of prescribed script. The emphasis is on the spontaneous creativity of the minister; there is no established form for communion and no prescribed format for the Table Prayer. We see in these celebrations the influence of the free churches and the evangelical movement. In contrast

Celebrating the Lord's Supper

with the ecumenically oriented movement that underscores the value of style and format and of ancient words that are part of the Christian tradition, the emphasis is on subjective expression and individual experience. A minister has the freedom to speak in paraphrase about the meaning of communion; she can use contemporary words that she has chosen, without the formulas of tradition. This freedom of expression is also found in the Table Prayer. In some countries, particularly in the United States, this type of celebration is gaining ground.[1] The established churches look at this process with much suspicion. Ronald P. Byars points to the impoverishment that occurs when ministers give their own form to the Eucharistic prayer, without being fully aware of the rich tradition of the Table Prayer:

> The Eucharistic prayer, the Great Prayer of Thanksgiving, has often been reduced to a purely private prayer of the presider's own composition. An extemporaneous prayer of thanksgiving is not a problem in and of itself, except when the presider is ignorant of, or indifferent to, the way the church has historically framed its prayer at the holy table. The Trinitarian form and content is often lost. Neither is a general prayer with allusions to the institution of the Supper or a simple blessing at the table sufficient to convey the fullness of the gift God offers in the sacrament.[2]

According to Robert Webber, this type of free celebration has the following characteristics: (1) the important role of free, spontaneous prayer, (2) the extensive role of "songs and choruses," and (3) an informal style.[3] We must indeed not underestimate the role of the songs in the liturgy of the Lord's Supper. Songs and hymns contribute to the emotional involvement and strengthen the intensity of the communion with Christ. During the singing of a song that is repeated several times, bread and wine are brought to the table. The song is intended as a call to worship and as an invitation to the celebration. The minister exhorts the people to participate in the communion service, or, if she has not already done that at the beginning of the service (in line with 1 Cor. 11), she calls upon the people to examine their hearts. The minister then offers a prayer of thanksgiving that is followed by the congregational singing of a contemporary Sanctus. The Words of

---

1. Robert Webber, *Planning Blended Worship: The Creative Mixture of Old and New* (Nashville: Abingdon Press, 1998), p. 145.
2. Ronald P. Byars, *The Future of Protestant Worship: Beyond the Worship Wars* (Louisville: Westminster John Knox Press, 2002), p. 68.
3. Webber, *Planning Blended Worship*, p. 144.

Institution (Matt. 26:26-28) are usually repeated verbatim. When the words "This is my body" are spoken, the bread is elevated and broken. Then often follow words of invitation (for instance, "Come, taste, and see that the Lord is good," while the bread and the cup are elevated). While the people come to the front to receive the bread and the wine, hymns are sung that testify of the communion with Jesus, of healing and wholeness and of salvation and newness of life. Among these well-known hymns we often hear "Abba, Father, Let Me Be Yours and Yours Alone" and *"Ubi caritas et amor, ubi caritas, Deus ibi est."*[4] During communion, small prayer circles may be formed (to pray for health and healing, for instance). The participants experience the singing and praying as important signs of God's presence. According to Webber, "Contemporary charismatic churches testify to the experience of unusual signs, wonders, gifts of knowledge and wisdom, and prophecies during this part of the service. Other contemporary churches, particularly in the Pentecostal tradition, often sing and dance after communion for twenty or thirty minutes."[5] The celebration is then concluded with an expression of praise, either spoken or sung.

Even though in the traditional Protestant churches the classical traditions (Reformed and ecumenical) have a moderating influence on these more spontaneous ways of celebrating the Lord's Supper, we do see the development of new styles. The free expression of the minister and the choice of hymns and song texts determine to a large degree the style of the celebration. In line with the Protestant tradition, this mix of styles continues to emphasize communion itself. The hymns and music underscore the intimate communion with Christ during the Lord's Supper. But in the texts of the hymns the emphasis is shifting towards the *experience* of salvation. This salvation becomes almost palpable and visible. As a result, these celebrations are characterized by joy and praise. This shows a bond with the Protestant ecumenical tradition. The celebration is *Eucharist,* thanksgiving. The accent is not on the crucified Christ and the forgiveness of sin (as in the classical Reformed approach), but on the risen Lord, who allows us to experience his redemptive presence, particularly during communion. The hymns that are sung during communion testify to the power of the resurrection and the breaking through of the new life, of healing and deliverance. The triumphant Christ fills worshippers' hearts and for a moment pulls away the curtain that still veils the end of time. All this happens in the context of continuous singing and prayer.

---

4. *Evangelische liedbundel,* no. 376, no. 219 (Zoetermeer: Boekencentrum, 1999).
5. Webber, *Planning Blended Worship,* p. 146.

The Origin of the Reformed Liturgy of the Lord's Supper

In Chapter 4 we already saw that the Reformed praxis of the Lord's Supper shows a rupture with the traditional sacrifice of the mass. This brings us to an important question: How did the Reformed praxis of communion receive its eventual format? When we dealt with baptism, we discovered the important role played by the refugee churches in London and Frankenthal (the Paltz) in shaping the classical Reformed liturgy. This is also true with regard to the liturgy of the Lord's Supper. Petrus Dathenus translated both the Baptismal Form and the Communion Form of the church order of the Paltz into Dutch. The first edition appeared in 1566, in the same booklet as Dathenus's psalter and Heidelberg Catechism. The Synod of Dordt abbreviated the Baptismal Form, but the Communion Form remained unchanged. To get a good picture of the classical Reformed communion praxis, we must understand the enormous changes that the Reformers implemented. Luther and Zwingli severely criticized the *Canon Missae*. With their first reforms (in 1523) they still remained within the traditional structure of the mass. But this changed within a few years. They rejected the prayer structure that highlights the element of sacrifice in the mass. From then onward, the Words of Institution were cited as Scripture reading, and all emphasis was on the communion of the bread and the wine. The citing of the Words of Institution and communion were brought together as closely as possible. These changes came about within just a few years. In 1525, just prior to Easter, radical Reformers in Zurich demanded a new liturgy for the Lord's Supper that conformed to the Scriptures. Zwingli then came into the picture with his *Action oder Brauch des Nachtmahls* ("Action or Use of the Lord's Supper"). The minister read the Words of Institution before the bread and the wine were distributed. In other European cities this happened around this time in the same manner.

Strasbourg and Geneva

If we want to have a good understanding of the Reformed communion praxis, we must first take a look at the developments in Geneva and Strasbourg. Even before Calvin arrived in Geneva and Strasbourg, the first reforms of the Roman mass had taken place. In Strasbourg, the first mass in the German language was celebrated by a priest named Schwartz *(Die teutsche Mesz)*. In actual fact, this was nothing but a literal translation of the Roman mass that was current — but it left out all sacrificial terminology. This liturgy went through a number of printings, and the priests probably used the proposed wording with a great deal of personal freedom. T. Brienen comments, "When surveying the liturgical developments in Strasbourg, one must conclude that Schwartz and his group started with the missal, as it was in use in Strasbourg around 1520. This missal was the basis for the 'Teutsche Messe.' There is a clear line from the medieval liturgy to this Protestant liturgy. . . . The structure of the mass is retained; it is cleansed from unbiblical elements, and gradually the restoration of the original order of worship comes about, in accordance with the église ancienne (the ancient church)."[6]

The report of a French student, Gérard Roussel, who attended a service in 1525, has been preserved:

> On the *Sunday*, which they have kept as their only holy day . . . , they celebrate *the Lord's Supper*. They do that in this way: A table is placed in an open area in the church, so that it is visible to all. It is not referred to as an altar, to avoid any similarity with those who have made the Supper of the Lord into a sacrifice. But there is no difference with common altars. The *servant* stands close to the table, but in such a way that his face is turned towards the people, and not his back, as has been customary, as the priests who bring the sacrifice preferred to show the people their back and not their face — as if they were sacrificing in front of them some appearance of God. When he sits down at the table, with his face towards the people, while all eyes are directed towards him, he says a few prayers that have been taken from the Bible. Next they all sing a psalm together. When this is finished and the servant has spoken a few other prayers, he ascends the pulpit and reads in a manner that the entire audience can understand the portion of Scripture that he wants to explain. He then gives a rather extensive explanation while citing also other related texts of Scripture. . . . After the sermon he returns to the table. All sing the confession of faith. Then he explains for what purpose Christ has given us his Communion, unfolding in a few words the merciful deed of Christ's death and of His blood that was shed for us. Following this, he cites the Words of Institution of Christ, as they have been recorded by the evangelists or Paul. Then he gives to all who want to approach the table (for no one is forced, even though all are invited) *bread and wine, the true symbols (symbola) of the body and blood of Christ, in remembrance of His death,* as he had charged His disciples to do. While the communion takes place and each person receives the meal,

---

6. T. Brienen, *De liturgie bij Johannes Calvijn* (Kampen: Kok, 1987), p. 51.

the *Kyrie Eleison* is sung by all, as a song of praise to thank for the gracious gift that has been received. The Supper is celebrated in such a way that the servant eats and drinks last, and then closes the service.[7]

In the cathedral of Strasbourg, the Lord's Supper was celebrated every Sunday during the main service. In the other parish churches in the city, it was done once every month or once every eight weeks. The same is true for the villages around Strasbourg. Calvin met this liturgical practice when he arrived in Strasbourg in 1538, after having been exiled from Geneva.

Four years later, he left for a new stay in Geneva. In 1542 he published the liturgy that was in use in Geneva at that time. It may have been a revision of the Francophone Strasbourg liturgy that took into account the customs that had developed in Geneva. The title of the publication is *La Forme des Prieres et Chantz Ecclesiastiques, avec la maniere d'administrer les Sacraments, and consacrer le Mariage: selon la coustume de l'Eglise ancienne* (1542). In the introduction he writes, "The Lord has commanded us three things, namely: the preaching of His Word, public solemn prayers, and the administering of the sacraments." What did the liturgy of the Lord's Supper look like?

On the Sunday, prior to the Sunday of the Communion, it is announced that there will be a Communion service, so that all may make preparations in order to be worthy to receive it; that children will not be admitted unless they have been thoroughly instructed and have confessed their faith in the church; and that strangers may make themselves known so that they may receive instructions about participation in the Lord's Supper. At the end of the sermon the servant reminds the people what our Lord had in mind when He gave us the Communion, and how we must receive it.

The liturgy of Lord's Supper had the following elements:

Prayers and intercessions
Apostolic Confession of Faith
Words of Institution from 1 Corinthians 11
Excommunication of those who were erring in what they believed and how they lived
Self-examination and encouragement of the believers
Sursum Corda

---

7. Quoted in Brienen, *De liturgie bij Johannes Calvijn*, p. 52.

Communion, while psalms were sung and a Bible reading took place
Prayer of Thanksgiving or Nunc Dimittis (from 1549 onwards)
Blessing.[8]

This order of the Lord's Supper shows a remarkable shift when compared with the earlier orders of the early Reformers. In these older orders the citing of the Words of Institution was almost immediately followed by the distribution of the bread and the wine (communion). Calvin did not follow this order. The Words of Institution were followed by an extensive instructional explanation that had a ring of praise and adoration to it. During the instruction the excommunication of the godless took place, and an appeal was made for self-examination, while the believers were encouraged and exhorted:

> Let us listen to the institution of the Holy Supper by Jesus Christ, as narrated by St. Paul in the eleventh chapter of the First Epistle to the Corinthians:
> For I have received, he says . . . and so on.
> We have heard, brethren, how our Lord celebrated his Supper with his disciples, thereby indicating that strangers, and those who are not of the company of the faithful, ought not to be admitted. Therefore, in accordance with this rule, in the name and by the authority of our Lord Jesus Christ, I excommunicate all idolaters, blasphemers, despisers of God, heretics, and all who form private sects and break the unity of the Church, all perjurers, all who rebel against their parents or their superiors, all who are seditious, mutinous, quarrelsome, or brutal, all adulterers, fornicators, thieves, ravishers, misers, drunkards, gluttons, and all who lead a scandalous and dissolute life. I declare that they must abstain from this holy table, for fear of defiling and contaminating the holy food which our Lord Jesus Christ gives only to His household and believers.[9]

So, after the Words of Institution, there was first of all a rejection of the unrepentants. Calvin argued that this rule was derived from the fact that

---

8. See G. J. Jasper and R. C. D. Cuming, *Prayers of the Eucharist* (New York: Oxford University Press, 1980), pp. 213-18; see also Brienen, *Die Liturgie bij Johannes Calvijn*, p. 101.

9. I have used the translation provided by Jasper and Cuming, *Prayers of the Eucharist*, p. 216.

Celebrating the Lord's Supper

Jesus held the supper exclusively with his disciples. The minister ("and I, in the name of and at the command of . . .") next proceeded to excommunicate the hardened sinners. They could not partake of the meal of the Lord. Then there was the self-examination of the believer and the invitation to come with true faith and partake of the bread and the wine:

> Therefore, in accordance with the exhortation of St. Paul, let each man prove and examine his conscience, to see whether he has truly repented of his faults, and is dissatisfied with his sins, desiring to live henceforth a holy life and according to God's will. Above all, let each man see whether he puts his trust in the mercy of God, and seeks his salvation entirely in Jesus Christ; and whether, renouncing all hatred and rancor, he truly intends and resolves to live in peace and brotherly love with his neighbors.
>
> If we have this testimony in our hearts before God, let us have no doubt at all that He claims us as His children, and that the Lord Jesus addresses His words to us, to invite us to His table, and to present to us this holy sacrament which He communicated to His disciples.
>
> And although we may feel within ourselves much frailty and misery from not having perfect faith, but being inclined to unbelief and distrust; . . . let us all be assured that the sins and imperfections which remain in us will not prevent Him from receiving us, and making us worthy to partake of this spiritual table.[10]

After this invitation, the actual communion is introduced by a didactic comment on the *Sursum Corda*. In several places the tone is rather polemic and apologetic (for example: "as if He were enclosed in the bread or the wine"):

> With this in mind, let us raise our hearts and minds on high, where Jesus Christ is, in the glory of His Father, and from whence we look for Him at our redemption. Let us not be bemused by these earthly and corruptible elements which we see with the eye, and touch with the hand, in order to seek Him there, as if He were enclosed in the bread or the wine. Our souls will only then be disposed to be nourished and vivified by His substance, when they are thus raised above all earthly things, and carried as high as heaven, to enter the kingdom of God where He dwells. Let us therefore be

---

10. I have used the translation provided by Jasper and Cuming, *Prayers of the Eucharist*, pp. 216-17.

content to have the bread and the wine as signs and evidences, spiritually seeking the reality where the word of God promises that we shall find it.[11]

This is followed by the distribution and communion.

The Dutch Variant

The classical Reformed Communion Form that found its way from the Paltz to the Netherlands and there has taken root is Calvinistic as far as tone and content are concerned, but it has its own character and differs in some aspects from the order of Geneva that dates from 1542. In the classical Reformed Dutch Form, the self-examination of the believers comes before the excommunication of those who do not repent. Calvin has the inverse order. Moreover, the excommunication of the godless does not have the same sharpness of tone in the classical Reformed Form:

Words of Institution

Beloved in the Lord Jesus Christ, attend to the words of the institution of the Holy Supper of our Lord Jesus Christ, as they are delivered by the holy Apostle Paul. . . .

Self-examination

That we may now celebrate the Supper of the Lord to our comfort, it is above all things necessary,

First. Rightly to examine ourselves. *Secondly.* To direct it to that end for which Christ hath ordained and instituted the same, namely, to his remembrance.

The true examination of ourselves consists of these three parts:

First. That every one consider by himself, his sins. . . . *Secondly.* That every one examine his own heart, whether he doth believe this faithful promise of God, that all his sins are forgiven him only for the sake of the passion and death of Jesus Christ. . . . *Thirdly.* That everyone examine his own conscience, whether he purposeth henceforth to show true thankfulness to God in his whole life. . . .

---

11. I have used the translation provided by Jasper and Cuming, *Prayers of the Eucharist*, p. 218.

Proclamation of God's grace and excommunication of the unrepentant

All those, then, who are thus disposed, God will certainly receive in mercy, and count them worthy partakers of the table of his Son Jesus Christ. On the contrary, those who do not feel this testimony in their hearts, eat and drink judgment to themselves.

Therefore, we also, according to the command of Christ and the Apostle Paul, admonish all those who are defiled with the following sins, to keep themselves from the table of the Lord, and declare to them that they have no part in the kingdom of Christ; such as all idolaters, all. . . .[12]

Admittedly, this part of the form undoubtedly derives from Calvin. At that time, the theologians in the Paltz (e.g., Olevianus) corresponded frequently with Calvin. There also is a clear similarity with the London liturgy of Marten Micron (who was also influenced by Calvin). J. A. M. Mensinga says, "In studying in further depth the origin (of the classical Reformed Form), we find that a small part coincides with Micron, and a larger part, especially of the first section that deals with self-examination, is borrowed from Calvin's Form, that had also inspired the people in London. . . . The summaries that have been taken from Calvin do not so much represent changes, but rather a different sequence or with new connections."[13]

There is yet another element in the liturgy that has been directly taken from Calvin: the wording of the *Sursum Corda*, just prior to communion. The polemical tone of Calvin may have disappeared, but the substance is still there:

> That we may now be fed with the true heavenly bread, Christ Jesus, let us not cleave with our hearts unto the external bread and wine, but lift them up on high in heaven, where Christ Jesus is our Advocate, at the right hand of his heavenly Father, . . . not doubting, but we shall as certainly be fed and refreshed in our souls through the working of the Holy Ghost, with his body and blood, as we receive the holy bread and wine in remembrance of him.[14]

---

12. Excerpts from the Reformed Communion Form.
13. J. A. M. Mensinga, *Verhandeling over de liturgische schriften der Nederlandse Hervormde Kerk* (The Hague: Thierry en Mensing, 1851), p. 214.
14. "Form for the Administration of the Lord's Supper," in *The Psalter: With Doctrinal Standards, Liturgy, Church Order, and Added Chorale Section* (Grand Rapids: Wm. B. Eerdmans, 1984), pp. 60-63.

The classical Reformed Form (as it originated in the Paltz) is based on three sources:

1. The order that was used by Calvin. This is evident, in particular, in the first part of the form about the self-examination and the excommunication of the unrepentant, and the didactic treatment of the *Sursum Corda*.
2. The influence of the liturgy of the Dutch refugee church in London. After the dispersion of the London refugee church across Europe, Micron's liturgy was used in different churches. Micron also distinguished three aspects in the self-examination process: reflections on one's sins, the fact that God forgives these sins through His grace, "as if we had suffered death in our own person on the wood of the cross," and the intent towards genuine improvement.
3. The influence of the Lutheran *Agende von Württemberg* (which was in use before the Elector of the Paltz converted to Reformed Protestantism). This contains the passage "as we have been pressed together from many different ways of life to become one wine and one drink" ("like one wine and one drink flows from the pressing together of many berries"). This is an expression that underscores the unity of the church and an admonition to show brotherly love.[15]

Communion takes place after the pronouncement of the *Sursum Corda*. The words of distribution are borrowed from the London liturgy:

> *In breaking and distributing the bread, the Minister shall say:*
> The bread which we break is the communion of the body of Christ.
> *And when he giveth the cup:*
> The cup of blessing, which we bless, is the communion of the blood of Christ.

The London liturgy is also quoted when the cup is given:

> The cup of thanksgiving, over which we pronounce the prayer of thanksgiving, is the communion with the blood of Christ. Take, drink from it, remember, and believe that the precious blood of our Lord Jesus Christ has been shed for a complete atonement of our sins.[16]

---

15. A. F. N. Lekkerkerker, *Kanttekeningen bij het Hervormde Dienstboek*, vol. 3 (The Hague: Boekencentrum, 1952), pp. 134-48.

16. Excerpts from the "Form for the Administration of the Lord's Supper," in *The Psalter*, pp. 62, 63.

After communion comes the Thanksgiving (the so-called post-communion). Texts from Psalm 103 are used for this. G. van der Leeuw states that this is "Thanksgiving in the scriptural form, unique in the reformed worship service and the most beautiful part of our liturgy."[17]

> Beloved in the Lord, since the Lord hath now fed our souls at this table, let us therefore jointly praise his holy name with thanksgiving, and everyone say in his heart, thus:
>
> Bless the Lord, O my soul; and all that is within me, bless his holy name. Bless the Lord, O my soul, and forget not all his benefits. Who forgiveth all thine iniquities; who healeth all thy diseases. Who redeemeth thy life from destruction, who crowneth thee with loving kindness and tender mercies. The Lord is merciful and gracious, slow to anger and plenteous in mercy. . . .
>
> Who hath not spared his own Son, but delivered him up for us all, and given us all things with him. . . . Therefore shall my mouth and heart show forth the praise of the Lord from this time forth forever more. Amen.

Theology and Piety in the Reformed Communion Praxis

We have already seen how in the classical Reformed communion praxis the emphasis is on communion. The liturgical acts — mostly performed at the table — form the main aspect of the celebration. The breaking of the bread and the blessing of the cup are followed by the distribution to each other and the eating and drinking. Prior to this is an anamnetic instruction. On the one hand, this instruction is *contemplative* — that is to say, it calls the worshipper to remember and consider. On the other hand, it is characterized by *adoration* and praise: God is praised for his atoning work. The liturgical performance, the distribution of the bread and the wine, and the eating and drinking are directly linked to the work of the Holy Spirit. Here the communion with Christ is realized.

There is a strong awareness of God's active role during the celebration in the praxis that has been shaped by the classical Reformed Communion Form. This explains why the term "Holy Communion" is often used. The thinking is that God himself feeds the believers, and refreshes them with the food of bread and wine. God is not merely present. In the sacrament

---

17. G. van der Leeuw, *Liturgiek* (Nijkerk: Callenbach, 1946), p. 155.

he "feeds and refreshes" the church that celebrates his meal. He seals his promise by uniting the believers with Christ. The celebration of the Holy Communion takes place before the face of God. Like the Roman Catholic celebration, a Reformed celebration has a sacramental connotation. However, the climax is not the moment of consecration, but the communion. The rite of consecration does not change the bread and the wine into the mystery of Christ, but the communal act of the eating and drinking results in the communion with Christ. The *epiclesis* and the *Sursum Corda* play an important role in realizing the communion with Christ.

The *epiclesis* begins as follows:

> O most merciful God and Father, we beseech thee, that thou wilt be pleased in this Supper to work in our hearts through the Holy Spirit, ... that our afflicted and contrite hearts, through the power of the Holy Ghost, may be fed and comforted with his true body and blood; yea, with him, true God and man. ...

The *Sursum Corda* is spoken at the table just before communion:

> That we may now be fed with the true heavenly bread, Christ Jesus, let us not cleave with our hearts unto the external bread and wine, but lift them up on high in heaven, where Christ Jesus is our Advocate, at the right hand of his heavenly Father. ...[18]

Because of the emphasis on the aspect of self-examination, the participant plays an important role in the Reformed communion praxis. Indeed, the weight that is given to self-examination may even cause a certain imbalance. It is understood that the consecration as such does not create the sacred. But the stress on self-examination may lead to a situation in which the liturgical acts as such become inferior to the personal experience of the *unio cum Christo*. This would make everything turn around the subjective experience of salvation. In itself, the full enjoyment of salvation is a legitimate aspect of the celebration. In the acts of bread and wine God *gives* us his salvation: he distributes it. At the same time, this salvation is appropriated when the congregation eats and drinks. The eating and drinking are also an act, something that is done. In that act we accept Christ

---

18. Excerpts from the "Form for the Administration of the Lord's Supper," in *The Psalter*, pp. 62, 63.

and give ourselves to God. And this enables Calvin to state that in the act of bread and wine we enjoy Christ. This is more than an encounter; it is a union and an exercise of communion. In this connection, A. A. van Ruler speaks about the human being and the effectuation of the communion of God in Christ. On the one hand, when we eat the piece of bread and drink the wine, it fully penetrates into our hearts and minds that we live in communion with the Redeemer. But, on the other hand, effectuation — "realization" — also means that we allow it to become full reality. We celebrate our redemption; it is a festive occasion; we are lifted up towards the kingdom of God. This is the element that is accentuated in the evangelical and charismatic churches: salvation is realized in a visible and palpable manner. For Calvin, however, this is primarily a spiritual experience rather than an actual realization.[19]

In Calvin's liturgy, the element of celebration and enjoyment is clearly present in the prayer after the sermon, prior to the instruction and the celebration itself. Through faith we savor Christ's presence, and he lives in us:

> And since Jesus not only sacrificed His body and His blood that one time on the cross, for the forgiveness of our sins; but also gave these for food and drink, with a view towards eternal life, so may You, O God, help us, through Your mercy, that we receive such a great and gracious deed, such a precious gift, with a genuine desire and full attention; that is: that we through the certainty of our faith find complete joy in His body and blood, yes, in He Himself, truly God and truly man, the only true heavenly bread; that we therefore will no longer live according to our evil, sinful nature; but that He lives in us, and produces in us a holy, blessed, and eternal life.... O heavenly Father, give us today that we may have and celebrate the glorious and blessed remembrance of Your dear Son; that we concentrate ourselves on this, and may proclaim the great deed of His death, so that we, through faith in You, may be continuously increased and be strengthened in all good things, and thus, being comforted, may even more convincedly call upon You as our Father, and glorify Your name. Amen.[20]

19. A. A. van Ruler, *Reformatorische opmerkingen in de ontmoeting met Rome* (Hilversum: Paul Brand, 1965), pp. 220, 221.

20. The original French can be found in Bruno Bürki, "La Sainte Cène Selon l'Ordre de Jean Calvin 1542," in Irmgard Pahl, ed., *Coena Domini I. Die Abendmahlsliturgie der Reformationskirchen im 16./17. Jahrhundert* (Freiburg: Universitätsverlag Freiburg Schweiz, 1983), pp. 355-56.

How real is the living and genuine relationship with Christ? Calvin is convinced that in the celebration of the Lord's Supper something actually happens between Christ and believers. Yet, it is not so simple to describe what happens. It remains a mystery, a secret. Calvin says that we are dealing with a "hidden union between Christ and the believers." Through "the physical things set forth in the Sacrament we are led by a sort of analogy to spiritual things."[21] In the Lord's Supper the promise is not only pictured but is actually delivered. Receiving it is not just a matter of insight and imagination, but of "enjoying true participation in Him."[22] Without the work of the Holy Spirit, the sacrament remains empty and idle; but the sacrament has great power when "the Spirit works and manifests His power" in it.[23]

Calvin holds a middle position, between the sacrament as an objective means of grace and the sacrament as having subjective-psychological impact. He does not pay much attention to the ecclesial act as a rite, yet he does not want to spiritualize the sacrament, either. Is this eating and drinking, he wonders, "merely" a matter of faith? There are those who maintain that the eating of Christ's flesh and the drinking of his blood are nothing but believing in *Christ himself*. However, I tend to think that Calvin says that Christ wanted to teach us something of deeper meaning in this expression: that by truly communing with him, we receive new life. This is more than just cognition. He is the bread of life, and true communion with him brings his life *in us and becomes ours,* just as the bread, when it is taken as food, strengthens us.

Comparison with the Sacrifice of the Mass

Ronald Byars complains about the fact that "the tone of the Genevan Eucharistic service, hedged around with solemn warnings, tends to accentuate the penitential at the expense of thanksgiving." He continues,

> This, in fact, is not so terribly different from the tone of the pre-Reformation Roman mass. Calvin had inherited from the piety of the medieval church a very sober, grave understanding of the Eucharist, inter-

---

21. John Calvin, *Institutes of the Christian Religion,* 4 vols. (London: SCM Press, 1961), Book IV.17.3, p. 1363.
22. Calvin, *Institutes of the Christian Religion,* Book IV.17.11, p. 1372.
23. Calvin, *Institutes of the Christian Religion,* Book IV.14.19, p. 1284.

preted primarily in terms of Christ's *Last* Supper, with little or no attention to the themes of resurrection and eating or drinking with the risen Lord. The resurrection themes, present in Scripture (e.g., Luke 24, John 21) and prominent in the Eucharistic celebrations of the early centuries of the church, had been obscured in the medieval Eucharistic celebration and continued to be eclipsed in the Reformed rites.[24]

We may indeed conclude that the classical Reformed rites are based on Jesus' celebration of the Last Supper, the evening before the passion night. This influences the tone of the celebration. The *suffering* Christ occupies the central place. For Calvin as well as for other Reformers, the suffering is connected with the *once-and-for-all* aspect as well as with the *vicariousness* of Christ's suffering. So, where is the difference with Rome? The debate is not about the central meaning of *hamartology* — the suffering and the atonement as such. Rather, the question is how radical an understanding we have of the sacrifice on the cross, and, even more, how we share in this sacrifice. The Reformation objects to the sacrifice of the mass (and to the large number of mysterious acts and gestures that are used to perform the sacrifice of the mass). G. J. Jasper and R. C. D. Cuming comment, "The first generation of continental Reformed liturgies strongly resisted the idea that the Eucharist is itself a sacrifice: there is only one sacrifice — that is the sacrifice of Jesus on Calvary — even though the opinions about the relationship between that sacrifice and the Eucharist and the presence of Christ in the Eucharist varied greatly."[25]

If we want to get an idea of the situation during that era, we must realize that, as Jasper and Cuming point out, believers seldom participated in communion. Communion was pushed aside by looking at the elevation and adoration of the consecrated elements. The mass had been turned into a mysterious spectacle, surrounded by all kinds of ceremonies that the early church did not yet know; it was a holy sacrifice in addition to the sacrifice of Christ on Calvary.[26] The Reformers believed that the Eucharist in the early church was a simple, transparent act and not an elaborate ritual. They wanted to return to the *meal* and to what Jesus himself did in the context of the Last Supper. This consisted of four things: *taking, blessing, breaking,* and

---

24. Ronald P. Byars, *Lift Your Hearts on High: Eucharistic Prayer in the Reformed Tradition* (Louisville: Westminster John Knox Press, 2005), p. 31.
25. Jasper and Cuming, *Prayers of the Eucharist*, p. 179.
26. Jasper and Cuming, *Prayers of the Eucharist*, p. 177.

distributing. Jesus commanded his disciples to also do these things, and he placed these acts in the context of the remembrance, the *anamnesis*. As a result, the Reformers emphasized — in contrast to the Roman mass of that time — these four acts and communion. They resolutely rejected the idea that the Eucharist as a liturgical act is, in fact, a sacrifice. They referred to such texts as Hebrews 9:12: Christ "entered once for all into the Holy Place." Calvin commented, "This is indeed very certain: that the cross of Christ is overthrown as soon as the altar is set up."[27]

The Roman Catholic liturgy *(Missale Romanum)* that we refer to in connection with the Reformation dates from 1570. It is a product of the Council of Trent (1545-1563). But the history of the development of the Roman rite goes back much further. In the time of the Reformation (before the Council of Trent), there existed no singular, normative liturgy. There were regional variations, and the bishops made their own decisions in these matters. But the new *Missale Romanum* of 1570 was intended as normative.[28] Only after Vatican II was a new missal published with important renewals: (a) the vernacular was to be used during the entire celebration; (b) the congregation was to actively participate; (c) the service of the Word was to be an independent element beside the Eucharist; (d) a new lectionary was supplied with Old Testament readings; and (e) the possibility was raised of the communion consisting of both bread and wine.

Therefore, the mass that was strongly resisted in the early Reformation liturgies was the mass that was current in the period before Trent. But, eventually, during the Council of Trent the idea of sacrifice was officially confirmed.[29] J. A. Jungmann says that the mass that received its form during the Council of Trent is really a sacrifice that liturgically emphasizes the sacrifice of the church: "The mass is a celebration of remembrance of the suffering, the resurrection, and the ascension of our Lord, of the sacrifice that redeemed us and is accepted by the heavenly Father *(Unde et memores)*. And further: The mass itself is a *sacrifice,* and not just a sacrifice that Christ brings, but a sacrifice that *we may bring together with Him* (offerimus). The sacrifice that Christ has brought does indeed constitute the foundation of the sacrifice, but when it is performed in the liturgy, the sacrifice of the Church is in the foreground."[30]

---

27. Calvin, *Institutes of the Christian Religion,* Book IV.18.3, p. 1431.
28. J. A. Jungmann, *Missarum Sollemnia,* vol. 1 (Kasterlee: De Vroente, 1966), p. 157.
29. Jungmann, *Missarum Sollemnia,* p. 152.
30. J. A. Jungmann, *The Mass of the Roman Rite: Its Origins and Development* (New York: Benzinger, 1951-55).

Celebrating the Lord's Supper

This is also clear from the prayers that constitute the *Canon*. We will look at several prayers in which the idea of sacrifice is present, beginning with the first prayer about the offerings:[31]

> To You, therefore, most merciful Father, we make humble prayer and petition through Jesus Christ, Your Son our Lord, that You accept and bless these gifts, these offerings, these holy and unblemished sacrifices....[32]

In this opening prayer, the offerings are referred to with three different names: *dona, munera,* and *sancta sacrificia illibata.* The elements on the altar are not just offerings; they become blameless sacrifices. After this prayer come prayers of intercession, and, before the consecration takes place, there are two more prayers for the offerings *(Hanc igitur and Quam oblationem)*:

> Therefore, Lord, we pray: graciously accept this oblation of our service, that of Your whole family; order our days in Your peace, and command that we be delivered from eternal damnation and counted among the flock of those You have chosen. Through Christ our Lord. Amen.[33]

The sacrificial theme, which has been interrupted by various intercessory prayers, is emphasized anew: "Graciously accept this oblation...." The prayer underscores the fact that in the celebration of the mass, Christ is the atoning sacrifice. This sacrifice will deliver believers from eternal damnation:

> Be pleased, O God, we pray, to bless, acknowledge, and approve this offering in every respect; make it spiritual and acceptable, so that it may become for us the Body and Blood of Your most beloved Son, our Lord Jesus Christ.[34]

---

31. The English translation here and following in this section is from en.wikipedia.org/wiki/Text_and_rubrics_of_the_Roman_Canon.

32. Te igitur, clementissime Pater, per Jesum Christum, Filium tuum, Dominum nostrum, supplices rogamus, ac petimus, uti accepta habeas et benedicas, haec dona, heac munera, haec sancta sacrificia illibata ...

33. Hanc igitur oblationem servitutis nostrae, sed et cunctae familiae tuae, quaesumus, Domine, ut placates accipias: diesque nostros in tua pace disponas, atque ab aeterna damnatione nos eripi, et in electorum tuorum jubeas grege numerari. Per Christum Dominum nostrum. Amen.

34. Quam oblationem tu, Deus, in omnibus, quaesumus, benedictam, adscriptam, ratam, rationabilem, acceptabilemque facere digneris; ut nobis Corpus, et Sanguis fiat dilectissimi Filii tui Domini nostri Jesu Christi.

This prayer ends the series of prayers that precede the consecration. Jungmann feels that we could call this final prayer a consecration *epiclesis*. God's power is invoked over the offerings that will be consecrated. With the verbosity of a Roman lawyer, the attributes are listed that believers ask for in their offerings, in order that they may be acceptable to God: they must be sacrifices that are blessed, that are dedicated to God, and that are given juridical value; they must also be perfectly spiritual sacrifices.

In the prayer that follows, the Words of Institution are recited as the formula of consecration:

> On the day before He was to suffer, He took bread in His holy and venerable hands, and with eyes raised to heaven to You, O God, His almighty Father, giving You thanks, He said the blessing, broke the bread, and gave it to His disciples, saying: Take this, all of you, and eat of it: for this is My body, which will be given up for you.
>
> In a similar way, when supper was ended, He took this precious chalice in His holy and venerable hands, and once more giving You thanks, He said the blessing, and gave the chalice to His disciples, saying: Take this, all of you, and drink from it: for this is the chalice of My Blood, the Blood of the new and eternal covenant, which will be poured out for you and for many for the forgiveness of sins. Do this in remembrance of Me.[35]

Remarkably, the words do not exactly coincide with the biblical version. There is, for instance, Christ taking the bread in "His holy and honorable hands" and looking "heavenward, unto You, His all-powerful Father." In addition, there is a reference to a "precious" or magnificent cup. And, of course, there is the exclamation "*mysterium fidei*." Jungmann points out that the texts developed over a considerable period of time, and also that some liturgical texts already existed before the Bible originated.

According to the classical way of thinking, as the words "this is My body" are spoken, the independent substance of the bread changes into the

---

35. Qui pridie quam pateretur, accepit panem in sanctas ac venerabiles manus suas, et elevatis oculis in caelum ad te Deum, Patrem suum omnipotentem, tibi gratias agens, benedixit, fregit, deditque discipulis suis, dicens: accipite,et manducate ex hoc omnes.Hoc est enim corpus meum. Simili modo postquam coenatum est, accipiens et hunc praeclarum Calicemin sanctas ac venerabiles manus suas: item tibi gratias agens, benedixit, deditque discipulis suis, dicens: accipiter, et bibite ex eo omnes. Hic est enim calix sanguis mei, novi et aeterni testamenti: mysterium fidei:qui pro vobis et pro multis effundetur in remissionem peccatorum. Haec quotiescumque feceritis, in mei memoriam facietis.

body and blood of Christ — that is to say, into the living God-man who is now in heaven. The consecration is a *sacrificial deed* of Christ. However, we should not lose sight of the fact that here we are dealing with the relationship between Christ and the believers. The believers are involved with what happens at the altar. "For that reason," says Z. de Korte, "we must, in that moment, unite ourselves as fully as possible with that act of Christ; in His own person He also sacrifices us, and our communion with Him as sacrifice must be experienced intensely."[36]

What then can we conclude about the Reformed celebration of the Lord's Supper when we compare it with the Roman mass at the time of the Reformers? Luther's remark that the smell of a sacrifice penetrates the entire *Canon* is quite pertinent. It makes sense that he saw no other option but to eliminate the *Canon* in its entirety. During the first phase of the Reformation, new prayers were composed in which the sacrificial terminology was no longer used. The Reformers were convinced of the radical significance of the *sacrifice on the cross*. Jesus came and died once and for all for the sins of the world. But the Reformers were also convinced that we humans who live in the here and now will participate in the salvation and redemption in Christ. Even though the Reformation removed the altar from the church, it did not reject the atonement in Christ. Our human participation in the Christ event and the effective presence of Christ here and now are not pushed aside. Admittedly, as Paul Tillich justly remarked, Protestantism is inclined to secularize these crucial points. But for Calvin, and in the classical Reformed communion rite, the doctrine of atonement, the salvation from "damnation" (a word that also occurs in the Roman mass), and the communion with Christ do play a very important role. The difference, in particular, is that for the Reformers the communion with Christ is an *act of faith*. The human self is fully involved in this. It is personal and spiritual. The basis for the celebration of the Lord's Supper is found in the four acts of Jesus himself. When the church performs those deeds, we share in the crucified Savior in a spiritual way, through the work of the Holy Spirit.[37] The Roman mass also acknowledges the effective presence of the sacrifice on the cross, but through the ecclesial *ritual* execution of the sacrifice of the mass. Therein Christ himself comes to believers in the emblems of bread and wine. With regard to this point, the Reformers take a new path.

---

36. Z. de Korte, *De misliturgie* (Antwerp: G. Tielenburg, 1949), p. 328.
37. W. F. Dankbaar, *De sacramentsleer van Calvijn* (Amsterdam: H. J. Paris, 1941), p. 188.

From a theological perspective, the mystery of the communion with Christ, and the remarkable exchange (justification for the godless) on which this is based, form the heart of the classical Reformed communion liturgy. This mystical emphasis originates in the vicarious death of Christ. The somber notes of penitence and repentance, the emphasis on self-examination, the existential tension between the holy God and sinful humankind, the bitter suffering of Jesus, the images from Isaiah 53 — all these emphases evoke the mystery of faith. Easter motifs and the eschatological dimension echo in the background. In the Reformed celebration of communion, the emphasis is on the atonement in Christ. Calvin refers to it as a "strange exchange," and his words have put their stamp on the classical Reformed communion rite:

> That by His descent to earth, He has prepared an ascent to heaven for us; that, by taking on our mortality, He has conferred His immortality upon us; that, accepting our weakness, He has strengthened us by His power; that, receiving our poverty unto Himself, He has transferred His wealth to us; that, taking the weight of our iniquity upon Himself (which oppressed us), He has clothed us with His righteousness.[38]

In the remembrance (classical Reformed form), it is confessed that Jesus Christ, on the night on which He was delivered,

> ... where he was bound that we might be freed from our sins; that he afterwards suffered innumerable reproaches, that we might never be confounded; that he was innocently condemned to death, that we might be acquitted at the judgment-seat of God; yea, that he suffered his blessed body to be nailed on the cross — that he might fix thereon the handwriting of our sins; and hath also taken upon himself the curse due to us, that he might fill us with his blessings: and hath humbled himself unto the deepest reproach and pains of hell, both in body and soul, on the tree of the cross, when he cried out with a loud voice, "My God, my God! why hast thou forsaken me?" that we might be accepted of God and never be forsaken of him. . . .[39]

---

38. Calvin, *Institutes of the Christian Religion*, Book IV.17.2, p. 1362.
39. "Form for the Administration of the Lord's Supper," in *The Psalter*, p. 61.

Contemporary Praxis

A Brief History

The current diversity in the way in which we celebrate the Lord's Supper has its roots in the history of the Protestant churches. Two aspects play an important role in this: first, the theological criticism regarding the interpretation of the remembrance of Christ in the classical Reformed communion rite, and, second, the rise of the ecumenical movement in the twentieth century.

Through the centuries the criticism regarding the Reformed emphasis on instruction increased. The classical doctrine of atonement in particular, as expressed in the "remembrance of Christ," was a key issue in this criticism. The emerging liberal theology no longer felt at ease with the "atonement through the cross of Christ." Because of the ongoing disenchantment with reality, there was little appreciation for the unique meaning of ritual acts. The liberal Protestants distanced themselves further and further from the Roman Catholic tradition and became Zwinglian in their view of the sacrament.

Liturgical renewal movements, however, underscored the value of the ecclesial tradition and appealed to the early church. In the twentieth century, ecumenical encounters contributed to the new appreciation for classical liturgical forms, particularly with regard to the Lord's Supper. In the Netherlands a Protestant ecumenical praxis of communion developed. The ecumenical movement played an important role in this. The first attempts in this direction are found in the *Dienstboek voor de Nederlandse Hervormde Kerk in ontwerp* that dates from 1955. But a completely new Protestant ecumenical liturgy appeared only with the publication of the *Oecumenisch Ordinarium* in 1968. These two documents, the *Dienstboek* from 1955 and the *Oecumenisch Ordinarium* from 1968, are significant milestones that allow us to understand the current praxis.

The Dutch Reformed *Dienstboek* of 1955 contains five different communion liturgies. The diversity, therefore, has a long tradition. The Dutch Reformed Church knew a number of different ways to celebrate the Lord's Supper. In addition to the classical Reformed rite, the *Dienstboek* presents a very short liturgical rite (Order 2) in which the didactic element is quite short. It cites only the Words of Institution and a new, brief, reformulated remembrance of Christ. According to A. F. N. Lekkerkerker, this rite has its roots in the liberal tradition.[40] The typical Calvinistic self-examination

---

40. Lekkerkerker, *Kanttekeningen bij het Hervormde Dienstboek*, vol. 3, p. 175.

with the excommunication of the unrepentant has disappeared. The remembrance of Christ is maintained, but is formulated through other theological concepts. Remarkably enough, the liturgical format of the celebration remains intact. Apparently, there were few major objections to the way in which the celebration itself was formatted. It seems that the criticism was particularly focused on the self-examination and the manner in which the remembrance was formulated. In this new rite (Order 2 in the *Dienstboek*), the remembrance is expressed in these words:

> Therefore, brothers and sisters, we shall eat the bread and drink the wine, with praise and thanks to Him, who shed His blood for us and suffered death for us, so that through the Holy Spirit we might enjoy true communion with Him, and, while expecting the coming of God's kingdom, might already now share in eternal life, as children of God and as partakers in this glory; also, that through the Spirit we might be members of one body, united together in brotherly love. To that purpose, may the almighty, merciful God and Father of our Lord Jesus Christ help us through His Holy Spirit. Amen.[41]

In these words the emphasis is indeed on the suffering and death of Christ, but not in terms of sacrifice and atonement for sin. The eschatological expectation is expressed in terms of eternal life, and of being children of God. The unity is confessed in terms of brotherly love. The remembrance is formulated in a humanizing terminology, avoiding doctrinal vocabulary. It should be noted, however, that the theological criticism regarding the didactic part of the classical Reformed communion rite did not originate in the twentieth century.[42] In the liberal congregations of the Dutch Reformed Church, the "supper" was celebrated only on Good Friday, and the remembrance, very intentionally, was no longer placed in the context of the despised "blood theology." C. B. Burger says, "The worshippers assembled around the table in order to experience something of Jesus' suffering on the cross, and to focus their thoughts especially on the tragic aspects, on the elements of innocence and example." Crucial aspects of the celebration were that it took place around the table and that it was close to Good Friday. Some liberal churches went still further by limiting their observance even more or by doing away with it altogether, as Burger explains: "While they did not know what to do with

---

41. Order 2, *Dienstboek* (1955), p 93.
42. See, for instance, E. F. Kruijf, *Liturgiek* (Groningen: Wolters, 1901), pp. 153-59.

Celebrating the Lord's Supper

the doctrine of the church and the evangelical kerygma, the abhorrence of magical ritual and irrational symbolism resulted in the fact that in many such liberal congregations the Communion was given only a very limited role, if it was not discontinued altogether. Some of these liberal congregations were consistent and no longer celebrated the Lord's Supper."[43]

Order 3 in the *Dienstboek* shows how some experimentation was allowed in the development of an ecumenical format. The *Prefatio* (as Table Prayer), preceded by the salutation and the *Sursum Corda*, is introduced, with the possibility of using different wordings, depending on the Sunday of the Christian Year. There is more room for texts that are sung, such as the Sanctus and the Agnus Dei. It should be noted that in 1955 the Words of Institution did not yet function as part of the Table Prayer; they were read as a Scripture quotation.

The *Oecumenisch Ordinarium* appeared in 1968 in Amsterdam. It was not an official publication of the church; it was initiated by the Van der Leeuw Foundation. A special characteristic of the liturgical order is the attention given to the musical element. The *Ordinarium* manifests a number of differences. The major change, when compared to the Reformed communion tradition, is that the remembrance of Christ and the Words of Institution in this rite have become part of the Table Prayer. This is theologically supported by referring to "anamnetic prayer." At the same time, as a result of the stress on the Israelite character of prayer, the emphasis shifts towards thanksgiving, away from the Roman Catholic idea of consecration: "Remembering through thanksgiving means that we survey the great deeds of God and contemplate in depth the history of salvation. . . ."[44] The thought is that, with the introduction of the Table Prayer, an ancient ecclesial tradition is restored. Simultaneously, a correction is made with regard to the Roman Catholic liturgy by emphasizing the Jewish roots of Christian worship. The structure of the Lord's Supper is as follows:

- Invitation
- Table Prayer (the main thanksgiving)
    Responsive statements
    Prefatio

---

43. C. B. Burger, "Hoe staan de vrijzinnigen tegenover het avondmaal?," in *Jaarboek voor de eredienst* (The Hague: Boekencentrum, 1959), pp. 73-74.

44. *Proeve van een oecumenisch ordinarium. Toelichting en verantwoording* (Amsterdam: Prof. Dr. G. van der Leeuw Stichting, 1968), p. 35.

>   Closing with Sanctus and Benedictus
>   Words of Institution
>   *Anamnesis* (issuing into the *Maranatha*)
>   *Epiclesis*
>   Our Father
> - Salutation
> - Agnus Dei (during the breaking of the bread)
> - Communion of bread and wine
> - Psalm 103 or hymn of Simeon
> - Dismissal and blessing

A new milestone is reached in the liturgy of the Lord's Supper in the Protestant churches in the Netherlands with the publication of the *Dienstboek een proeve. Schrift, maaltijd, gebed* (1998). This book contains two detailed liturgies for the Lord's Supper. First, it presents the Protestant ecumenical celebration in the form of the Table Prayer, and, second, it offers an instructional form inspired by the classical Reformed tradition. In the theological argumentation, two motifs which are characteristic of the liturgical movement in the Netherlands are once again prominent: emphasis on the anamnetic thanksgiving and attention to the Jewish roots. "The Supper of the Lord is characterized by remembering with thanksgiving, to which the Scriptures constantly admonish us and by which the church moves in the tracks of the synagogue. God's salvific acts are in the center."[45] Apparently, in this tradition there is little understanding of the Hellenistic background of the Lord's Supper.

Communion in Keeping with the Mystery of Christ

Both the classical Reformed format and the Protestant ecumenical format for the celebration of the Lord's Supper follow a set pattern. This is particularly true for the classical Reformed celebration, since the liturgical texts and acts are almost unchanged and are a part of every celebration. The hymns and the Scripture readings may vary, but the instruction, the wording of the prayers, and the texts used at the distribution are fixed. In the Protestant ecumenical celebrations, the structure is fixed and some prescribed wording is used, but

---

45. *Dienstboek een proeve. Schrift, maaltijd, gebed* (Zoetermeer: Boekencentrum, 1998), Comments, p. 885.

considerable variation is possible with regard to the Table Prayer (depending on the Sunday of the Christian Year). In the classical Reformed tradition, the symbolic meaning of the act with bread and wine is less ambiguous. The instruction — as repeated with every celebration — provides for the interpretation of the remembrance of Christ and the sacramental act.[46] The document provides an unequivocal *hermeneutical rule* (and excludes in any case the idea that the Lord's Supper is a sacrificial act by the church). Still, we should not regard the classical Reformed Form as a purely hermeneutical rule. It also introduces a *holy act*. It describes the required attitude for participation in communion and the spiritual impact of communion. Because of the unequivocality of the stipulated interpretation, a strong tradition is established. The frequent repetition establishes an environment that regulates and shapes the personal experience. In a similar way this also occurs in the *Missale Romanum*. The set formulas of the *Canon* prayer and the ever-repeated ceremonial acts (such as making the sign of the cross and using incense) are fixed identifications for believers and provide a structure for piety. In that respect, the Protestant ecumenical celebration has a much more flexible structure. In contrast with the classical Reformed celebration, there is no set pattern for the interpretation of the remembrance of Christ. The explicit instruction is lacking. The remembrance of Christ, of course, is not absent, but it has become part of the Table Prayer and thus does not primarily function as providing the correct interpretation. Moreover, the Table Prayers vary, depending on the Christian Year, which results in a broader variety of meaning being attached to the remembrance. Unlike the Roman Catholic Eucharist, the Protestant ecumenical celebration does not have a strong sacramental tradition in the consciousness of the congregation. As a result, there is little idea of communion as a sacred ritual act.

In the Protestant churches, the variation only continues to increase. There still exist fixed communion traditions — in particular, classical Reformed celebrations and "high church" Protestant ecumenical celebrations — but mixed forms are now most common. In addition, we see an increasing number of celebrations with a minimum of prescribed texts, while the minister speaks of the remembrance of Christ in words of her own choice that often have a personal ring to them. This not only means that there are many different versions of how the remembrance of Christ is interpreted; it also raises the question of the devotion of those who partake. What happens,

---

46. Cf. Rainer Volp, *Liturgik*, vol. 1 (Gütersloh: Gütersloher Verlagshaus Gerd Mohn, 1994), pp. 135, 136.

from a religious perspective, when communion is celebrated? What is the specifically religious dimension in the communion liturgy and in the actual communion? How do people experience communion with Christ?

When the congregations assemble, the texts, symbols, and acts have a special kind of impact. Manfred Josuttis points out that we should not interpret this effect purely hermeneutically. By participating in a worship service, people enter the sphere of the sacred.[47] Celebrating the Lord's Supper together is a performative act that evokes and realizes a religious effect. This impact is directly related to Jesus Christ. In Chapter 3 we saw that the Christ event is a mystery, and that the *pneuma* is the connecting link of Christ's active presence in our midst. This implies that the appropriation of Christ, his involvement in the human sphere, the contextual relevancy of atonement, and so on are at issue in the liturgical acts with bread and wine. This demands diversity, a plurality of forms and a palette of different colors. Eating and drinking are social activities, and this social dimension must not be fossilized in a ritual act. In the celebration of the Lord's Supper, the mystery of Christ acquires a *living presence.* This happens in a receptivity of faith. However, it remains important that the liturgical acts put Christ in the spotlight. In that sense the communion liturgy has confessional characteristics. The celebration is about the true God and about the remembrance of Christ. Therefore, the Table Prayer must in any case have a Trinitarian structure, and the instructional part of the liturgy must cite the Words of Institution and focus on the remembrance of Christ. These are the constitutive elements of how the church celebrates the Lord's Supper. That is why the free, spontaneous formatting of the Table Prayer and of the remembrance of Christ carries a great risk. For it raises the question of whether the confession of the church is given adequate attention. Indeed, could the subjective intention not easily become prominent at the expense of the institutional ecclesial connection? This question must continuously be asked. At the same time, it illustrates the vulnerability of the Protestant position. We have noted that the early Reformation rites eliminated the *Canon* (and thus the Table Prayer). The Words of Institution were followed immediately by communion. Prior to the citing of the Words of Institution, a short instruction was given and a few prayers were offered. Because of the emphasis on communion, there was no elaborate cycle of prayers and no fixed text for the remembrance. The liturgy of Zwingli in his *Action* (1525) was particularly sober. Later, Calvin

---

47. Manfred Josuttis, *Die Einführung in das Leben. Pastoraltheologie zwischen Phänomenologie und Spiritualität* (Gütersloh: Kaiser Verlag, 1996), pp. 95-99.

added the self-examination and provided extensive instructions regarding the remembrance of Christ. As a result, the celebration became more stylized. This meant that those Protestants who wanted a more informal way of celebrating the Lord's Supper might find support in the early Reformation liturgy, specifically in that of Zwingli.

I would, however, like to add a final remark. The celebration of the Lord's Supper finds its center in the mystery of the communion with Christ. It is all about participation in an event that supercedes the subjective faith experience and the tangible emblems of bread and wine. We are touched by a transcendent reality: salvation in Christ. For that reason we can speak of the *Holy* Communion. This does not imply that the liturgical acts are in themselves holy acts, but *the sacred does happen — it touches us* in the sense that the congregation that celebrates the Lord's Supper participates in the redemption in Christ. The cross and the resurrection are the foundation; the kingdom of God forms the horizon. The communion liturgy — whether in the format of an instruction embedded in praise or in that of the Table Prayer — must ensure that the celebrating church remains focused on the *mystery of Christ*. This is the church's responsibility that finds expression in the liturgical format of the Lord's Supper. When this awareness is present, form and freedom, and script and Spirit, are no longer played off against each other, but are mutually enriching.

Bibliography

Aland, K. *Die Säuglingstaufe im Neuen Testament und in der Alten Kirche.* Munich: Kaiser Verlag, 1961.
Albrecht, Christoph. *Einführung in die Liturgik.* Göttingen: Vandenhoeck & Ruprecht, 1989.
———. *Schleiermachers Liturgik.* Göttingen: Vandenhoeck & Ruprecht, 1963.
Allen, Ronald J. *Hearing the Sermon: Relationship/Content/Feeling.* St. Louis: Chalice Press, 2004.
———. "Teaching." In *The New Interpreter's Handbook of Preaching,* ed. Paul Scott Wilson. Nashville: Abingdon Press, 2008.
———. *The Teaching Sermon.* Nashville: Abingdon Press, 1995.
Allen, Ronald J., and John S. McClure, eds. *Listening to Listeners: Homiletical Case Studies.* St. Louis: Chalice Press, 2004.
Allmen, J. J. von. *Worship: Its Theology and Practice.* London: Oxford University Press, 1965.
Althaus, Paul. *Der Brief an die Römer. Das Neue Testament Deutsch.* Göttingen: Vandenhoeck & Ruprecht, 1949.
Audi, Robert. "Belief, Faith, and Acceptance." *International Journal of Philosophy of Religion* 63 (2008): 87-102.
Baelz, Peter. *Does God Answer Prayers?* London: Darton, Longman & Todd, 1982.
Baptism, Eucharist, and Ministry, 1982-1990. Geneva: World Council of Churches, 1982.
Barnard, Marcel. "Doop en belijdenis." In *De weg van de liturgie. Tradities, achtergronden, praktijk,* ed. M. Barnard and F. G. Immink. Zoetermeer: Meinema, 2008, pp. 281-302.
———. "Late Modern Rhythm and the Renewal of Worship." In *At the Crossroads of Art and Religion,* ed. Hetty Zock. Leuven: Peeters, 2008, pp. 173-87.
Barth, Karl. *Church Dogmatics.* 4 vols. Ed. Thomas F. Torrance, trans. Geoffrey W. Bromiley. Edinburgh: T&T Clark, 1936-1969.

Bibliography

———. *The Doctrine of God.* In *Church Dogmatics,* II.i. Ed. Thomas F. Torrance, trans. Geoffrey W. Bromiley. Edinburgh: T&T Clark, 1976.
———. *The Doctrine of of God.* In *Church Dogmatics,* II.ii. Ed. Thomas F. Torrance, trans. Geoffrey W. Bromiley. Edinburgh: T&T Clark, 1970.
———. "Die Gemeindemässigkeit der Predigt." In Gert Hummel, *Aufgabe der Predigt.* Darmstadt: Wissenschaftliche Buchgesellschaft, 1971, pp. 165-78.
———. *Predigten 1914.* Republished by Ursula and Jochen Fähler. Zurich: Theologischer Verlag, 1974.
Bartow, Charles L. *God's Human Speech: A Practical Theology of Proclamation.* Grand Rapids: Wm. B. Eerdmans, 1997.
Bass, Dorothy C., and Craig Dykstra, eds. *For Life Abundant: Practical Theology, Theological Education, and Christian Ministry.* Grand Rapids: Wm. B. Eerdmans, 2008.
Bavinck, H. *Reformed Dogmatics.* Grand Rapids: Baker Academic, 2003-2008.
Becking, Bob, and Marjo C. A. Korpel, eds. *The Crisis of Israelite Religion: Transformation of Religious Tradition in Exilic and Post-Exilic Times.* Leiden: Brill, 1999.
Beker, J. Christiaan. *Paul the Apostle: The Triumph of God in Life and Thought.* Minneapolis: Fortress Press, 1980.
Berkhof, Hendrikus. *Christian Faith,* rev. ed. Grand Rapids: Wm. B. Eerdmans, 1986.
Best, Thomas F., and Dagmar Heller. *Eucharistic Worship in Ecumenical Context: The Lima Liturgy — and Beyond.* Geneva: WCC Publications, 1998.
Bieritz, Karl-Heinz. *Das Kirchenjahr. Feste, Gedenk- und Feiertage in Geschichte und Gegenwart.* Munich: C. H. Beck, 1991.
Bieritz, Karl-Heinz, and Hans Christoph Schmidt-Lauber, eds. *Handbuch der Liturgik. Liturgiewissenschaft in Theologie und Praxis der Kirche.* Göttingen: Vandenhoeck & Ruprecht, 1995.
Blankenburg, Walter, and Karl Ferdinand Müller, eds. *Leiturgia.* Volumes 1 & 2. Kassel: Stauda, 1954.
Boendermaker, Joop. "Maaltijd van de Heer; Oecumenisch Protestant." In *De weg van de liturgie. Traditles, achtergronden, praktijk,* ed. M. Barnard and F. G. Immink. Zoetermeer: Meinema, 2008.
Bohren, Rudolf. *Predigtlehre.* Munich: Kaiser Verlag, 1971.
Boon, R. *De joodse wortels van de christelijke eredienst.* Amsterdam: Prof. G. van der Leeuw Stichting, 1973.
Braaten, Carl E. *That All May Believe: A Theology of the Gospel and the Mission of the Church.* Grand Rapids: Wm. B. Eerdmans, 2008.
Brakel, Wilhelmus à. *Redelijke Godsdienst,* vol. 1. Nijkerk: n.p., 1870.
Brienen, T. *De liturgie bij Johannes Calvijn.* Kampen: Kok, 1987.
Bronsveld, A. W. *De evangelische gezangen, Verzameld in de Jaren 1803-1805, en in gebruik bij de Nederlandse Hervormde Kerk. Historisch-letterkundig onderzoek.* Utrecht: Kemink & Zoon, 1917.

BIBLIOGRAPHY

Brueggemann, Walter. *An Introduction to the Old Testament: The Canon and Christian Imagination.* Louisville: Westminster John Knox Press, 2003.

———. "The Preacher as Scribe." In *Inscribing the Text: Sermons and Prayers of Walter Brueggemann,* ed. Anna Carter Florence. Minneapolis: Fortress Press, 2004, pp. 5-19.

———. *Theology of the Old Testament: Testimony, Dispute, Advocacy.* Minneapolis: Fortress Press, 1997.

———. *The Threat of Life: Sermons on Pain, Power, and Weakness.* Ed. Charles L. Campbell. Minneapolis: Fortress Press, 1996.

Brunner, Peter. "Zur Lehre vom Gottesdienst der im Namen Jesu Versammelten Gemeinde." In *Leiturgia,* vol. 1, ed. Karl Ferdinand Müller and Walter Blankenburg. Kassel: Stauda, 1954, pp. 83-361.

Bultmann, Rudolf. *Das Evangelium des Johannes.* Göttingen: Vandenhoeck & Ruprecht, 1968.

———. *Glauben und Verstehen.* Tübingen: J. C. B. Mohr, 1960.

Burger, C. B. "Hoe staan de vrijzinnigen tegenover het avondmaal?" In *Jaarboek voor de eredienst.* The Hague: Boekencentrum, 1959, pp. 72-81.

Bürki, Bruno. "Gottesdienst im Reformierten Kontext." In *Handbuch der Liturgik. Liturgiewissenschaft in Theologie und Praxis der Kirche,* ed. Karl-Heinz Bieritz and Hans Christoph Schmidt-Lauber. Göttingen: Vandenhoeck & Ruprecht, 1995, pp. 162-74.

Buttrick, David. *Homiletic: Moves and Structures.* Philadelphia: Fortress Press, 1987.

Buttrick, George Arthur. *Prayer.* Nashville/New York: Abingdon-Cokesbury Press, 1941.

Byars, Ronald P. *The Future of Protestant Worship: Beyond the Worship Wars.* Louisville: Westminster John Knox Press, 2002.

———. *Lift Your Hearts on High: Eucharistic Prayer in the Reformed Tradition.* Louisville: Westminster John Knox Press, 2005.

Calvin, John. *Institutes of the Christian Religion.* 4 vols. London: SCM Press, 1961.

Campbell, Charles L. *Preaching Jesus: New Directions for Homiletics in Hans Frei's Postliberal Theology.* Grand Rapids: Wm. B. Eerdmans, 1997.

"The Catechism, or Method of Instruction in the Christian Religion." In *The Psalter: With Doctrinal Standards, Liturgy, Church Order, and Added Chorale Section.* Grand Rapids: Wm. B. Eerdmans, 1984, pp. 1-18.

Childers, Jana. *Performing the Word: Preaching as Theater.* Nashville: Abingdon Press, 1999.

Childs, Brevard. *Biblical Theology of the Old and New Testaments.* London: Xpress Reprints, 1993.

Clements-Jewery, Philip. *Intercessory Prayer: Modern Theology, Biblical Teaching, and Philosophical Thought.* Aldershot/Burlington: Ashgate, 2005.

Cobb, Peter G. "The History of the Christian Year." In *The Study of Liturgy,* ed. Ches-

lyn Jones, Geoffrey Wainwright, and Edward Yarnold, S.J. London: Oxford University Press, 1987, pp. 403-18.
Constitution on the Sacred Liturgy: Sacrosanctum Concilium.
Craddock, Fred B. *As One without Authority: Essays on Inductive Preaching.* Nashville: Chalice Press, 1979.
Crichton, J. D. "A Theology of Worship." In *The Study of Liturgy,* ed. Cheslyn Jones, Geoffrey Wainwright, and Edward Yarnold, S.J. London: Oxford University Press, 1987, pp. 1-30.
Cullmann, Oscar. *Christ and Time: The Primitive Christian Conception of Time and History.* London: SCM Press, 1951.
Dalmais, Irénée Henri. "The Liturgy as Celebration." In *Primary Sources of Liturgical Theology,* ed. Dwight W. Vogel. Collegeville, Md.: Liturgical Press, 2000, pp. 18-26.
Dankbaar, W. F. *De sacramentsleer van Calvijn.* Amsterdam: H. J. Paris, 1941.
———. *Hervormers en Humanisten.* Amsterdam: T. Bolland, 1978.
Davis, Henry Grady. *Design for Preaching.* Philadelphia: Muhlenberg Press, 1958.
Dienstboek een proeve: Schrift, maaltijd, gebed. Zoetermeer: Boekencentrum, 1998.
Dienstboek voor de Nederlandse Hervormde Kerk in ontwerp. The Hague: Boekencentrum, 1955.
Dingemans, G. D. J. *Als hoorder Onder de hoorders . . . Een hermeneutische homiletiek.* Kampen: Kok, 1991.
Dodd, C. H. *The Interpretation of the Fourth Gospel.* Cambridge: Cambridge University Press, 1978.
Doop en belijdenis: Proeven voor de eredienst, aflevering 3. Zoetermeer: Boekencentrum, 1993.
Drews, Paul. "'Religiöse' Volkskunde: eine Aufgabe der Praktischen Theologie." In *Seelsorge. Texte zum gewandelten Verständnis und zur Praxis der Seelsorge in der Neuzeit,* ed. F. Wintzer. Munich: Gütersloher Verlagshaus, 1978, pp. 54-61.
Dykstra, Craig, and Dorothy C. Bass. "A Theological Understanding of Christian Practices." In *Practicing Theology: Beliefs and Practices in Christian Life,* ed. Miroslav Volf and Dorothy C. Bass. Grand Rapids: Wm. B. Eerdmans, 2002, pp. 13-32.
Edwards, O. C., Jr. *A History of Preaching.* Nashville: Abingdon Press, 2004.
Evangelische liedbundel. Zoetermeer: Boekencentrum, 1999.
"Form for the Administration of Baptism." In *The Psalter: With Doctrinal Standards, Liturgy, Church Order, and Added Chorale Section.* Grand Rapids: Wm. B. Eerdmans, 1947, 1984, pp. 55-58.
"Form for the Administration of the Lord's Supper." In *The Psalter: With Doctrinal Standards, Liturgy, Church Order, and Added Chorale Section.* Grand Rapids: Wm. B. Eerdmans, 1927, pp. 60-63.
Forsyth, P. T. *The Soul of Prayer: A Christian Interpretation of the Old Testament.* 1916; reprint: London, 1998.

BIBLIOGRAPHY

Frederikse, Th. C., ed. *Klare wijn*. The Hague: Boekencentrum, 1967.
Gennep, F. O. van. "Het is beslist." In *Waarlijk opgestaan! Een discussie over de opstanding van Jezus Christus*, ed. F. O. van Gennep and R. Zuurmond. Baarn: Ten Have, 1989.
―――. *Naam geven wat ik zoek, preken*. Baarn: Ten Have, 1991.
Gerretsen, J. H. *Liturgie*. Nijmegen: Ten Hoet, 1912.
Grözinger, Albrecht. *Homiletik*. Gütersloh: Gütersloher Verlagshaus, 2008.
Guardini, Romano. "An Open Letter." In *Foundations in Ritual Studies: A Reader for Students of Christian Worship*, ed. Paul Bradshaw and John Mellow. Grand Rapids: Baker Academic, 2007, pp. 3-8.
―――. *Liturgie und Liturgische Bildung*. Mainz/Paderborn: Grünewald Schöningh, 1992.
―――. *De geest de liturgie*. Turnhout: Brepols, 1944. ET: *The Spirit of the Liturgy*. New York: Crossroad, 1998.
Gunning, J. H., Jr. *Blikken in de Openbaring*, vol. 3. Rotterdam: Höveker, 1929.
―――. *De gezangenkwestie in de Nederlandse Hervormde Kerk*. Utrecht: Oosthoek, 1910.
―――. *Onze eredienst. Opmerkingen over het liturgisch element in den gereformeerden cultus*. Gröningen: Wolters, 1890.
Hageman, Howard G. *Pulpit and Table*. Richmond, Va.: Wipf & Stock, 1962.
Hartly, Peter. *Interpersonal Communication*. London/New York: Routledge, 1999.
Hartog, J. *Geschiedenis van de predikkunde in de protestantse kerk van Nederland*. Utrecht: K. H. Schadd, 1887.
Heering, G. J. *Geloof en openbaring*, 2 vols. Arnhem: Van Loghum Slaterus, 1935-1937.
Heiler, Friedrich. *Mysterium Caritatis. Predigten für das Ganze Kirchenjahr*. Munich: Reinhardt Federmann Verlag, 1949.
―――. *Prayer: A Study in the History and Psychology of Religion*. New York: Oxford University Press, 1958.
Heimbrock, Hans-Günther. *Spuren Gottes Wahrnehmen. Phänomenologisch Inspirierte Predigten und Texte zum Gottesdienst*. Stuttgart: Kohlhammer, 2003.
Hengel, Martin. *Paulus und Jakobus. Kleine Schriften* iii, Wissenschaftliche Untersuchungen zum Neuen Testament. Tübingen: Mohr Siebeck, 2002.
Heppe, Heinrich, and Ernst Bizer. *Reformed Dogmatics*. London: Allen & Unwin Ltd., 1958.
Herbst, Wolfgang, ed. *Evangelischer Gottesdienst. Quellen zu seiner Geschichte*. Göttingen: Vandenhoeck & Ruprecht, 1992.
Hermelink, Jan. "Ausmahlen und Hindurchsehen. Das diskurssemiotische Konzept des 'Mentalen Bildes' in der Predigtarbeit." In *Predigen im Plural. Homiletische Aspekte*, ed. U. Pohl-Patalong and F. Muchlinsky. Hamburg: Eb-Verlag, 2001, pp. 36-45.
Hilkert, Mary Catherine. *Naming Grace: Preaching and the Sacramental Imagination*. New York: Continuum, 1997.

Bibliography

Hoekstra, T. *Gereformeerde homiletiek.* Wageningen: Zomer & Keuning, 1926.
Hogan, Lucy. "Creation of Form." In *Teaching Preaching as a Christian Practice,* ed. Thomas G. Long and Leonora Tubbs Tisdale. Minneapolis: Fortress Press, 1997, pp. 134-48.
———. "Rethinking Persuasion." *Homiletic: A Review of Publications in Religious Communication* (Winter 1999).
Hogan, Lucy Lind, and Robert Reid. *Connecting with the Congregation: Rhetoric and the Art of Preaching.* Nashville: Abingdon Press, 1999.
Hurtado, Larry W. *Lord Jesus Christ: Devotion to Jesus in Earliest Christianity.* Grand Rapids: Wm. B. Eerdmans, 2003.
Hyperius, Andreas. *De Formandis Concionibus Sacris, Sive De Interpretatione Scripturam Populari.* Basel, 1579.
Immens, Petrus. *De godvruchtige avondmaalsganger.* Nijkerk: I. J. Malga, 1874.
Immink, F. Gerrit. "Homiletics: The Current Debate." *International Journal of Practical Theology* 8, no. 1 (2004).
———. "Een methode van preekvoorbereiding." In *Als een leerling leren preken. Preekvoorbereiding stapsgewijs,* ed. Henk van der Meulen. Zoetermeer: Boekencentrum, 2008, pp. 9-20.
———. *Faith: A Practical Theological Reconstruction.* Grand Rapids: Wm. B. Eerdmans, 2005.
———. "Heilig avondmaal: klassiek-gereformeerd." In *De weg van de liturgie,* ed. M. Barnard and F. G. Immink. Zoetermeer: Meinema, 2008, pp. 245-56.
———. "In gesprek met de 'New Homiletic.' Literatuurbericht Homiletiek." *Praktische Theologie* 3 (2001): 370-93.
———. "Introduction: Bearer of the Word." In *The New Interpreter's Handbook of Preaching,* ed. Paul Scott Wilson. Nashville: Abingdon Press, 2008, pp. 433-35.
———. "Kun je alles aan God vragen? Praktisch-theologische notities bij het vraaggebed." *Praktische Theologie* 4 (2004).
———. "'Missio Dei' in Preaching: God Language and Human Receptivity." In *Preaching as God's Mission,* ed. Tsuneaki Kato. Tokyo: Kyo Bun Kwan, 1999, pp. 116-35.
———. "Theological Concepts in Empirical Research." In *Dreaming the Land: Theologies of Resistance and Hope,* ed. Friedrich Schweitzer and Hans-Georg Ziebertz. Berlin: LIT Verlag, 2007, pp. 190-98.
Iwand, Hans-Joachim. *Predigt-Meditationen I.* Göttingen: Vandenhoeck & Ruprecht, 1977.
Jasper, G. J., and R. C. D. Cuming. *Prayers of the Eucharist.* New York: Oxford University Press, 1980.
Jenny, Markus. *Die Einheit des Abendmahlsgottesdienstes bei den Elsässischen und Schweitzerischen Reformatoren.* Zurich: Zwingli Verlag, 1968.
Jeremias, J. *Die Kindertaufe in den Ersten Vier Jahrhunderten.* Göttingen: Vandenhoeck & Ruprecht, 1958.

Jeter, Joseph R., Jr. "Preaching in a Diverse World." In *The New Interpreter's Handbook of Preaching,* ed. Paul Scott Wilson. Nashville: Abingdon Press, 2008.
Jonge, H. J. de. "The Early History of the Lord's Supper." In *The Earliest History of the Christian Gathering,* ed. Valery A. Alikin. Leiden: Brill, 2010.
———. "Ontstaan en ontwikkeling van het geloof in Jezus' opstanding." In *Waarlijk opgestaan! Een discussie over de opstanding van Jezus Christus,* ed. F. O. van Gennep and R. Zuurmond. Baarn: Ten Have, 1989.
Jonge, Marinus de. *Jesus, the Servant-Messiah.* New Haven: Yale University Press, 1991.
Jonker, H. *En tóch preken.* Nijkerk: Callenbach, 1973.
Josuttis, Manfred. *Der Weg in das Leben. Eine Einführung in den Gottesdienst.* Munich: Kaiser Verlag, 1991.
———. *Die Einführung in das Leben. Pastoraltheologie zwischen Phänomënologie und Spiritualität.* Gütersloh: Kaiser Verlag, 1996.
———. *Religion als Handwerk. Zur Handlungslogik Spiritueller Methoden.* Gütersloh: Kaiser Verlag, 2002.
Jüngel, Eberhard. ". . . ein Bißchen Meschugge . . ." In *Predigten und biblische Besinnungen.* Stuttgart: Radius Verlag, 2001.
Jungmann, Josef Andreas. *De eredienst van de Katholieke Kerk.* Roermond: Romen, 1959.
———. *Missarum Sollemnia,* vol 1. Kasterlee: De Vroente, 1966.
Kay, James F. *Christus Praesens.* Grand Rapids: Wm. B. Eerdmans, 1994.
———. *Preaching and Theology.* St. Louis: Chalice Press, 2007.
Kittel, Gerhard. *Theological Dictionary of the New Testament.* Grand Rapids: Wm. B. Eerdmans, 1985.
Kloppenburg, Wim. "Het kerklied." In *De weg van de liturgie. Tradities, achtergronden, praktijk,* ed. M. Barnard and F. G. Immink. Zoetermeer: Boekencentrum, 2008, pp. 266-80.
Kohlbrugge, H. F. *Is het ongelooflijk dat God de doden opwekt?* 1862; reprint: Zoetermeer: Boekencentrum, 1996.
Koopmans, J. *Het kerkelijk jaar.* Wageningen: Veenman, 1941.
Kooten, George H. van. *Het oecumenisch leesrooster (1977-2010): Geschiedenis, filosofie en impact.* Gröningen: Instituut voor Liturgiewetenschap, Rijksuniversiteit Gröningen, 2007.
———. *Paul's Anthropology in Context.* Tübingen: Mohr Siebeck, 2008.
Kooten, Geurt Henk van. *Paulus en de kosmos. Het vroege christendom te midden van de andere Grieks-Romeinse filosofieën.* Zoetermeer: Boekencentrum, 2002.
Korte, Z. de. *De misliturgie.* Antwerp: G. Tielenburg, 1949.
Kruijf, E. F. *Liturgiek.* Gröningen: Wolters, 1901.
Kuyper, Abraham. *Our Worship.* Grand Rapids: Wm. B. Eerdmans, 2009.
Lange, Ernst. *Die Verbesserliche Welt: Möglichkeiten Christlicher Rede Erprobt an der Geschichte vom Propheten Jona.* Berlin: Kreuz Verlag, 1968.

Leeuw, G. van der. *Liturgiek*. Nijkerk: Callenbach, 1946.
———. *Sacramentstheologie*. Nijkerk: Callenbach, 1949.
Lekkerkerker, A. F. N. *Kanttekeningen bij het Hervormde Dienstboek*, 4 vols. The Hague: Boekencentrum, 1952-1956.
Lietaert Peerbolte, L. J. *Over heilige teksten en heilige huisjes*. Amsterdam: Vrije Universiteit, 2009.
Lietzmann, Hans. *Mass and the Lord's Supper: A Study in the History of the Liturgy*. Leiden: Brill, 1979.
Lindbeck, George A. *The Nature of Doctrine: Religion and Theology in a Postliberal Age*. Philadelphia: Westminster John Knox Press, 1984.
Linden, Carel ter. *Haghepreken*. Zoetermeer: Meinema, 1999.
Lischer, Richard. *The End of Words: The Language of Reconciliation in a Culture of Violence*. Grand Rapids: Wm. B. Eerdmans, 2005.
———. *A Theology of Preaching*. Eugene, Ore.: Wipf & Stock, 1992.
———. "Why I Am Not Persuasive." *Homiletic: A Review of Publications in Religious Communication* (Winter 1999).
Long, Thomas G. "A New Focus for Teaching Preaching." In *Teaching Preaching as a Christian Practice*, ed. Thomas G. Long and Leonora Tubbs Tisdale. Louisville: Westminster John Knox Press, 2008, pp. 3-17.
———. *The Witness of Preaching*. Louisville: Westminster John Knox Press, 1989.
Lose, David J. *Confessing Jesus Christ: Preaching in a Postmodern World*. Grand Rapids: Wm. B. Eerdmans, 2003.
Lowry, Eugene. *The Homiletical Plot: The Sermon as Narrative Art Form*. Louisville: John Knox Press, 2001.
Lukken, Gerard. *Rituals in Abundance: Critical Reflections on the Place, Form, and Identity of Christian Ritual in Our Culture*. Leuven: Peeters, 2005.
Luther, Martin. *D. Martin Luthers Werke: Kritische Gesamtausgabe*, vols. 45-49. Weimar: Böhlau, 1921.
———. *The Ninety-five Theses and Three Primary Works by Dr. Martin Luther*. Grand Rapids: Christian Classics Ethereal Library, 1885.
———. *Predigten über die Christusbotschaft*. Gütersloh: Gütersloher Verlagshaus Mohn, 1979.
McClure, John S. *Otherwise Preaching: A Postmodern Ethic for Homiletics*. St. Louis: Chalice Press, 2001.
Mensinga, J. A. M. *Verhandeling over de liturgische schriften der Nederlandse Hervormde Kerk*. The Hague: Thierry en Mensing, 1851.
Michel, Otto. *Der Brief an die Hebräer*. Göttingen: Vandenhoeck & Ruprecht, 1966.
———. *Der Brief an die Römer*. Göttingen: Vandenhoeck & Ruprecht, 1963.
Micron, Marten. *De Christlicke Ordinancien der Nederlantscher Ghemeinten te Londen (1554)*. Re-edited by Dr. W. F. Dankbaar. The Hague: M. Nijhof, 1956.
Miskotte, K. H. *De weg van het gebed*. The Hague: Boekencentrum, 1962.
———. *Het waagstuk der prediking*. The Hague: D. A. Daamen, 1941.

———. *Om het levende woord. Opstellen over de praktijk der exegese.* Kampen: Kok, 1973.
Moehn, W. H. Th. *God roept ons tot zijn dienst.* Kampen: Kok, 1996.
Mouw, Richard J., and Mark A. Noll, eds. *Wonderful Words of Life: Hymns in American Protestant History and Theology.* Grand Rapids: Wm. B. Eerdmans, 2004.
Muis, J. "The Truth of Metaphorical God-talk." *Scottish Journal of Theology* 63 (2010): 142-62.
Müller, Theophil. *Evangelischer Gottesdienst. Liturgische Vielfalt im Religiösen und Gesellschaftlichen Umfeld.* Stuttgart: Kohlhammer, 1993.
Mulligan, Mary Alice, Ronald J. Allen, Diane Turner-Sharazz, and Dawn Ottoni Wilhelm, eds. *Believing in Preaching: What Listeners Hear in Sermons.* St. Louis: Chalice Press, 2005.
Nauta, R. *Ik geloof het wel. Godsdienstpsychologische studies over mens en religie.* Assen: Van Gorcum, 1995.
Nicol, Martin. *Einander ins Bild Setzen. Dramaturgische Homiletik.* Göttingen: Vandenhoeck & Ruprecht, 2002.
Niebergall, A. "Die Geschichte der Christlichen Predigt." In *Leiturgia,* vol. 2, ed. Walter Blankenburg and Karl Ferdinand Müller. Kassel: Stauda, 1954, pp. 181-354.
Niebergall, Friedrich. "Die Moderne Predigt." In *Die Aufgabe der Predigt,* ed. Gert Hummel. Darmstadt: Wissenschaftliche Buchgesellschaft, 1971, pp. 9-74.
Niebuhr, H. Richard. *Faith on Earth.* New Haven: Yale University Press, 1989.
Nieman, James. "Why the Idea of Practice Matters." In *Teaching Preaching as a Christian Practice,* ed. Thomas G. Long and Leonora Tubbs Tisdale. Louisville: Westminster John Knox Press, 2008, pp. 18-40.
Noordmans, O. *Verzamelde werken,* vol. 8. Kampen: Kok, 1980.
Noort, E. "Reconstructie van de geschiedenis van Israël." *Nederlands Theologisch Tijdschrift* 58 (2004).
Onze hulp. Een gemeenteboekje. Amsterdam: Prof. Dr. G. van der Leeuw Stichting, 1978.
Oosterzee, J. J. van. *Practische theologie. Een handboek voor jeugdige godgeleerden.* Utrecht: Kemink, 1877.
Otto, Gert. *Rhetorische Predigtlehre. Ein Grundriss.* Mainz: Matthias Grünewald Verlag, 1999.
———. *Sprache als Hoffnung.* Munich: Kaiser Verlag, 1989.
Otto, Rudolf. *The Idea of the Holy: An Inquiry into the Non-Rational Factor in the Idea of the Divine.* London: Oxford University Press, 1958.
Parker, T. H. L. *Calvin's Preaching.* Louisville: Westminster John Knox Press, 1992.
Peels, H. G. L. "Helder en onbevangen. Een recent pleidooi voor een ambachtelijke exegese van het Oude Testament." *Theologia Reformata* 46 (2003).
Pleizier, Theo. *Religious Involvement in Hearing Sermons: A Grounded Theory Study in Empirical Theology and Homiletics.* Delft: Eburon, 2010.

Bibliography

Plüss, David. *Gottesdienst als Textinszenierung. Perspektiven einer Performativen Ästhetik des Gottesdienstes.* Zurich: Theologischer Verlag Zürich, 2007.
Pollanus, Valerandus. *Liturgia Sacra (1551-1555).* Newly published and edited by Dr. A. C. Honders. Leiden: Brill, 1970.
Proeve van een oecumenisch ordinarium. Toelichting en verantwoording. Amsterdam: Prof. Dr. G. van der Leeuw Stichting, 1968.
The Psalter: With Doctrinal Standards, Liturgy, Church Order, and Added Chorale Section. Grand Rapids: Wm. B. Eerdmans, 1947, 1984.
Ratzinger, Joseph (Pope Benedict XVI). *Jesus of Nazareth: From the Baptism in the Jordan to the Transfiguration.* New York: Doubleday, 2007.
Redman, Robb. *The Great Worship Awakening: Singing a New Song in the Postmodern Church.* San Francisco: Jossey-Bass, 2002.
Rengstorf, Carl Heinrich. "Didaskoo." In *Theological Dictionary of the New Testament,* ed. Gerhard Kittel. Grand Rapids: Wm. B. Eerdmans, 1985.
Ricoeur, Paul. *Interpretation Theory: Discourse and the Surplus of Meaning.* Fort Worth: Texas Christian University Press, 1976.
Rienstra, Debra, and Ron Rienstra. *Worship Words: Disciplining Language for Faithful Ministry.* Grand Rapids: Baker Academic, 2009.
Riesebrodt, Martin, and Stevan Rendall. *The Promise of Salvation: A Theory of Religion.* Chicago: University of Chicago Press, 2010.
Roest, Henk de. *Een huis voor de ziel. Gedachten over de kerk voor binnen en buiten.* Zoetermeer: Boekencentrum, 2010.
Rose, Lucy. *Sharing the Word: Preaching in the Round Table Church.* Louisville: Westminster John Knox Press, 1997.
Roukema, Riemer. *Jesus, Gnosis, and Dogma.* London: T&T Clark, 2010.
Ruler, A. A. van. *Ik geloof.* Nijkerk: Callenbach, 1971.
———. *Reformatorische opmerkingen in de ontmoeting met Rome.* Hilversum: Paul Brand, 1965.
———. "Structuurverschillen tussen het christologisch en het pneumatologisch gezichtspunt." in *Theologisch werk,* vol. 1. Nijkerk: Callenbach, 1969, pp. 175-90.
Schillebeeckx, Edward. *Jesus: An Experiment in Christology.* New York: Crossroad, 1985.
Schleiermacher, Friedrich. *Die Praktische Theologie nach den Grundsätzen der Evangelischen Kirche im Zusammenhang Dargestellt.* Berlin: Jacob Frerich, 1850; photographic reprint: Berlin/New York: De Gruyter, 1983.
———. *On Religion: Speeches to Its Cultured Despisers.* Cambridge: Cambridge University Press, 1996.
Scholten, J. H. *De leer der Hervormde Kerk in hare grondbeginselen, uit de bronnen voorgesteld en beoordeeld,* vol. 1. Leiden: P. Engels, 1874.
Schweitzer, Albert. *Die Mystik des Apostels Paulus.* Tübingen: Mohr Siebeck, 1930.
Schweitzer, J. *Reformierte Abendmahlsgestaltung in der Schau Zwinglis.* Basel: Reinhardt, 1954.

BIBLIOGRAPHY

———. *Zur Ordnung des Gottesdienstes in den nach Gottes Wort Reformierten Gemeinden der Deutschsprachigen Schweitz.* Zurich: Zwingli Verlag, 1944.
Second Helvetic Confession. Grand Rapids: Christian Classics Ethereal Library, n.d.
Seters, Arthur Van. *Preaching as a Social Act: Theology and Practice.* Nashville: Abingdon Press, 1988.
Smart, Ninian. *The Concept of Worship.* London: St. Martin's Press, 1972.
Stählin, Rudolf. "Die Geschichte des Christlichen Gottesdienstes." In *Leiturgia,* vol. 1, ed. Walter Blankenburg and Karl Ferdinand Müller. Kassel: Stauda, 1954, pp. 1-82.
Stählin, Wilhelm. "Der Wille zur Form" (1921). In *Evangelischer Gottesdienst. Quellen zu seiner Geschichte,* ed. Wolfgang Herbst. Göttingen: Vandenhoeck & Ruprecht, 1992, pp. 231-33.
Stewart, Robert B., ed. *The Resurrection of Jesus: John Dominic Crossan and N. T. Wright in Dialogue.* Minneapolis: Fortress Press, 2006.
Talstra, Eep. *Oude en nieuwe lezers. Een inleiding in de methoden van uitleg van het Oude Testament.* Kampen: Kok, 2002.
Taylor, Barbara Brown. *Home by Another Way.* Cambridge: Cowley Publications, 1999.
Taylor, Charles. *A Secular Age.* Cambridge: Belknap Press, 2007.
———. *Wat betekent religie vandaag?* Kapellen/Kampen: Pelckmans, 2003.
Theissen, Gerd. "Exegese und Theologie. Über Bedeutung und Funktion der Exegese in der Theologie." *Nederlands Theologisch Tijdschrift* 58 (2004).
Thiemann, Ronald F. *Revelation and Theology: The Gospel as Narrated Promise.* Notre Dame: University of Notre Dame Press, 1985.
Thompson, James W. *Preaching like Paul: Homiletical Wisdom for Today.* Louisville: Westminster John Knox Press, 2001.
Thurneysen, Eduard. "Die Aufgabe der Predigt." In *Die Aufgabe der Predigt,* ed. Gert Hummel. Darmstadt: Wissenschaftliche Buchgesellschaft, 1971, pp. 105-18.
Toorn, K. van der. *Scribal Culture and the Making of the Hebrew Bible.* Cambridge: Harvard University Press, 2007.
Troeger, Thomas. *Imagining the Sermon.* Nashville: Abingdon Press, 1990.
Troost, A. F. *Dichter bij het geheim. Leven en werk van Willem Barnard/Guillaume van der Graft.* Zoetermeer: Boekencentrum, 1998.
Tubbs Tisdale, Leonora. *Preaching as Local Theology and Folk Art.* Minneapolis: Fortress Press, 1997.
Vinet, A. *Homiletics; Or, The Theory of Preaching.* Edinburgh: T&T Clark, 1853.
Volp, Rainer. *Liturgik. Die Kunst Gott zu Feiern,* vol. 2: *Theorien und Gestaltung.* Gütersloh: Gütersloher Verlagshaus Gerd Mohn, 1994.
Vos, Cas. "Liturgische taal als metaforische taal." In *Nieuwe wegen in de liturgie,* ed. Marcel Barnard and N. A. Schuman. Zoetermeer: Meinema, 2002, pp. 80-89.
Vriezen, Th. C. *Hoofdlijnen der theologie van het Oude Testament.* Wageningen: H. Veenman, 1966.

Bibliography

Vrijlandt, M. A. *Liturgiek*. The Hague: Commissie voor de kerkmuziek, 1987.

Ward, Richard F. "Performative Language." In *The New Interpreter's Handbook of Preaching,* ed. Paul Scott Wilson. Nashville: Abingdon Press, 2008, pp. 234-38.

———. *Speaking of the Holy: The Art of Communication in Preaching*. St. Louis: Chalice Press, 2001.

Webber, Robert. *Planning Blended Worship: The Creative Mixture of Old and New.* Nashville: Abingdon Press, 1998.

Wegman, H. A. J. *Riten en mythen: Liturgie in de geschiedenis van het christendom.* Kampen: Kok, 1991.

White, James F. *Documents of Christian Worship: Descriptive and Interpretive Sources.* Louisville: Westminster John Knox Press, 1992.

Wilbur, Ellen, ed. *The Consolations of God: Great Sermons of Phillips Brooks*. Grand Rapids: Wm. B. Eerdmans, 2003.

Wilson, Paul Scott. *The Four Pages of the Sermon: A Guide to Biblical Preaching.* Nashville: Abingdon Press, 1999.

———. *The Practice of Preaching*. Nashville: Abingdon Press, 1995.

———, ed. *The New Interpreter's Handbook of Preaching*. Nashville: Abingdon Press, 2008.

Witvliet, John D. *Worship Seeking Understanding: Windows into Christian Practice.* Grand Rapids: Baker Academic, 2003.

Wright, N. T. *The Resurrection of the Son of God*. Minneapolis: Fortress Press, 2003.

Index of Subjects and Names

anamnesis, 145, 158, 220, 240, 248
atonement, 5, 39, 45, 51, 52, 92, 101, 103, 138, 154, 156, 157, 159, 165, 175, 216, 234, 239, 243, 244-46, 250

baptism, xiii, 15, 16, 50, 64, 82, 85, 119-39, 142, 179, 199, 227, 252, 255, 261; infant baptism, 94, 126-29, 132, 139
Barth, Karl, 32, 46, 69, 116, 165, 168-72, 174, 207
Beker, J. Christiaan, 78, 79, 91
Bible, vii, 12, 13, 14, 22, 38, 40, 45, 47, 54, 63, 65, 103, 126, 128, 131, 146, 148, 151, 152, 163, 166, 167, 175, 183, 185-93, 197, 211, 221, 228, 230, 242; authority of, 93, 94, 106, 107, 111-15; metaphor in, 54, 66, 67, 71, 134, 158, 167, 196
Brueggemann, Walter, 180, 181, 183, 194
Buttrick, David, 174, 198, 214-16

Calvin, John, 12, 17, 18, 43, 47, 54, 95, 96, 99-101, 107, 110, 111, 116, 124, 135, 138, 145, 155, 156, 207, 208, 227, 229, 230, 232, 233, 237-40, 244, 250
Canon Missae, 13, 95, 96, 227
communion with Christ, ix, xi, xii, 29, 34, 35, 36, 61, 81, 83, 84, 88, 101, 139, 225, 236, 243, 244, 250, 251
confession of sin, 97, 146, 152-57, 160
covenant, 87, 104, 130, 131, 136, 138, 151, 152, 204, 220, 242

creation, 32, 38, 44, 48, 79, 81, 86, 90, 91, 99, 119, 122, 141, 147, 151, 161, 171, 179, 182, 202, 203, 204, 210, 221

Didache, 104, 105, 123
divine presence, xii, 2, 16-18, 24, 28-32, 39, 47, 50, 52-54, 57-61, 71-73, 76, 79, 88, 93, 96, 102, 103, 113, 141, 143, 182, 183, 186, 220, 222, 226, 237, 239, 243, 250

epiclesis, xii, 36, 37, 47, 52-56, 93, 96, 110, 186, 236, 242, 248
eschatology, 69, 78, 116
Eucharist, viii, xi, 1, 33-37, 50, 55, 93-98, 105, 133, 138, 144, 196, 199, 225, 226, 230-32, 238-40, 249, 252-54, 257
exegesis, 74, 183-201, 217

God's promises, 59, 107, 108, 112, 116, 129-32, 137-39, 145, 159, 187, 189, 208, 232, 236, 238
grace, xi, 3, 17, 18, 28, 34, 43, 53, 57, 59, 85, 91, 108, 115, 129-31, 139, 145, 146, 148, 153, 154, 157, 181, 202, 204, 206, 207, 220, 222, 233, 234, 238
Guardini, Romano, 7, 9, 58, 149

Holy Communion, 38, 133, 235, 236, 251
Holy Spirit, xii, 15, 18, 20, 27, 29, 36, 43, 47, 51, 52, 55, 57-61, 88, 106, 108, 111, 130, 133, 134, 147, 154, 159, 182, 183, 246

Index of Subjects and Names

Holy Supper, 13, 230, 232
hymn, ix, x, 1-6, 9, 12, 13, 16, 18, 21, 23, 27, 38, 50, 60, 64, 89, 91, 93, 121, 143, 144, 168, 186, 225, 226, 248

illumination, 53, 54, 58, 153, 175, 223
Intercession, xiii, 149, 160, 162

kerygma, 45, 46, 78, 110, 116, 166, 167, 185, 186, 203-8, 219, 220, 247
Kuyper, Abraham, 7, 10, 16, 17, 21, 31, 150
Kyrie, xiii, 11, 67, 91, 156, 159, 160, 229

Leeuw, G. van der, 7, 9, 10, 36, 55, 137, 149, 235, 247
Lord's Supper, vii, ix, xi, xiii, 8, 13, 14, 36, 51, 53-55, 64, 93-96, 99-105, 121, 200, 224-32, 236, 238, 242, 243, 245, 247-51
Luther, Martin, 2, 3, 40-43, 46, 96, 99, 107, 111, 185, 227

Messiah, 37, 44, 76, 86, 90, 168, 189, 200, 202, 207
minister, ix, xi, xiii, 1, 5, 9, 12, 16, 18-25, 32, 36, 37, 53, 58, 60, 62-64, 92, 95, 100, 106, 112-22, 126, 130, 143, 148, 151, 153-55, 160-63, 165, 167, 173, 174, 176, 178, 183-95, 197, 201, 209-11, 214-19, 222-31, 234, 249
Miskotte, K. H., 32-34, 145, 159, 185, 186
Missale Romanum, 96, 240, 249
mystery, xi, xii, 10, 35, 39, 56, 58, 68-81, 83-91, 103, 115, 151, 172, 209, 220, 236, 244, 248, 250, 251

New Homiletic, 164, 212, 214
Noordmans, O., 28, 51, 52, 85

parousia, 78, 162
participation: in worship, 2, 3, 6, 7, 12, 33, 39, 57-62, 95, 163, 164, 166, 174; in the sacraments, 14, 105, 133, 137, 238, 243, 251
pneuma, 37, 42, 44-46, 81-84, 180, 199, 205, 250; pneumatological, 54, 57, 59, 61

praise, 2-6, 23, 56, 59, 89-91, 95, 106, 141, 144, 148, 151, 154, 158, 160, 186, 187, 226, 229, 230, 235, 246, 251
prayer, ix, x, xii, 3-5, 7, 9, 11-23, 27, 28, 32, 38, 43, 47, 50, 52-62, 64, 67, 89-104, 113, 120-26, 134, 135, 140-62, 168, 211, 224-34, 237, 241-43, 247-51; liturgical prayer, 21, 143, 144, 146, 148, 150, 161
preaching, vii, ix, xi-xiii, 12, 24, 33, 53, 62, 63, 71, 89, 97-100, 110-23, 135, 154, 163-223, 229; and rhetoric, ix, x, xiii, 20, 25, 61-63, 117-21, 163, 188, 201, 214-17
prefatio, 14, 247
Pronaus, 96, 98, 99
Protestant, vii, xi-xiii, 1-7, 9, 11, 12, 14, 16, 20, 21, 24, 27-37, 40, 43, 45-47, 51, 55, 57, 71, 79, 80, 93-97, 102, 103, 106, 107, 109, 112, 115, 125, 127, 129, 132, 133, 146, 148, 156, 183, 201, 217, 224-28, 234, 243, 245, 248, 249-51
psalter, 3, 6, 21, 126, 227

redemption, 39, 40, 45, 52, 69, 86, 90-92, 107, 156, 159, 201, 202, 204, 216, 220, 231, 237, 243, 251
Reformed: Reformed communion, 11, 103, 106, 227, 232, 233, 235, 236, 243-47; Reformed liturgy, 14, 101, 126, 154; Reformed worship, 12, 21, 146, 235
ritual, xi, 24, 45, 57, 123, 133, 243, 245, 247, 249, 250
Ruler, A. A. van, 39, 57, 237

sacrament, 34, 45, 85, 87, 93, 129, 136, 138, 196, 231, 235, 238
salvation, xii, 17, 33, 34, 36-47, 57, 61, 69, 70, 81, 86, 88, 89, 91, 109, 110, 115, 116, 129, 130, 136, 146-48, 151, 152, 160-62, 170, 183, 184, 186, 193, 198, 202, 204, 205, 220, 226, 231, 236, 237, 243, 250, 251
Sanctus, 11, 14, 225, 247, 248
Schleiermacher, Friedrich, 30, 31, 121
sermon, vii, ix, x, xiii, 3, 12, 21, 24, 25, 32, 34, 52, 53, 60, 63-67, 70-72, 93, 94, 97-99, 106, 109, 110, 113-23, 154, 163-

265

INDEX OF SUBJECTS AND NAMES

223, 228, 229; and eloquence, 24, 94, 116-21, 203; and listeners, xiii, 62, 63, 118, 119, 121, 213, 215, 222; plot of, 118, 212-14, 216
soul, 83, 122, 144, 147
Sunday, vii, viii, x, xii, 11, 23, 27, 38, 47, 48, 50, 59, 93, 94, 96, 98, 100, 113, 131, 152, 160, 188, 201, 229, 247, 249

Table Prayer, 14, 95, 99, 224, 247, 249, 250, 251
thanksgiving, 14, 95, 144, 145, 148, 225, 230, 235, 247, 248
Tillich, Paul, 33, 34, 37, 243

votum, 11, 16-18, 152

Word of God, 33, 54, 106, 109, 110, 112, 113, 117, 121, 163, 232

Words of Institution, 100, 105, 224, 227-30, 242, 245, 247, 250
worship: agenda of, viii, xii, 10-12, 20, 22, 23, 27, 88, 143, 150; blended, xiii, 4, 6, 225, 226; and emotion, 4-6, 16, 27, 59, 62-64, 73, 88, 122, 140, 143, 147-49, 161, 206, 211, 222, 223, 225; and the human self, 22, 23, 39, 57-59, 64, 88, 89, 243; and involvement, xii, 26, 59, 60, 62, 73, 85, 92, 101, 140, 161, 166-67, 173, 175, 186, 222, 223, 225; script of, vii, viii, xii, xiii, 1, 7, 10, 12-15, 22, 27, 135, 143, 148, 150, 158, 198, 209, 251
worship service, vii-xii, 1-38, 46, 57-65, 85, 89, 90, 93, 96-100, 106, 111, 115, 118, 121, 145, 148, 160-63, 183, 190, 191, 235; and performance, 2, 4, 6, 7, 9, 12, 13, 15, 16, 22, 24-29, 39, 57-64, 89, 118, 146, 163, 164, 183, 201, 211, 212, 219, 222, 235

www.ingramcontent.com/pod-product-compliance
Lightning Source LLC
Chambersburg PA
CBHW021138230426
43667CB00005B/163